Mega-Events

This book brings together different perspectives of mega-event bidding, hosting and legacies. Their impact is considered through an international range of mega-events in terms of land use, political and socio-economic change, and the placemaking processes that accompany these area-based regeneration projects. From city-regions that have not been successful or withdrawn from mega-event selection, to contemporary Olympic, Football World Cup and Expo host cities whose legacy is still unfolding, to event sites whose legacy is now established, the global appeal of the mega-event is apparent from this collection.

The book interrogates the mega-event phenomenon in ten countries, from North and South America, and Australia, to Western and Eastern Europe. Drawing on their historical evolution and antecedents, and following recurrent themes of urban regeneration and resistance, the book highlights the importance of major events and festivals to the creation and marketing of place through branding and regional growth.

In considering a range of mega-events critically and in different national and geopolitical contexts, the book will be of interest to policy and decision-makers at local, regional, national and international levels, and will be of particular interest to professionals, scholars and students working in planning, urban studies, sport and leisure studies, and in event and festival management.

Graeme Evans is Professor of Creative & Cultural Economy, University of the Arts London. He is a widely published expert on creative cities and the phenomenon of mega-events and regeneration, and advises cultural agencies on cultural planning, creative industries, and mega-event impacts and strategies.

Mega-Events

Placemaking, Regeneration and City-Regional Development

**Edited by
Graeme Evans**

Routledge
Taylor & Francis Group

LONDON AND NEW YORK

First published 2020 by Routledge

2 Park Square, Milton Park, Abingdon, Oxon, OX14 4RN
605 Third Avenue, New York, NY 10017

Routledge is an imprint of the Taylor & Francis Group, an informa business

First issued in paperback 2020

British Library Cataloguing in Publication Data
A catalogue record for this book is available from the British Library

Library of Congress Cataloging-in-Publication Data
A catalog record has been requested for this book

ISBN: 978-1-138-60828-3 (hbk)
ISBN: 978-0-367-77710-4 (pbk)

Typeset in Times New Roman
by Taylor & Francis Books

Contents

Figures

Tables

Contributors

Patricia Aelbrecht is Lecturer in Urban Design at the School of Geography and Planning, Cardiff University. Her research focuses on the social dimension of urban design, in particular on how social practices and activism in public space shape and redefine the meanings and uses of public spaces in a wide range of cultural and social contexts in Europe. Recent work also investigates mega-events as catalysts of urban regeneration and the contested regeneration of post-war modernist cityscapes. She holds a PhD in Urban Studies and an MSc in International Planning from University College London, and a BArch and MArch from the Technical University of Lisbon.

Anne-Marie Broudehoux is Associate Professor at the School of Design of the University of Quebec at Montreal, where she has been teaching since 2002. She received her doctoral degree in architecture from the University of California at Berkeley in 2002. She is the author of *Mega-Events and Urban Image Construction: Beijing and Rio de Janeiro*, published by Routledge in 2017. She has given several conference papers and published multiple articles and book chapters on the socio-spatial impacts of sporting mega-events on the process of urban image construction, especially with respect to the instrumentalisation of culture, the development of tourism spaces and the invisibilisation of poverty. Her book, *The Making and Selling of Post-Mao Beijing*, also at Routledge, was awarded the International Planning History Society book prize in 2006. Her current research is concerned with the spatialisation of the memory of the Atlantic slave trade in the Americas, more especially in Rio de Janeiro.

Stefano Di Vita holds a PhD in Urban, Regional and Environmental Planning and an MSc in Architecture and is Assistant Professor in Urban Planning and Design at the Architecture and Urban Studies Department of the Politecnico di Milano. His main research interests address spatial dynamics and planning tools for urban phenomena extended at a regional scale, by focusing specifically on the sustainability of urban transformation and regeneration processes aimed at fostering economic development and innovation: from mega-events to digitalisation of urban spaces and productions.

Graeme Evans is Professor Creative & Cultural Economy at the University of the Arts London. He convened the Regional Studies Association Mega Events Research Network hosting a number of workshops and conference sessions in the UK, Italy, the Netherlands and the USA. He has undertaken research and evaluation as part of Capital of Culture bids and festivals, and for the London 2012 Olympics and legacy development, including AHRC-funded projects on Cultural Mapping, Cultural Ecosystems and the East London Fashion District in and around the Olympic Park. Publications include *Cultural Planning: An Urban Renaissance?* and *Designing Sustainable Cities.*

John R. Gold is Professor of Urban Historical Geography in the Department of Social Sciences at Oxford Brookes University, Special Appointed Professor in the Graduate School of Governance Studies at Meiji University (Tokyo, Japan) and Editor (with Margaret Gold) of the journal *Planning Perspectives.* A frequent radio and television broadcaster, he is the author or editor of 23 books on architectural and cultural subjects. These include *Cities of Culture: Staging International Festivals and the Urban Agenda, 1851–2000* (2005), *The Practice of Modernism: Modern Architects and Urban Transformation, 1954–1972,* (2007), *Olympic Cities: City Agendas, Planning, and the World's Games, 1896–2016* (three editions: 2007, 2011, 2016), *The Making of Olympic Cities* (2012) and *Festival Cities: Culture, Planning and Urban Life since 1918* (2019–2020). Many have appeared in foreign language translations.

Margaret M. Gold lectures in cultural tourism and events management at London Metropolitan University and at Goldsmiths, University of London. She is Editor (with John Gold) of the journal *Planning Perspectives.* Her books include *Imagining Scotland* (1995), *Cities of Culture: Staging International Festivals and the Urban Agenda, 1851–2000* (2005) *Olympic Cities: City Agendas, Planning, and the World's Games* (three editions: 2007, 2011, 2016), a four-volume edited collection on *The Making of Olympic Cities* (2012), and *Festival Cities: Culture, Planning and Urban Life since 1918* (2019–2020). Her current research interests include heritage interpretation and cultural festivals.

Dr Luke Juran is faculty in the Department of Geography and at the Virginia Water Resources Research Center at Virginia Tech. His research investigates socio-political dimensions of infrastructure and land use development.

Mathias Kuhlmann has been a social scientist, consultant and journalist since 1994 within European strategies and programmes comprising a wide range of policies such as building, housing, regional and urban development, economic promotion, employment, education, migration and social integration. He has been involved in many transnational exchange activities funded by the EU and the OECD such as ESF Innovative Actions, EQUAL, ESF Learning Networks, INTERREG, LEED Forum on Partnerships, URBAN and URBACT. When his hometown Hamburg applied in 2015 to host the Olympic and Paralympic Games 2024, he started his work on mega-events and urban development including HafenCity Hamburg.

Robert Oliver is Associate Professor in the Department of Geography at Virginia Tech, USA. His research examines the intersections of public space, symbolism and entrepreneurial urbanism, with a particular emphasis on how various claims to urban space are rendered visible during mega-event planning and hosting processes.

Erik Olson recently completed graduate studies in the Department of Geography at Virginia Tech. His thesis investigated the trepidation about the value of the Olympic Movement and the Olympic Games in Stockholm, Sweden over the past two decades.

Sven Daniel Wolfe is a researcher and doctoral candidate at the Department of Geography and Sustainability at the University of Lausanne. He is an urban and regional geographer interested in mega-events, geopolitics, and the Global East, and he investigates how global processes are implicated in the individual and the everyday. His doctoral thesis is concerned with the motivations and meanings of the 2018 men's football World Cup in Russia, focusing on how this mega-event is governed and deployed, what narratives carry the event to the population, and what effects hosting has on everyday life.

Acknowledgements

This edited collection arose out of the Regional Studies Association (RSA) Research Network on *Mega-Events Regeneration and Regional Development*, so thanks are due to the staff and for support of the RSA and the RSA international network. Particular thanks are also due to my fellow conveners, including Bas van Heur, Peter Peters, Philip Lawton, Lauren Andres – and special thanks to Ozlem Edizel who assisted me in organising the series of workshops, conference sessions and dissemination activities and for her research on the London 2012 Olympics and mega-events in Turkey. I would also like to thank Greg Richards and the ATLAS Events research group, John and Maggie Gold, and the numerous researchers, activists and officials who have shared their knowledge and perspectives on this phenomenon and generously hosted me at various points in the planning, operation and legacy stages of their respective mega-events.

1   Introduction

Graeme Evans

The phenomenon of mega-events, once distinguished as 'special' or 'hall-mark' events, has arguably become normalised, reflecting their universal and thus ubiquitous nature – and their longevity. Despite the excessive cost, controversy and corruption associated with their selection, delivery and post-event legacies – cities, regions, as well as nation states continue to vie for the honour of hosting international mega-events.

These event-based urban imaginaries have a long trajectory. Universal Expositions and World Fairs, the forerunner of today's Expos, date from the 1700s, early examples of globalisation and capitalism through respective Franco-British empires, converging in the exemplar Great Exhibition in 1851 (Greenhalgh, 1988). The Olympics movement was resurrected in 1894 with the first modern Olympics symbolically held in Athens in 1896, although the early twentieth-century Olympics were treated as a sideshow to the fairground, employing them as additional but subsidiary attractions to the already established World's Fairs. For instance, Paris 1900 treated its Olympics as an indistinguishable component of the 'Exposition Universelle' whereas St Louis in 1904 followed the same formula (Gold and Gold, 2010; Evans, 2019). By the 1930s, however, host nations had also started to use the Olympics as a stand-alone opportunity to advertise their country and regimes, notably Berlin's 'Third Reich' 1936 Games. By 1964 Tokyo was promoting its Games as an important medium for conveying Japan's credentials as a modern country and for signifying its re-emergence onto the international stage after World War II, a modernisation strategy later adopted in Seoul, Beijing and Rio (see Broudehoux Chapter 6), and most recently in Sochi, Russia (see Wolf, Chapter 6). Versions of this international cultural diplomacy and branding exercise can also be seen in the FIFA Football World Cup and other competitions hosted by developing regions such as in the Middle East (e.g. Qatar) and South Africa. Old world cities also return to the bidding table, often revisiting their earlier experiences and sentiments (e.g. London's post-War Olympics in 1948 and London 2012). Even when associated with cost overruns, corruption and displacement of residents and businesses, as in the case of Tokyo (1964), this city (having lost out to Rio in 2016), sought and won the 2020 Olympics. Tokyo had been awarded the organisation of the 1940 Summer Olympics, but this honour was subsequently passed to Helsinki, because of Japan's invasion of China, before ultimately being cancelled because of World War II. The late Zaha Hadid – also architect of London 2012's Aquatic Centre – and original designer for the Tokyo 2020 Olympic stadium oversaw the original budget of £707 million rise to £1.37 billion, which led to her replacement and the appointment of a Japanese design firm working with a revised budget of £843 million.

The history of these special events therefore predates the post-industrial urban renewal and competitive city eras. For example, a year prior to the first revived Olympics, the inauguration of the International Art Exhibition, or Venice Biennale, took place in 1895. Although a biannual art exhibition would not in itself be considered a mega-event as such, as the event has grown in size and importance – cultural, symbolic, economic – it has expansively evolved into a permanent spectacle, with the national pavilions of the Giardini sitting alongside the temporary exhibitions in the Arsenale dockside complex (another regeneration project waiting to happen – Figure 1.1), and now spread across other venues and sites in Venice.

Today, over 150 art biennales are now held across the globe. Venice is not unlike the Edinburgh International Festival in this respect, established in 1947, and which has spawned the now much larger Fringe and associated festivals (12 distinct festivals including literature, jazz, etc. – BOP, 2012), and

Figure 1.1 Venice Arsenale dock, Architecture Biennale, 2014
Source: author.

also the annual Milan Design Feira, again with a larger off-site fringe exhibition programme. This international design fair attracts over 160 countries and 2,000 exhibitors – more than International Expos. Public sports, exhibitions and festivals are therefore supplemented by commercial trade shows which in countries like Germany and China which occupy semi-permanent sites, e.g. International Building Exhibitions (IBAs – see Kuhlmann on Hamburg, Chapter 9) and Garden Festivals, often linked to regeneration and re-use of industrial sites. The serial festival represented by the *European City of Culture* first hosted by Athens in 1984 also draws on the expansive Venice Biennale. Like these notable major festivals these events have widened in scope and scale over time, expanding their footprint and transforming what was once a prosaic one-off event into a cyclical mega-celebration of culture and commerce, and fast track route to regeneration and redevelopment.

What these historical antecedents provide is not only a longitudinal reference and perspective on this contemporary phenomenon but a commentary on urban spectacle, city development (and therefore regimes) and cultural identity, at various scales. Scale has become an important factor in mega-event development since they claim – and seek to reconcile – the local and the global, with the intensive site-based developments associated with Olympic venues, villages, Expo sites and major culture-led regeneration used to project collective visions and host qualities. This is most apparent through the worldwide media dissemination which dominates major sporting events, notably Olympics and World Cups, but also through the self-conscious themes adopted to provide International Expos with the gravitas they otherwise lack (at their most basic, a series of national tourism board theme sheds).

Even Cities/Capitals of Culture have increasingly felt it necessary – particularly during the bidding stage – to emulate these utopian missions coupled with the local and regional economic development and political ambitions of their proponents. This has also seen their political and spatial scope (and ambitions) extend to regional and cross-border events such as Aix-en-Provence combining with Marseille for the 2013 French Capital of Culture (Andres and Gresillon, 2014) and Maastricht's (unsuccessful) bid for the first Euroegional Festival in 2018, combining with Liege in Belgium and Aachen in Germany (Evans 2012; Lawton, 2014).

Mega-events: cities of renewal

Writing over 25 years ago, Hall located the rationale for hosting what until then had been termed hallmark events, within the fourth era of World's Fairs running from the early 1960s – namely 'the city of renewal' (1992, 29). Today's mega-events are no exception to this 50-year trajectory, which has hardened in recent years toward major cities hosting and bidding for the 'greatest show on earth'. National capitals such as Madrid, Paris, Stockholm (Olson et al., Chapter 8) and Tokyo, and cultural capitals Amsterdam, Los Angeles, New York, Rio (Broudehoux, Chapter 6), Sydney, Istanbul and Toronto (Oliver,

Figure 1.2 Mascot, Shanghai Expo 2010
Source: author.

Chapter 10) have competed for hosting major international events such as Expos and Olympics, despite their escalating cost and now-predictable controversies and dubious legacy effects (Evans, 2010; Grix, 2014). Re-presenting and re-imaging major cities through these mega-events is therefore both a competitive strategy (Ward and Jonas, 2004) and a reflection of the 'festivalisation of the city' (Richards and Palmer, 2010). These once-in-a-lifetime events also present a dualistic challenge to their hosts – between the temporal/ ephemeral nature of the event and the permanent legacy, and between the 'host' audience and the outside world. The latter includes visitors/tourists, global media, commercial sponsors, and institutional 'brand' holders who also impose their design controls on the event organisers (Evans, 2019).

Large-scale festivals and sporting competitions make up the majority of what are considered contemporary hallmark or mega-events. Early studies into the phenomenon tended to view them as simply 'special' (i.e. not regular/ annual) large-scale events. However, subsequent studies (Hall, 1989) identified short-term staged events also, such as carnivals and festivals. Such events can be of significant economic and social importance, which may not only serve to attract visitors but also assist in the development or maintenance of community or regional identity (Getz, 2012). The term 'hallmark event' is not therefore confined to the large-scale events that generally occur within cities and major towns. Community festivals and local celebrations can be described as hallmark events in relation to their regional and local significance. Such an observation highlights the importance of the economic, social and spatial context within which these events take place. However, the term 'mega-event' has far more specific application. Mega-events, such as World's Fairs – or 'Expos' (Olds, 1988) and the Olympic Games (Ritchie and Yangzhou, 1987), are events which are expressly targeted at the international market – global media, tourists and investors, as well as local and national participants. They also entail major capital investment in venues, facilities and transport and drive a number of planning imperatives.

More recently, Müller (2015) has revisited the definitional ambiguity of the mega-event concept which brings together the key, but still quantitative factors, which distinguish them from other hallmark or special events. In his analysis, in order to be considered as mega-events, they should:

1 Attract a large number of visitors.
2 Have a large mediated reach.
3 Come with large costs.
4 Have large impacts on the built environment and the local-regional population.

Although, in the past, visitor numbers were an indication of the size of the event, in order to experience a sporting mega-event today it is no longer essential to travel and watch it in situ. In fact, the widespread broadcasting of sporting competitions since the 1980s has meant that the vast majority of those who watch an event do so on TV or other media (Horne, 2007); Sugden and Tomlinson, 2012). From Montréal 1976 to the London 2012 Olympics, the value of broadcasting rights for the Summer Games has risen from $34.9 to $2,569 million – almost 23 times in real terms. This is an indication of the evolution of the global media economy, but also of the commercialisation of large events. According to the International Olympic Committee (IOC), about half of the world's population, 3.64 billion, saw at least one minute of coverage of the 2012 Summer Games (IOC, 2014). From Barcelona 1992 to London 2012, the number of accredited media personnel almost doubled to more than 24,000 – more than two media representatives per athlete (Chappelet, 2014). This growth underscores the extent to which large events are mediated rather than directly experienced. This has also meant that their design focus has widened from the facilities and site itself to branding and communication design, merchandising, and sponsorship (Evans, 2019).

Non-sporting events are, however, more fundamentally experiential and festival in nature. In these cases. size still matters in mega-event positioning, particularly in Asian countries where their appeal and more regimented social system guarantees very high levels and reach of attendance (e.g. Japan's Aichi Expo 2005 attracted over 22 million visits, albeit with a budget of $3.3 billion). As Shanghai – 'the culmination of a 30-year process of opening and re-integrating with the world' – boasts (Land, 2010, 14):

Figure 1.3 China Pavilion at Shanghai Expo, 2010
Source: author.

World expo tends naturally to stupendous scale, but never like this. Expo 2010 is by far the largest ever staged in almost every conceivable respect. It has far more participants and visitors than any expo has attracted before, drawn to most expansive site, developed by the most enormous urban development process the world has ever seen. It takes place in the largest city in the world's most populous country. It is not only the first china expo but also the first Expo in the developing world.

This contrasts with European events, notably Hanover's Expo in 2000 which failed to attract even half of its 44 million target – even after cutting entrance ticket prices – posting a loss of $1.3 billion for the regional government. In the same year London hosted the Millennium Festival at Greenwich Peninsula (Evans, 1995), which also failed to achieve it's 12 million visitor target by over 50%.

The mega-event phenomenon sits generally within urban and regional studies and also alongside other forms of urban regeneration – *housing, industry, science & technology* (including 'smart' and 'tech city') and *culture*-led (Evans, 2001), with all the tensions and issues that arise – from gentrification to globalisation. As the examples of mega-event legacies included in this book reveal, all these variants of regeneration feature in post-event site development (see Aelbrecht on Lisbon, Chapter 4), whilst the festival nature of these situates

Figure 1.4 Dutch pavilion at Shanghai Expo, 2010
Source: author.

major events as a particular form of culture and culture-led regeneration. This has important implications for cultural policy since decisions to host (and even just bid for) such extravagant events create significant opportunity costs for other cultural and social investment, as other budgets are raided to finance bidding and hosting expenditure. For example, London2012's excessive budget resulted in National Lottery and other public funds being diverted from arts, sports and heritage projects nationwide for several years. From Bilbao to Buenos Aires, these international events are given priority over supporting existing cultural and economic initiatives through 'hard branding' the city of consumption (Evans, 2003; Dinardi, 2017).

Book rationale and scope

As well as adding to the literature and stock of knowledge on this subject, the impetus for this book has been the need for both a historical-contemporary perspective on mega-events and their trajectory over time and space, and a wider disciplinary consideration in a field that has been dominated by economic and short-term impacts primarily of sporting events – or historical-sociological analyses (Roche, 2000; Horne and Manzenreiter, 2013). Growing bodies of work also focus on the legacy attaching to specific mega-events (i.e. Olympics), as the passing of time affords a longer-term view of the actual land-use, economic and social changes (Cohen and Watt, 2017), whilst others document various resistance movements, including artist interventions (Powell and Marrero-Guillamón, 2012) – reflecting socially engaged practice in the field of urban and community development (Leeson, 2017).

The opportunity for a more spatial lens on mega-events also responds to their expansive footprints and regional scope, which has widened their political, land-use/planning and city-regional impact. For instance China's foray into mega-events represented by the Beijing Olympics in 2008 and the 2010 Asian Games in Guangdong saw these temporary stimuli prolonging the cycle of regional growth. Here as in other countries, 'mega-events have been used as instruments (ab)used by city governments to expedite land sales, relocate old industries, and drive migrant workers and the urban underclass out of the city centre' (Lin et al. 2018, 24). This city-regional dimension led to the establishment of the Regional Studies Association (RSA) *Research Network on Mega Events, Regeneration and Regional Development*, convened by the editor, and colleagues in Birmingham, London and Maastricht. Since 2011, a series of research seminars, conferences and sessions have been organised at international symposia, including the Regional Studies Association (RSA), Association of American Geographers (AAG) and Royal Society of Geographers (RGS). Several contributors to this book participated in these exchanges and a larger constituency contributed to the debate and discussions, some of whose work is captured in RSA (*Regions*, 2014) and in other publications (Richards, de Brito and Wilks, 2013; Kassens-Noor, nd), and also on the network's website: www.megaevents.org.

Chapter themes

The important historical perspective on mega-events is reflected in the initial chapters, commencing with John and Maggie Gold's critique of brownfield land usage for urban Olympics held in New York (1932) and London (2012) respectively. This planning and political device has been used repeatedly in other cities to guide location and to rationalise investment and planning decisions through land reclamation and regeneration, avoiding conflicts from more developed/populated areas. This has also facilitated a notable feature of mega-event based regeneration – the extension of the city-region and associated gentrification effects.

This regeneration and legacy theme continues in Evans' chapter on London 1851/2012, again rationalised through brownfield 'redevelopment' [*sic*] and land remediation (e.g. canals). In fact the current site has been largely been built on and around post-industrial green space and waterways, with an Olympic Park – much of it hard-landscaped and subject to further building – providing less open/green space than prior to the Olympic makeover (Evans, 2014, 2016). The legacies in this case compare London South Kensington's museum quarter, or *Albertopolis*, of the mid-nineteenth century (from the 1851 Great Exhibition) with the presiding Mayor's vision for London 2012, which he coined

Olympicolis, thus emulating this Victorian era's cultural and education quarter through satellite campuses of several universities and cultural institutions (conveniently ignoring the fact that there were already incumbent universities and cultural venues in and around Stratford).

A more near-historical case is provided by Patricia Aelbrecht (Chapter 4), of the Lisbon Expo which was held over 20 years ago in 1998, providing a longer post-event assessment of this mega-event, and seemingly more successful than many of its comparators. More contemporary examples are then considered, starting with Milan's 2015 Expo (Di Vita, Chapter 5) which had a distinctive city-regional identity and strategy, but which was accompanied by familiar political conflicts and corruption, as regimes shifted during the event development and delivery process. An observation from these (and other) mega-events, is that the bidding, development and event delivery process needs to be viewed over a longer-term period in order to assess the impact and legacy that have been generated over time (and also the opportunity costs arising from the decision to host such mega-events).

This common issue reflects the reality of these major events – the long duration of the pre-planning, positioning and consensus building leading to a successful or unsuccessful selection (and the political fall-out from both of these outcomes). And then if awarded, a further lengthy development phase leading to the event itself, which too often compromises the original aims and excessive optimism associated with the bidding and award process. This disappointment, as the experience of the event itself fades, then intensifies over a further protracted period in the 'legacy' phase, as post-event use of the event facilities and supposed benefits to host communities fail to materialise. The cycle of broken and false promises, change of leadership (national and city-regional government, e.g. mayors) and crises in delivery organisations in the construction phase, combined with the uncontrollable economic and global changes that undermine even then best laid plans and budgets, suggest that these mega-events should be avoided. Counterfactually however, cities and nation states repeatedly continue to put themselves forward to host and finance these projects, effectively taking a zero base rather than an evidence-based approach.

Reasons for this are complex and also reflect what can be termed through the somewhat clichéd phrase the 'universal and the particular'. International awarding bodies (e.g. IOC, UIE, FIFA, EU) govern, control and brand these mega-events, to ensure their global status and familiarity, including their operational consistency (e.g. access, design, layout, image, identity) and sponsorships (including 'naming') rights. Aspiring host cities seek and often struggle to adapt their own rationale and their cultural and place-based specificities to these hegemonic and geopolitical systems. Not surprisingly these tensions lead to resistance and in some cases rejection by residents (Hayes and Karimachas, 2012), as in the case of Stockholm (Olson, Chapter 8) and Hamburg (Kuhlmann, Chapter 9). Where governance is weak (or autocratic, depending on the perspective), the pro-development rhetoric is able to override other concerns, such as social justice, displacement and environmental degradation, as is apparent in the case of Rio de Janeiro (Broudehoux, Chapter 6). On the other hand, boosterism is the overriding approach used to justify and leverage public funding where lesser known regions seek the international recognition and level of public diplomacy that would otherwise bypass them. This is the case with Russia's Sochi Winter Olympics as discussed by Wolfe (Chapter 7), from the perspective of road and rail development.

The opportunity to upgrade and invest huge amounts of public money in new transport infrastructure is a prosaic, but important aspect of mega-events, since the level of transport investment involved can outstrip the direct costs of the event facilities themselves (Evans and Shaw, 2001). This is critical given the fact that Olympic budgets consistently over-run (on average over 170% – London 2012 was over 300% over the original capital budget – Evans, 2010) and Expos likewise exceed their original budgets. As Wolfe (Chapter 6) documents in the recent case of Sochi's Winter Olympics, this Russian event could be seen (to misquote the V&A Museum's infamous advertising campaign) as an 'ACE transport system with a nice Winter Olympics attached'. Reputedly costing Russia over $50 billion, this mega-project topped Beijing's Summer Olympics spend of $40 billion (Zimbalist, 2015). The costs and benefits of hosting a short-term event can therefore be rationalised through the connectivity that new transport infrastructure brings to a region or sub-region, enabling access for employment, tourists and providing an essential element in placemaking. Mega-events involving major transport investment therefore provide the rare opportunity to extend the city-region, including establishing new quarters or zones of the city, such in Beijing (2008 Olympics), Shanghai (2010 Expo) and Milan (2015 Expo), as well as London 2012's grand placemaking project to extend the city's economy and growing population eastwards to Stratford.

Non-event

Each mega-event case history is therefore a product of the 'path dependency' of each city-region, with the mega-event punctuating what can be a deeply symbolic and historic trajectory and city growth agenda. This is clearly apparent where cities repeatedly bid to host mega-events either successively or periodically returning to earlier attempts after failing to be selected, or withdrawing from the process. For every successful mega-event there are therefore a long and shortlist of failed bidders and the mega-event literature tends to ignore these by focusing solely on the winners (for an exception regarding failed Olympics bids – see Oliver and Lauermann, 2017). As the experience of bidding, winning, hosting and delivering mega-events accumulates and knowledge is transferred (including via international networks and resistance movements which mobilise around contested mega-event sites), cities and citizen's scepticism is reinforced. For example, Boston's 'No Olympics' movement successfully resisted the Boston 2024 organising committee's efforts, in a city that had experienced decades of disruption from the 'Big Dig' transportation project – the largest ever in the USA – with a now-familiar overspend, of five times the original $2.6 billion budget.

Three examples of 'failed' mega-event bids are therefore included here, starting with Stockholm's successive if ambivalent attempts to bid to host the Winter Olympics Games (Olson, Chapter 8). This is followed by a practitioner's view of the fascinating process which led to Hamburg's bid for the Summer Olympics being voted down by residents of HafenCity, in a rare example of democratic decision-making (Kuhlmann, Chapter 9). Meanwhile this same HafenCity saw the erection of a new Elbphilharmonie concert hall (in this case not the subject of a referendum), designed by the architects Herzog & de Meuron (also responsible for the 'birdsnest' stadium for the Beijing Olympics), and whose budget went from €77 million to €789 million. In the final Chapter (10), Bob Oliver presents the case of Toronto, a repeat bidder and aspiring host for the Summer Olympics and other hallmark events.

These 'non-event' examples provide both insights to the bidding and political processes involved, but also of the alternative strategies pursued by these cities, including other event hosting and ongoing area-based regeneration – and further attempts at mega-event bidding. Clear examples then, of the seductive power of mega-events as subjects of political imagineering and as preferred routes to enhanced place branding and realisation of often long held, if problematic, regeneration plans.

References

Andres, L. and Gresillon, B. (2014) 'European Capital of Culture': A leverage for regional development and governance? The case of Marseille Provence 2013', *Regions*, 295(3), 8–10.

BOP (2012) *Edinburgh Festivals Impact Study.* London: Burns Owens Partnership.

Chappelet, J.-L. (2014) 'Managing the size of the Olympic Games', *Sport in Society*, 17, 581–592.

Cohen, P. and Watt, P. (eds) (2017) *London 2012 and the Post-Olympics City: A Hollow Legacy?* Basingstoke: Palgrave Macmillan.

Dinardi, C. (2017) 'Cities for sale: Contesting city branding and cultural policies in Buenos Aires', *Urban Studies*, 54(1), 85–101.

Evans, G.L. (1995) 'Planning for the British Millennium Festival: Establishing the visitor baseline and a framework for forecasting', *Festival Management and Event Tourism*, 3, 183–196.

Evans, G.L. (2003) 'Hard branding the City of Culture: From Prado to Prada', *International Journal of Urban & Regional Studies*, 27(2), 417–440.

Evans, G.L. (2010) 'Cities of Culture and the Regeneration Games', *Journal of Tourism, Sport and Creative Industries*, 6, 5–18.

Evans, G.L. (2012) 'Maastricht: From treaty town to European Capital of Culture'. In C. Grodach and D. Silver (eds) *The Politics of Urban Cultural Policy Global Perspectives.* London: Routledge, 264–285.

Evans, G.L. (2014) 'Designing legacy and the legacy of design: London 2012 and the Regeneration Games', *Architectural Review Quarterly*, 18(4), 353–366.

Evans, G.L. (2016) 'London 2012'. In J. Gold and M. Gold (eds) *Olympic Cities: City Agendas, Planning and the Worlds Games, 1896–2016*. London: Routledge.

Evans, G.L. (2019) 'Design of Contemporary Mega Events'. In A. Massey (ed.) *Blackwell Companion to Contemporary Design*. Blackwell: Oxford.

Evans, G.L. and Shaw, S. (2001) 'Urban leisure and transport: Regeneration effects', *Journal of Leisure Property*, 1(4), 350–372.

Getz, D. (2012) *Event Studies: Theory, Research and Policy for Planned Events*. London: Routledge.

Gold, J. and Gold, M. (eds) (2010) *Olympic Cities: City Agendas, Planning and the Worlds Games, 1896–2016*. London: Routledge.

Greenhalgh, P. (1988) *Ephemeral Vistas: The Expositions Universelles, Great Exhibitions and World's Fairs, 1851–1939*. Manchester: Manchester University Press.

Grix, J. (2014) *Leveraging Legacies from Mega-Events: Concepts and Cases*. Basingstoke: Palgrave Macmillan.

Hall, C.M. (1989) 'The definition and analysis of hallmark tourist events', *GeoJournal*, 19(3): 263–268.

Hayes, G. and Karimachas, J. (2012) *Olympic Games, Mega-Events and Civil Societies*. Basingstoke: Palgrave Macmillan.

Horne, J. (2007) 'The four "knowns" of sports mega-events', *Leisure Studies*, 26, 81–96.

Horne, J. and Manzenreiter, W. (2013) 'An introduction to the sociology of sports mega-events', *The Sociological Review*, 54, 1–24.

IOC (2014) *Olympic Marketing Fact File*. Lausanne: International Olympic Committee.

Kassens-Noor, E. (Series Editor) (nd) Mega Event Planning Pivot Series. Basingstoke: Palgrave Macmillan. Available online at: https://www.palgrave.com/gp/series/14808, accessed 18 July 2019.

Land, N. (ed.) (2010) *Urbanatomy: Shanghai World Expo Guide*. Shanghai: China Intercontinental Press.

Lawton, P. (2014) 'After the event: Continuity and change in Euregio Meuse-Rhine', *Regions*, 295, 16–18.

Leeson, L. (2017) *Art: Process: Change: Inside a Socially Situated Practice*. London: Routledge.

Lin, C.S., He, C., Li, X. and Wu, Y. (2018) 'Empowering regional economy with a spectacular space: Mega-events, over-drafted capital and momentary growth in China's metropolises', *Area Development and Policy* 3(1), 24–41.

Müller, M. (2015) 'What makes an event a mega-event? Definitions and size', *Leisure Studies*, 34(6), 627–642.

Olds, K. (1988) 'Planning for the housing impacts of a hallmark event: A case study of Expo 86'. Unpublished MA thesis, School of Community and Regional Planning, University of British Columbia, Vancouver.

Oliver, R. and Lauermann, J. (2017) *Failed Olympic Bids and the Transformation of Urban Space*. Basingstoke: Palgrave Macmillan.

Powell, H. and Marrero-Guillamón, I. (2012) *The Art of Dissent: Adventures in London's Olympic State*. London: Marshgate Press.

Richards, G. and Palmer, R. (2010) *Eventful Cities: Cultural Management and Urban Revitalisation*. London: Routledge.

Richards, G., de Brito, M.P. and Wilks, L. (2013) *Exploring the Social Impact of Events*. London: Routledge.

Ritchie, J. and Yangzhou, J. (1987) 'The Role and Impact of Mega-events and Attractions on National and Regional Tourism: Conceptual and Methodological Overview'. In AIEST (ed.) *Proceedings of the 37 Annual Congress of the International Association of Scientific Experts in Tourism (AIEST) in Calgary (23–29 August)*. St Gallen: AIEST, pp. 17–58.

Roche, M. (2000) *Mega-Events and Modernity: Olympics and Expos in the Growth of Global Culture*. London: Routledge.

Sugden, J., and Tomlinson, A. (eds) (2012) *Watching the Olympics: Politics, Power, and Representation*. London: Routledge.

Ward, K. and Jonas, A. (2004) 'Competitive city-regionalism as a politics of space: A critical reinterpretation of the new regionalism', *Environment and Planning A: Economy and Space*, 36(12), 2119–2139.

Zimbalist, A. (2015) *Circus Maximus*. Washington DC: Brookings Institution.

Part I

Mega-events

Placemaking, regeneration and legacy

2 Pestilence, toxicity and all the fun of the fair

Brownfield sites, mega-events and areal regeneration, 1939–2012

John R. Gold and Margaret M. Gold

The Summer Olympic Games and the World's Fairs (Expositions Universelles, Expos) – the two festivals that truly possess the scale, impact and international visibility necessary to merit the title 'mega events' – share two important characteristics. First, unlike festivals that have permanent venues, the organisers of the Olympics and World's Fairs are perennially faced with the challenge of having to find sizable spaces for events that, at best, are unlikely to be repeated within several generations. Secondly and related, the spaces of temporary congregation thus acquired normally require conversion after the closing ceremony. Admittedly there are instances where cities have retained their Olympic Parks or Exposition showgrounds in states that admit the possibility of staging kindred events in the medium-to-long-term, but more often than not city managers recognise that their interests are better served by post-event site conversion that addresses more immediate and local needs. In the current era, that strategy increasingly means redeveloping event spaces in a manner that achieves a measure of urban regeneration as compensation for the high levels of expenditure incurred in land acquisition, infrastructure (transport, housing) and in staging the event in the first instance.

There are potentially five main strategies that have been employed over the years when finding locations for staging mega-events (Gold and Gold, 2018), but we confine the analysis here to one particular option: the use of brownfield sites. In the chapter that follows, we supply a contextual overview before examining three instances in which the prospect of large-scale mega-event investment opened up prospects of longer-term remediation and rehabilitation of blighted land. These respectively are: Flushing Meadow, the showground for New York's World's Fair (1939–1940); Homebush Bay, which housed the Olympic Park for Sydney 2000; and the Lower Lea Valley, which served the same function for London 2012. The final section concludes with commentary as to the wider narratives evoked when considering the deployment of brownfield sites as mega-event spaces.

The brownfield option

The recurrent movement from one host city to another, shared by both the World's Fairs and the Olympics, came about for different reasons. In the case of the World's Fairs it was not overall programmatic direction, given that the Bureau of International Expositions – the body that now oversees the staging of World's Fairs – was not founded until 1928. Rather, the ambulatory sequence of Fairs essentially reflected the unfolding of ambitions and competitive rivalries of cities around the world, which vied with one another to present their best face on the international stage. By contrast, the International Olympic Committee (IOC) deliberately opted for a peripatetic format rather than staging the Olympics at a permanent site, as had been the case with the classical Games that were held for almost 1,200 years at Olympia in Greece's Peloponnese. This decision was primarily ideological. In the 1890s, the nascent IOC saw its function as resuscitating an event that represented the quintessence of the ancient cultural achievement to which Western civilisation in general was heir, rather than the late nineteenth-century Greek state (Christensen and Kyle, 2014). That outlook, in turn, imbued the modern Olympics with an internationalist stance, able continually to move to new host cities without loss of purpose, rather than needing to return permanently to Greece as a geographic hearth in order to give the revived Games authenticity. Ceding control to the Greeks would have interfered with the freedom of action to pursue that policy (Gold and Gold, 2017b, 27) and might well have jeopardised the continued existence of the IOC.

To some extent, the characteristics that make for a desirable event space may differ slightly for World's Fairs as opposed to the Olympics. Exposition organisers nowadays primarily seek to acquire a single, large and undifferentiated site for a showground, whereas the Olympics may well be staged at venues situated in discrete clusters at points scattered throughout the city or beyond. Yet common features normally outnumber differences. Organisers of both events generally search for sites close enough to the heart of the city to fit into the mainstream of urban life but where land costs, particularly in the light of the extent of sequestrations and requisite compensations, are manageable. Both also recognise that the impacts of their festivals will extend well beyond the more immediate circumstances of staging the event and will need to be integrated into the future planning of their host cities.

This is particularly the case with infrastructural developments such as transport. The need for efficient movement of spectators and participants to and from the city centre and between venues has long prompted investment in transport systems. The 1900 Exposition Universelle, for instance, was credited with accelerating the development of the Parisian Metro (Mattie, 1998, 103); the Franco-British Exhibition and Olympic Games in 1908 with encouraging the Central London Railway to build an extension to serve the White City stadium (Jenkins, 2008). These early developments, of course, predated present-day pursuit of strategies that seek to fast-track infrastructural improvements by linking them to investment designed to meet mega-event deadlines, but they did indicate how such projects might leave positive outcomes for the host city from hosting these festivals.

That sentiment certainly underpins much twenty-first-century thinking about mega-event *legacy*, the loosely defined, all-embracing but flexible term that includes tangible or intangible, planned or unplanned, direct or indirect, short- or long-term, and positive or negative event-related outcomes (Gold and Gold, 2013, 3530). Embracing subjects ranging from 'city impacts to volunteers and workers, spatial politics and communities to gender discourse, and protest and publics' (Tomlinson, 2014, 137), legacy offers a credible comprehensive concept in a field where diversity abounds (Preuss, 2015; Tomlinson, 2016; Girginov, 2018). In particular, it has now become the standard frame of reference for planning and evaluating the options available when choosing the spaces where a mega-event will be held.

Over time, as shown in Table 2.1, five broad locational choices have been exercised when deciding on mega-event spaces. The first category, typical of the early days when the entire contents of Expositions could be housed in a single pavilion, was to employ *temporary* sites. This strategy was pioneered by London's 1851 Great Exhibition, where the organisers gained permission from the Crown to use a 26-acre plot of flat land in Hyde Park on condition that, post-event, they subsequently removed the 'Crystal Palace' and undertook remedial landscaping. Yet this strategy is not without equivalent in the modern era. The master plan for the 1996 Atlanta Summer Games enlisted facilities available at local universities to provide the major indoor arenas, with the main stadium being a temporary structure that was largely demolished after the event as part of plans for developing baseball in the city. Only Centennial Park, built as an area where visitors and spectators could congregate during the Games, remained as a tangible reminder.

The second category, where available land is found in *city centre* locations, was primarily associated with nineteenth-century festivals. Very occasionally, it could be found even in the twentieth century as with Seattle's 1962 Century 21 Exposition, for example, crammed into a 30-hectare site surrounding the Civic Auditorium. Yet more often recently, the much desired city centre option is only achieved by wholesale demolition of the existing urban fabric and mass evictions of people and businesses. In this context while precise figures are difficult to unravel from more general clearance policies occurring at the same time, the Geneva-based Center on Housing Rights and Evictions estimated that Seoul (South Korea) evicted 720,000 people for works connected with the 1988 Games, with roughly 300,000 people evicted by works specifically related to the 2008 Olympics.

Increasingly, since clearance on this scale can now only be seriously contemplated by authoritarian regimes, sites at the *urban fringe* – the third category – have gained attractiveness. Here availability of sufficient parcels of land (usually appropriated from existing agrarian or market garden uses), ease of construction, and lack of restrictive ordinances compensate for the new transport links required to connect with the urban core. However, expenditure on communications media can be linked to subsequent exercises in suburban or regional infrastructural development, as shown by Expos, such as Osaka 1970 and Hanover 2000 (Gold and Gold, 2005).

Table 2.1 Event space categories with representative examples

Event Space	City and Year	Event details	Post-event use
Temporary	London1851	Crystal Palace, Hyde Park	Returned to parkland
	Atlanta 1996	Olympic Stadium, temporary use of University facilities	Centennial Park, partial stadium demolition – creation of Turner Field
City centre	Paris 1867 *et seq.*	Champs de Mars, later Trocadéro, banks of Seine, Esplanade des Invalides	Permanent use, major attractions, e.g. Eiffel Tower
	Seattle 1962	Small site surrounding Civic Auditorium	Buildings mostly permanent structures
	Seoul 1988	Seoul Sports complex and Olympic Park	Retention as sporting venues and cultural quarter
	Beijing 2008	Clearance to allow creation of Olympic Green, north of city centre	Sports stadia; urban leisure and tourism centre.
Urban fringe	London 1908	White City stadium	Stadium in use until 1984
	Berlin 1936	Reichssportfeld, Maifeld	Sports complex
	Osaka 1970	Bamboo groves, rice paddies	National culture park
	Hannover 2000	Fairgrounds, formerly aircraft factory, hangers	Continuation as exhibition and congress site
Reclamations	Montreal 1967, 1976	Reclaimed islands from St Lawrence	Parkland, F1 motor racing circuit, tourist attractions
	Seville 1992	Reclaimed island	Science park, adventure theme park
Brownfield conversions	St Louis 1904	Forest Park and flood plain	University campus
	New York 1939-40	Corona Dumps	Flushing Meadow, parkland, tennis, museums
	Lisbon 1998	Industrial zone along River Tagus	Housing, parklands, gardens, casino, marina
	Sydney 2000	Homebush Bay	Newington, new suburb
	London 2012	Lower Lee Valley	Created E20: sports stadia, housing, business, creative industries, cultural quarter

Source: based on Gold and Gold (2018, 355).

The fourth category, *reclamations*, sees event spaces created by means of dredging and infill. The organisers of Expo '67 in Montreal, for instance, generated event spaces around islands in the Ste Laurence River by using spoil substantially obtained from tunnel borings undertaken when building the extension to the city's metro. Expo '92 in Seville took place on a show-ground formed by reclaiming land around La Cartuja, an island in the Guadalquivir River. In both cases, the post-event history of the sites proved problematic, primarily through medium-term difficulties in finding financially viable alternative uses.

Set against these other options, *brownfield conversions* offer distinctive sets of advantages and drawbacks. At the outset, it is important to recognise that the use of brownfield sites has a long and varied history. The 1904 Louisiana Purchase Exposition in St Louis, for instance, required the clearing of the heavily wooded Forest Park, draining its wetlands, rechannelling and treating the sewage-laden and flood-prone Des Peres River, and investing in a new water supply system. The 1939–1940 New York World's Fair took place in what was previously a seriously contaminated industrial dumping ground at Flushing Bay, New York. Yet care must be exercised when referring to 'brownfield' in this regard, since the term only dates from 1992. As coined by Charles Bartsch of the Northeast-Midwest Institute, an American economic think tank, the word referred specifically to industrial sites impaired by environmental contamination (Gemmill, 2012, 4). This emphasis persisted in US practice, with the influential Environmental Protection Agency, for example, defined brownfield land in 1997 as: 'Abandoned, idled, or under-used industrial and commercial facilities where expansion or redevelopment is complicated by real or perceived environmental contamination' (ibid.). Over time and in other contexts, however, usage has expanded to describe 'both spatially and formalistically everything from polluted industrial landscapes to former factory buildings, including vacant or abandoned properties usually found in older, declining sections of a city' (Loures and Vaz, 2018, 66). For example, the British Government's announcement in 1998 that 60 per cent of new homes would be constructed on brownfield sites within a decade (Alker et al., 2000, 49) was predicated on a conception of brownfield land that went well beyond contamination (the generic UK definition was 'previously developed land'). Rather, to meet that ambitious figure it was necessary also to include land that was idle, abandoned, vacant, derelict, redundant, underused, previously used, and affected by mining subsidence or prone to flooding.

Yet regardless of the imprecision with which the term is habitually used, it can broadly be said that brownfield land is generally shunned due to the costs of conversion. If adopted to serve as an event space, it is usually because, first, it offers the possibility of finding conveniently located land without the problems of mass evictions or, second, the promise of post-event productive remediation of marginal land is sufficient to offset the higher short-term preparation costs. The latter argument is frequently assisted by narratives that combine the utopian with the place promotional. These deploy a visionary

Table 2.2 Brownfield mega-event spaces and their characteristics

Site	Previous usage	Contaminants
Flushing Meadow – Corona Park, Queens, New York City	Dumping of industrial ash and household waste, port dredging	Fuel ash, street sweepings, household refuse
Homebush Bay, Sydney	Brick pits and brickworks; state abattoir; chemical industry, paint, gasworks, petroleum products, shipbreaking	Dumping of by-products, pesticides, dioxins, industrial and organic waste
Lower Lea Valley, East London	Heavy industry, chemicals, leather, confectionery, railway depot and works, dumping of toxic and organic waste	Heavy metals, radioactive waste, surface utilities, pylons, electricity cables

imagery replete with parklands and green open spaces, vibrant new communities and state-of-the-art social facilities, shining science parks and eco-friendly workplaces that, it is argued, will be the new face of areas seemingly lastingly scarred by noxiousness, dirt, waste, past greed and present-day neglect. Their transformation will redound to the lasting credit of the event and to the city that had the courage to stage it in this manner. To understand the unfolding of such narratives, however, it is important to consider the evidence supplied by three of the most notable instances in which the problems of procuring event spaces were solved by the brownfield option (see Table 2.2).

A valley of ashes

The first of these case studies was the location chosen in the north-central part of the borough of Queens in New York to serve as the showground for the city's 1939–1940 World's Fair. The site was a wedge-shaped strip roughly 3.5 miles (5.6 kilometres) long and 1.25 miles (2 kilometres) wide running south from Flushing Bay and centred on Flushing Creek, which comprised meadowland and a 'biodiverse tidal salt marsh which served as a natural filtration system for the area's waterways' (Montejo, 2017, 50). Transformation of the area gathered pace at the start of the twentieth century through urban encroachment, aided by New York City's decisions to deepen the creek to create a port and to sell portions of marshland to private owners. Waste tipping for the city's booming industries and household sector as well as disposal of spoil from building the Long Island Railroad saw landfill deposited in the tidal wetland to the north and the blocking of a river from Flushing Bay. The resulting pestilential backwater became a notorious breeding ground for malarial mosquitoes. The most polluted part of the 1,346-acre (544-hectare) site was the rat-infested 350-acre (141-hectare) portion known as the Corona Dump. Used for waste tipping, particularly dumping of coal ash, household refuge and 'street sweepings' (primarily horse manure) by the Brooklyn Ash Removal Company, it had grown dramatically since its opening in 1909, with mounds up to 90 feet high locally nicknamed the 'Corona Alps' (Kuhn, 1995, 420). Spectators on the New York subway marvelled at the scene of desolation memorably described by F. Scott Fitzgerald (1925, 16) in *The Great Gatsby* as a 'desolate area of land ... a valley of ashes – a fantastic farm where ashes grow like wheat into ridges and hills and grotesque gardens'.

Plans for remediation of the area had preceded any specific links with a World's Fair. There was already precedent within the USA for the creation of parks by landfill (Harnik et al., 2006) and, more specifically, the development of large parks was as significant as the creation of urban expressways in the thinking of the Parks Commissioner Robert Moses, whose broader town planning vision did so much to shape mid-twentieth-century New York (Ballon and Jackson, 2007). Robert Caro (1974, 1083) traced Moses' interest in developing the Flushing-Corona site as a park back to the 1920s. The attraction lay in its size, ease of access to major transport routes, position – a 'true Central Park' for the growing city of New York – and 'in some way the very ugliness of the meadows seemed to furnish inspiration, too' (ibid.). From 1930 onwards, Moses had the area rendered as prospective parkland on city maps and appropriated a quotation from Isaiah 61:3, 'to give unto them beauty for ashes', as a promotional slogan to put to potential backers.

The decision in 1934 to stage a World's Fair to celebrate the sesquicentenary of George Washington's first inauguration as first American President complemented the city's existing planning strategy. The city of New York had already begun purchasing portions of the dumping grounds from the Brooklyn Ash Company in 1934, with the contracts to dump ash being finally revoked two years later. It had also secured state and New Deal federal funds to initiate work to transform the marshlands and dump into an ordered landscape. Nevertheless, there is no doubt that the prospect of turning the area into an exposition showground drastically accelerated progress. The World's Fair Corporation relished the ample room available for the event – at 1,216 acres (492 hectares) it was the second-largest site ever made available for an Exposition – yet it would enjoy close links with downtown through excellent accessibility. Moreover, clearance could be presented as having few implications for existing private housing or property, with the forced eviction from Corona of a mostly Italian working-class community living on the eastern edge of the dump largely passing public notice (Montejo, 2017, 51). Under its agreement with the Fair Corporation, brokered by Moses, the city of New York agreed to fund the reclamation work within the time frame in return for receiving the site as municipal open space once the World's Fair was over. It would then be renamed Flushing Meadow Park (although was most often called Flushing Meadows).

Despite requiring the largest land reclamation project ever attempted in the eastern USA, the scheme was immediately attractive to the general public and city authorities alike

The large central portion of the site would house the main exhibit area and the narrower southern end, when developed around an artificial lake, offered good prospects for the amusement area (Santomasso, 1980, 30). The formal planning process began in January 1936 (Gold and Gold, 2005, 93–96). The city's mayor, Fiorello La Guardia, performed the groundbreaking ceremony on 19 June 1936. The contractors removed some of the ash to add to the hard core required for the highways being built in the vicinity of the park and levelled other mounds. Water mains and sewers were installed and the marshes drained. Difficult waterlogged or marshy areas were landscaped as lakes or water features (Steinberg, 2014). A series of associated infrastructural projects was undertaken to provide visitor access to the Fair, including constructing the Bronx-Whitestone Bridge and the Whitestone Expressway. Connections were needed to the recently built Grand Central Parkway, which ran alongside the showground. Other improvements included subway and railway extensions, new rail stations, a sewage plant for Bowery Bay, and La Guardia Airport (Kroessler, 1995, 1275). Dredging, which had been left incomplete in 1917, was recommenced to make Flushing Bay accessible by sea, with moorings for ocean-going vessels.

The immediate post-event history of the site proved complex. This was partly because of the outbreak of the Second World War, with the US Army occupying a swathe of the site's northern section, but rather more because the Fair's outstanding debts of £4.6 million – which caused the Fair Corporation to file for bankruptcy – prevented the city reinvesting the anticipated profits in order to realise Moses' grand parkland vision (Kroessler, 1995, 1276; Sabat, 2014). Unable to secure alternative finance, work began on a scaled-down version of 'Flushing Meadow Park'. The Fair's Beaux-Arts ground plan with its wide promenades was retained, along with some ceremonial architecture and elements of its landscaping. Most pavilions were demolished as planned, but a few were kept to house visitor attractions. The pedestrian bridges that had linked discrete sections of the showground were also retained (Montejo, 2017, 51).

The Park proved popular even in its incomplete state, although remained much less than the original conception. Hopes that a second New York World's Fair in 1964 (Stern et al. 1995, 1027–1057) might supply the profits for Park development that the first had failed to do were dashed when the latter produced an even larger deficit in comparative terms. While heavily used for recreation, the current layout remains much of the Exposition design. Nevertheless, the renamed Flushing Meadows-Corona Park did gain improved facilities, retained the 12-storey-high ceremonial model of the earth (Unisphere) from the 1964 show and gained some additional legacy features, such as the science museum and space park, the multipurpose Shea Stadium (1964–2008) and the stadium complex of the United States Tennis Association (1978-). As such, when audiences round the world tune in to watch the US Open tennis tournament, they see images of the Unisphere and its fountains – an annual reminder of Flushing Meadows' origins.

'The dioxin capital of the world'

In 1962, just six years after the successful Melbourne Summer Games, Sydney's Lord Mayor Henry Jensen argued that his city lacked the necessary major sports facilities that would allow it to stage major international competitions such as the Olympic or Commonwealth Games. To rectify this deficiency, Jensen proposed reclaiming a brickworks in St Peter's, a neighbourhood south of the city centre where, despite still producing bricks, the extensive clay pits had been used for landfill since 1948. His plan for sports investment would start with a stadium for the New South Wales rugby league team, followed by an athletics stadium, indoor arena, Olympic pool and cricket grounds (Little, 1997, 81). An Olympic bid was recognised as a way of leveraging the funds, with the idea gaining plausibility when the IOC ruled in 1965 that Olympic hosts henceforth would have to grant visas to admit East German athletes – something that Australia was prepared to do but that NATO countries had always refused to accept. Weighing up the prospects, the Australian Olympic Committee threw its weight behind the proposal to bid for the 1972 Summer Games.

The domestic timing, however, was not ideal. The Australian government was unwilling to commit to the bid given its problems with the severe cost overruns on the Sydney Opera House, on which construction had begun in March 1959. Internationally, too, the visa issue was resolved, thereby allowing bids from Montreal, Madrid and Munich (the eventual winner). Rehabilitation did occur in St Peter's but not for sports facilities. The land, purely brownfield now that all brick-making had ceased, was transferred to the city council in 1991, landscaped and transformed into a park containing wetlands, native species and remnant chimneys and kilns of the former brick works conserved as industrial heritage (City of Sydney, 2018).

The principle of looking to brownfield sites to achieve the multiple objectives of fast-tracking land reclamation and gaining world-class sports facilities through hosting a mega-event, however, had now been established. After fierce opposition arose to a campaign to bid for the 1988 Games with an Olympic Park based on the Moore Park-Centennial Park district, south east of downtown Sydney, the state government hired Walter Bunning, a leading architect-planner to consider the siting of a new sports complex. After evaluating 20 possible sites across the metropolitan area, Bunning's report recommended the development of surplus government land at Homebush Bay, another brownfield site situated approximately 9 miles (14 kilometres) west of Sydney's city centre on the Parramatta River (Freestone and Gunasekara, 2016, 320).

The bid for 1988 also foundered, but a further initiative to try to capture the 2000 Olympic Games emerged at the end of the 1980s. By this stage, other options had been set aside, with Homebush Bay as its clear focus. The bid was intended as much to address the host city's needs for infrastructural and environmental improvement as for seeking the prestige of hosting the mega-event. Key to its proposals was the objective of seeking a replacement for the

Royal Agricultural Society's outmoded showground at Moore Park and provide a cluster of modern world-class sports facilities. The bid also responded to the growing mood of environmentalism within Olympic circles, claiming that these would be a 'Green Games' expressing environmental responsibility in use of resources and design of facilities. At the outset, relative little was made of the proposal to reclaim brownfield land, which might well have been considered detrimental to the bid. Nevertheless, although reclamation of brownfield land was not yet highlighted as a positive feature of Olympic legacy as it would be for London 2012 (see below), it was relatively easy as the project developed to link the rhetoric of the Games as a force for good to the environmental transformation taking place at Homebush Bay.

Originally tidal wetlands and scrub, Homebush Bay had housed a remarkable mélange of noxious and polluting activities that covered around 395 acres (160 hectares). The area's occupants had included: large chemical-production companies built in the 1950s, which between them produced fertiliser, chlorine and, during the Vietnam War, Agent Orange; the country's largest abattoir, which had only closed in 1988; a saltworks; the state brickworks, which had left pits used for landfill that had included hazardous materials; and an armaments depot for the Navy. Some rehabilitation had already occurred (Cashman, 2008, 28), most notably, to produce the biodiverse Bicentennial Park, a technology park and an aquatic centre. Despite this, much of the area was still characterised as being 'one of Australia's worst toxic waste dumps' (Beder, 1993, 12) with many environmental problems being pervasive and resistant to treatment. Since the 1930s, the bay had regularly spawned algal blooms through contamination from waste products from the slaughterhouses and from the untreated household and industrial waste in the landfill sites. Some of the chemical plants dumped their pollutants directly into the harbour under lease from the former Maritime Services Board (Weirick, 1999, 76). Unpleasant smells habitually arose from materials trapped in the mangrove swamps. Perhaps of greatest significance was the presence of dioxins, highly toxic chemical compounds that pose serious risks for human health. Even at the time of the Games, the environmental group Green Games Watch still described the Olympic site at Homebush as 'the dioxin capital of the world' (Chipperfield, 2000).

When Sydney finally gained the nomination for the 2000 Games in September 1993, a key element in its candidacy was the promise to concentrate the Olympic venues in a central park at Homebush. Work to prepare the site started with human health and ecological risk assessments (Prasad, 1999, 84). These and other site surveys painted a picture of the site's complexity and fragility. They recognised the problems that stemmed from past interventions, for example, with areas of infill providing inadequate bases for siting the main stadia due to foundation problems and instabilities. Chemical remediation of the site proved more difficult than anticipated, with lingering doubts about the effectiveness of decontamination. Some applications of the more expensive aspects of green technology were omitted from the final scheme. Conscious of risk and timing, the Olympic Coordinating Authority bulldozed contaminated waste into four heaps, which were covered with clay and landscaped to provide grass-covered mounds that visitors could climb to gain views over the Park (Searle, 2012). The result, as one observer laconically noted, was that visitors would 'walk on nine million cubic metres of contaminated fill which has been buried beneath 'a metre of dirt and a mountain of public relations' (Chipperfield, 2000).

The experience of Sydney 2000 proved influential for subsequent games-makers in terms of their delivery (Cashman, 2008; Gold and Gold, 2017b, 53–55), operational organisation, memories of friendliness and for raising the international profile of the city, but questions surfaced in the medium-term about aspects of the Olympic Park. Besides problems over lack of affordable housing, the chequered history of the stadia and dashed hopes about the stimulus that the Games might give to Sydney's capabilities of drawing global investment and tourists, environmentalists have continued to question whether the decontamination of the toxic waste site had been fully tackled (Berlin, 2003). Above all, however, there were criticisms about the long delays in articulating a viable and comprehensive legacy plan. Three master plans appeared between 2002 and 2008 as the legacy agencies struggled to come to terms with post-event realities. An inevitable consequence was the lengthening of the time frame for delivering legacy from an initial 7–10 years to 22 years.

That lengthening of the timeframe has softened some of the criticisms. Stadia such as the Acer Arena (the former SuperDome indoor arena) have stabilised and expanded their customer bases and further rehabilitation works have improved lingering contamination. In his assessment of the first decade of progress, for example, Glen Searle (2012, 201) pointed out that the principal success: 'only very partially conceived before 2000, has been the ongoing development of a major employment and residential centre at Olympic Park that draws on the legacy of vacant remediated public land, rail access, sporting venues and abundant parkland left by the Games'. With the development of Newington and additional green space for the city's western suburbs, the major long-term positive legacy of staging the Olympic Games at Homebush lies in the benefits they have brought to Sydney's 'spatial structure rather than in any significant boost to overall economic development' (ibid., 202).

'A polluted wasteland'

A similar judgement might eventually be made for London 2012; the Games with which Sydney's experience most directly resonated. Like Homebush, the site of the main Olympic Park for London 2012 in the Lower Lea Valley was usable only with comprehensive detoxification. In addition, and notwithstanding its proximity to the financial heart of London a few miles to the west, the Lower Lea Valley also possessed an aura of marginality borne of its long association with heavy, sometimes noxious, industries and from being a dumping ground for waste products. Already a centre for milling and porcelain manufacture in the eighteenth century, London's nineteenth-century industrial expansion brought chemical industries, leather tanneries, cosmetic factories, match manufacturing, paint-making and the extensive locomotive depot and works of the Great Eastern Railway at Stratford. Sulphur, phosphorous, ammonia and coal products were stored onsite, with approved burial of toxic waste products. By the turn of the twenty-first century, much of this activity had gone due to relocation or closure. What remained was a strip of land exuding all the signs of deindustrialisation that ran roughly north–south on either side of the river and acted as a barrier to surrounding communities. Nevertheless, despite perhaps representing 'vast areas of nothing in particular' (Braden and Campany, 2016), it was far from being the *tabula rasa* that much early writing on London 2012 seemed to suggest. Comprising land still prone to waterlogging along its maze of meandering and water channels, it owed 'its integrity to its time as a polluted wasteland' (Read, 2017) and possessed an intricate matrix of small communities and unassuming economic activities. These included many small scale and a few larger business enterprises, scrap yards, utilities, a cluster of artists' studios in converted factory premises and a substantial social housing project at Carrs Lane, all alongside the redundant buildings and other characteristic remains of industrial decline.

The attractions quickly seen for nominating the Lower Lea Valley for use as an Olympic Park quickly revealed the extent to which ideas about future Games had moved on from the early 1990s. Thinking about staging a 'Green Games' with explicit concern for sustainability was still present, but the new emphasis on legacy, firmly embedded into IOC thinking from 2003 onwards, had come to the fore. That perception was clearly articulated in the bid documents and was a powerful factor behind proposals preferring East London rather than the West London locations favoured for the previous Games in 1908 and 1948. Development of the 607-acre (246-hectare) event space and the associated stadia, press and media centres and village would be made more expensive in the light of the costs of land remediation and site preparation. Nevertheless, if the proposal was accepted, the Lower Lea Valley could play a significant part in boosting the already ongoing regeneration of East London. In addition, the proposed Olympic Park was in the midst of predominantly multicultural districts that ranked among the England's poorest areas (Evans and Edizel, 2016). Developing an Olympic Park there might do more than just fast-track rehabilitation and urban regeneration, it could also mobilise mega-event investment as a vehicle to address multiple deprivation and social inequality.

Once London won the bid in July 2005, it was clear that land reclamation would receive the earliest attention. After completion of property acquisitions, a Global Remediation Strategy (GRS) was developed which:

> established the framework by which Site Specific Remediation Strategies (SSRS) were determined for each Olympic Park construction zone. Implementing this framework enabled sustainable soil and groundwater

remediation techniques to be planned and delivered and enabled more than 90 per cent of one million cubic metres of contaminated soil to be cleaned and reused on site. (OPDC, 2016)

Other planned works included rechannelling the water courses and removal of the electricity pylons that crisscrossed the park by burying the cables underground. As was inevitable for a site for which information about storage and tipping was incomplete, discoveries of unknown deposited materials were common. A 2010 report noted how a previously unrecorded quantity of toxic materials (vinyl chloride) and radioactive waste, illegally dumped by a firm that had left the area in 2006, had needed to be treated (Anon., 2010).

The close linkage between physical and social regeneration, however, would always be an essential part of London's emerging legacy plans. London indeed was the first Olympic city to set up a legacy body before staging its Games. Established in 2009, the Olympic Park Legacy Company (OPLC) had responsibility bounded by the limits of what would now be known as the Queen Elizabeth Olympic Park (QEOP). This was replaced in February 2012 by the London Legacy Development Corporation (LLDC), a body under the control of London's Mayor and with a remit to plan the redevelopment of the QEOP and the surrounding area in partnership with the private sector.

The original Legacy Master Plan identified the northern part of the Park as being characterised by waterways and landscaped parklands with the emphasis on outdoor recreation and biodiversity. By contrast, the southern area would contain the bulk of the housing and workplaces for the new inner-city district (postcode E20), with the only significant spaces there being leisure- and events-oriented. The conversion of the Athletes' Village, re-designated as the East Village, to offer 2,818 homes (with planning permission for a further 2500) would go ahead as soon as possible post-Games. A further five neighbourhoods, providing over 6,000 new homes, would subsequently appear, along with requisite educational and social facilities. Three new employment hubs would also appear, offering 7,000–8,000 new jobs.

Two key points relevant to the current debate have emerged from the legacy experience to date. First, the process of delivering the urban legacy has taken place in an environment where little or nothing is available from the public purse. Effective remediation of the land has converted the Lower Lea Valley into prime real estate. Hence despite the visions underpinning the grand plan-making, the need for private sector investment brings pressures that lead to compromise and change. Moreover, new ideas have crystalised that were not part of the original scheme. The decision to create a Cultural and Educational District on pieces of land wrapping around the Aquatics Centre ('Stratford Waterfront') has stymied the original plans for developing this as part of Marshgate Wharf, the largest of the five new neighbourhoods planned for the Park. This, in turn, has had implications for the quantity and character of new housing (see Evans, Chapter 3).

Secondly, critical attention is now firmly focused on the continuing inability to meet promises made about the social aspects of legacy, with profound suspicion that important elements will never be delivered. As recent literature indicates (e.g. Cohen and Watt, 2017; Evans, 2015), issues connected with the physical rehabilitation of the QEOP have now largely become taken-for-granted elements of the areas past (although construction on the periphery of Park not subject to the Olympic land clean-up continues to be hampered by polluted soil, e.g. at Hackney Wick). As such, they are increasingly absent from appraisals of progress relative to the consideration given to the perceived failings with reference to social legacy. This, in turn, is reflected in the narratives currently constructed with regard to the use of brownfield sites for mega-event spaces.

Narratives of transformation

These three case studies, spanning around 80 years of experience of using brownfield sites for event spaces, goes some way towards identifying underlying trends that transcend the idiosyncrasies of local experience. They also hint at broader narratives, raising questions about the plurality of histories constructed around the development and final disposition of event spaces and about the interests embodied in those histories (Burrow, 2009, xvi). In many ways, those narratives owe a debt to the 'Whig interpretation of history' (Butterfield, 1931) that has long dominated writings about both the Olympics and World's Fairs.

To elaborate, brownfield sites are seen from the viewpoint of an interpretative approach that selectively views the past in terms of the march towards ever greater achievement and enlightenment (Gold and Gold, 2011a, 123). Brownfield sites were 'badlands' in all senses of that word. Facing up to their problems decisively and building for the future could deliver not just improvement but also redemption.

For Robert Moses, this came with Biblical support. The short-term myopia of past policies had left a landscape despoiled by ash and toxic waste. His analogy, drawn as we have seen from Isaiah, saw the work necessary for the Fair as bringing about a garden to be enjoyed by all; redemption after the ravages of industrialisation. Homebush Bay had been a marginal place, providing 'dumping grounds for debris kept out of sight by being kept at a distance'. Now, however, it would be central through planned action to bring the 'focal point of Sydney's recreational activities to a rubbish dump at Homebush' (Coltheart, 2001, 6). The Lower Lea Valley in the official view was rendered as 'a polluted industrial site and a barrier to urban renewal' (OPLC, 2012, 3), a *tabula rasa* on which progress would be etched. Development would create 'places to live that are rooted in the ethos and fabric of East London's diverse and vital communities', places for 'Londoners who want to live and work without a long commute and raise a family in a stable urban community' and enjoy 'a healthy and sustainable lifestyle, anchored by sports and active living' (LLDC, 2014, 6, 12). Urban transformation brought by brownfield regeneration, then, was not just about improving the built environment, but it was also a vehicle for delivering the Good Life (Gold, 2008).

Writings on London, of course, were directly influenced by the legacy discourse and the sense that the future of the event space could be presented as being of co-equal importance with the staging of the Games. Similar ideas, however, were often expressed before, if not perhaps in precisely the same terms. For example, in a note written in 1964 (cited in Montejo, 2017, 48), Robert Moses suggested:

> The aftermath of a World's Fair is at least as significant as the Fair itself. Visitors to such an exposition carry away indelible impressions, lively lessons, enduring satisfactions and pleasant memories, but what finally remains on the ground when the pageant has faded, the brickbats have been removed by the wreckers and scavengers, and the park planners have gone to work, is of more concern to the next generation than any spectacle, however gorgeous.

Yet despite the sense of historic continuity that this conveys, notions concerning legacy, like any other story told about urban development, is based on a narrative, and narratives do change (Gold and Gold, 2011b). The lengthy time frame in which legacy is embedded – 80 years in the case of Flushing Meadows – means that evaluation of the use of brownfield land requires a lengthy longitudinal view. As with thinking about the festivals themselves, there is no guarantee that ideas about the planned outcomes of mega-events will not by then have moved on.

References

Alker, S., Joy, V., Roberts, P. and Smith, N. (2000) 'The definition of brownfield', *Journal of Environmental Planning and Management*, 43, 49–69.

Anon (2010) 'Clearing toxic waste from London 2012 site cost £12.7m'. Available online at: www.bbc.co.uk/news/uk-england-london-11750688, accessed 19 November 2018.

Ballon, H. and Jackson, K.T. (eds) (2007) *Robert Moses and the Modern City: The Transformation of New York*. New York: Norton.

Beder, S. (1993) 'Sydney's toxic green Olympics', *Current Affairs Bulletin*, 70(6), 12–18.

Berlin, P. (2003) 'What did the Olympics bring Sydney?' *New York Times*, 24 December. Available online at: www.nytimes.com/ 2003/12/24/news/24iht-t1_2.html, accessed 20 November 2018.

Braden, P. and Campany, D. (2016) 'Olympic legacy: Photographing the Lea Valley', *Guardian*, 7 December. Available online at: www.theguardian.com/artanddesign/ga llery/2016/dec/07/adventures-in-the-lea-valley-polly-braden-david-campany-photo graphy, accessed 20 November 2018.

Burrow, J. (2009) *A History of Histories*. Harmondsworth: Penguin.

Butterfield, H. (1931) *The Whig Interpretation of History*. London: George Bell and Sons.

Caro, R. (1974) *The Power Broker: Robert Moses and the Fall of New York*. New York: Knopf.

Cashman, R. (2008) 'The Sydney Olympic Park Model: Its Evolution and Realization'. In A. Hay and R. Cashman (eds) *Connecting Mega Events Cities: A Publication for the 9th World Congress of Metropolis*. Sydney: Sydney Olympic Park Authority, 21–39.

Chipperfield, M. (2000) 'Sydney in bad odour over toxic backyard for Olympic Games', *The Telegraph*, 27 August. Available online at: www.telegraph.co.uk/news/worldnews/australiaandthepacific/1367883/Sydney-in-bad-odour-over-toxic-backyard-for-Olympic-Games.html, accessed 19 November 2018.

Christensen, P. and Kyle, D.G. (2014) 'General Introduction', in P. Christensen and D. G. Kyle (eds) *A Companion to Sport and Spectacle in Greek and Roman Antiquity*. Chichester: Wiley Blackwell, 1–15.

City of Sydney (2018) History of Sydney Park. Available online at: www.cityofsydney. nsw.gov.au/learn/sydneys-history/people-and-places/park-histories/sydney-park, accessed 3 June 2018.

Cohen, P. and Watt, P. (eds) (2017) *London 2012 and the Post-Olympics City: A Hollow Legacy*. Basingstoke: Palgrave Macmillan.

Coltheart, L. (2001) *Making the Magic: An Outline History of the Olympic Coordination Authority NSW*. Sydney: Olympics Coordination Authority.

Evans, G.L. (2015) 'Designing legacy and the legacy of design: London 2012 and the Regeneration Games', *Architectural Review Quarterly*, 18(4): 353–366.

Evans, G. and Edizel, Ö. (2016) 'London 2012'. In J.R. Gold and M.M. Gold (eds) *Olympic Cities: City Agendas, Planning, and the World's Games, 1896–2016*. 3rd edition. London: Routledge, 359–389.

Fitzgerald, F.S. (1925) *The Great Gatsby*. New York: Charles Scribner's Sons.

Freestone, R. and Gunasekara, S. (2016) 'Sydney 2000'. In J.R. Gold and M.M. Gold (eds) *Olympic Cities: City Agendas, Planning, and the World's Games, 1896–2016*. 3rd edition. London: Routledge, 317–332.

Gemmill, J.H. (2012) 'The role of an agency in setting the policy agenda'. Unpublished PhD thesis, Auburn University, Auburn, AL. Available online at: https://etd.auburn.edu/bitstream/handle/10415/3125/GemmillDissertation%2005072012.final.pdf?sequence=2&ts=1437112033083, accessed 12 November 2018.

Girginov, V. (2018) *Rethinking Olympic Legacy*. London: Routledge.

Gold, J.R. (2008) 'Modernity and Utopia'. In P. Hubbard, T. Hall and J.R. Short (eds) *The Sage Companion to the City*. London: Sage, 67–86.

Gold, J.R. and Gold, M.M. (2005) *Cities of Culture: Staging International Festivals and the Urban Agenda, 1851–2000*. Farnham: Ashgate.

Gold, J.R. and Gold, M.M. (2011a) 'Introduction'. In J.R. Gold and M.M. Gold, *Olympic Cities: City Agendas, Planning, and the World's Games, 1896–2012*. 2nd edition. London: Routledge, 17–55.

Gold, J.R. and Gold, M.M. (2011b) 'The History of Events: Ideology and Historiography'. In S. Page and J. Connell (eds) *Routledge Handbook of Event Studies*. London: Routledge, 119–128.

Gold, J.R. and Gold, M.M. (2013) 'Bring it under the legacy umbrella': Olympic host cities and the changing fortunes of the sustainability agenda', *Sustainability*, 5, 3526–3542.

Gold, J.R. and Gold, M.M. (2017a) 'Introduction'. In J.R. Gold and M.M. Gold (eds) *Olympic Cities: City Agendas, Planning, and the World's Games, 1896–2020*. 3rd edition. London: Routledge, 1–17.

Gold, J.R. and Gold, M.M. (2017b) *Olympic Cities: City Agendas, Planning, and the World's Games, 1896–2020.* 3rd edition. London: Routledge.

Gold, J.R. and Gold, M.M. (2018) 'Urban Segments and Event Spaces: World's Fairs and Olympic Sites'. In C. Hein (ed) *The Routledge Handbook of Planning History.* London: Routledge, 348–363.

Harnik, P., Taylor, M. and Welle, B. (2006) 'From dumps to destinations: The conversion of landfills to parks', *Places*, 18, 83–88.

Jenkins, R. (2008) *The First London Olympics 1908.* London: Piatkus.

Kroessler, J.A. (1995) 'World's Fairs'. In K.T. Jackson (ed) *The Encyclopedia of New York City.* New Haven, CT: Yale University Press, 1275–1276.

Kuhn, J. (1995) 'Flushing Meadows-Corona Park'. In K.T. Jackson (ed) *The Encyclopedia of New York City.* New Haven, CT: Yale University Press, 420.

Little, C. (1997) 'From one brickpit to another: The ancient history of the Sydney Olympic bid', *Sporting Traditions*, 14, 79–90.

LLDC (London Legacy Development Corporation) (2014) *A Walk around the Olympic Park.* London: LLDC.

Loures, L. and Vaz, E. (2018) 'Exploring expert perception towards brownfield redevelopment benefits according to their typology', *Habitat International*, 72, 66–76.

Mattie, E. (1998) *World's Fairs.* New York: Princeton University Press.

Montejo, F. (2017) 'Life after mega-events: Strategically reusing legacy parks'. Unpublished masters dissertation in city planning, Massachusetts Institute of Technology, Cambridge, MA.

OPLC (Olympic Park Legacy Company) (2012) *Creating the Queen Elizabeth Olympic Park: Post-Games Transformation.* London: OPLC.

OPDC (2016) *Decontamination Strategy: Local Plan Supporting Study.* London: Old Oak and Park Royal Development Corporation / Mayor of London. Available online at: www.london.gov.uk/sites/default/files/old_oak_land_contamination_guida nce_vnov_new_cover.pdf, accessed 21 November 2018.

Prasad, D. (1999) 'Environment'. In R. Cashman and A. Hughes (eds) *Staging the Olympics: The Event and its Impact.* Sydney: University of New South Wales Press, 83–92.

Preuss, H. (2015) 'A framework for identifying the legacies of a mega sport event', *Leisure Studies*, 34, 643–664.

Read, S. (2017) *Cinderella River: The Evolving Narrative of the River Lee.* London: Hydrocitizenship. Available online at: http://eprints.mdx.ac.uk/23299/1/Cinderella% 20River%20-%20Low%20Resolution%20pr.pdf, accessed 20 November 2019.

Sabat, M. (2014) 'Panorama: Robert Moses' Modern City and the New York World's Fairs'. In L. Hollengreen, C. Pearce, R. Rouse and B. Schweizerin (eds) *Meet Me at the Fair: A World's Fair Reader.* Pittsburgh, PA: the Editors and the ETC Press, 281–288.

Santomasso, E.A. (1980) 'The Design of Reason: Architecture and Planning at the 1939/40 New York World's Fair'. In H.A. Harrison (ed.) *Dawn of a New Day: The New York World's Fair.* New York: Queen's Museum / New York University Press, 29–41.

Searle, G. (2012) 'The long term urban impacts of the Sydney Olympic Games', *Australian Planner*, 49, 195–202.

SOPA (Sydney Olympic Park Authority) (2009) *Master Plan 2030: A New Master Plan for Sydney's Newest Suburb.* Sydney: Sydney Olympic Park Authority.

Steinberg, T. (2014) *Gotham Unbound: The Ecological History of Greater New York.* New York: Simon & Schuster.

Stern, R.A.M., Mellins, T. and Fishman, D. (1995) *New York 1960: Architecture and Urbanism between the Second World War and the Bicentennial.* New York: Monacelli Press.

Tomlinson, A. (2014) 'Olympic legacies: Recurrent rhetoric and harsh realities', *Contemporary Social Science*, 9, 137–158.

Tomlinson, A. (ed.) (2016) *The Olympic Legacy: Social Scientific Explorations.* London: Routledge.

Weirick, J. (1999) 'Urban Design'. In R. Cashman and A. Hughes (eds) *Staging the Olympics: The Event and its Impact.* Sydney: University of New South Wales Press, 70–82.

3 From Albertopolis to Olympicopolis
Back to the future?

Graeme Evans

Introduction

The early Victorian *Albertopolis* project has been used by today's politicians and their agencies as an inspiration and model for a new cultural and education quarter to be developed in the Queen Elizabeth Olympic Park, coined *Olympicopolis* by the outgoing Mayor of London (2008–2016), Boris Johnson. There are a number of obvious, but also significant parallels to these examples of placemaking and culture-led regeneration (Evans, 2014). Both represent a paradigm of art and industry through technological and global cultural forces in eras of early and late capitalism, but which belie the claims, then and now, of cultural democracy and access that their proponents use in order to justify both public spending and support.

Great Exhibitions and culture-led regeneration

The 1851 'Great Exhibition of the Works of Industry of All Nations' generated a surplus of over £186,000. This was primarily used by Prince Albert to purchase nearly 90 acres of land stretching southwards from Kensington Gore in the area to be known as *Albertopolis* to house the complex of museums, colleges and institutions (today this includes the V&A Museum, Science Museum, National History Museum, Royal College of Art, Imperial College University, Royal College of Music, the Albert Hall and the Royal Geographic Society) that, it was hoped, would celebrate the interplay of the arts and science and technology and their application to industry, which the Exhibition itself had sought to catalyse and represent. In 1862 its sequel, the International Exhibition, was built on the newly constructed Cromwell Road, although less popular and less financially successful than its predecessor. Both exhibitions attracted over 6 million visits equivalent then to a third of the country's population, triggering the building boom which transformed the area from a rural landscape of farms, nurseries and market gardens into a prosperous metropolitan area (this compares with the 6.5 million visitors to the *Millennium Dome Experience* which ran for 12 months in 2000, and the 10 million visits to the Festival of Britain which ran from May to September 1951). Unlike in 1851 with the Crystal Palace in Hyde Park rebuilt

and extended in its new south east London location, the 1862 Exhibition structure was demolished two years later, to eventually be the site for the Natural
History Museum which opened in 1881, further expanding London's prime
museum quarter.

A Victorian example then, of what today is termed event or culture-led
regeneration (Evans, 2005; 2015), as is being played out in the Olympic Park and
adjoining neighbourhoods of Stratford and Hackney Wick in east London. Like
the Queen Elizabeth Olympic Park, this Victorian placemaking *grand projet* was
enabled by new transport links with the inexorable expansion of the railways
from the 1830s, which led to Lord Kensington selling his defunct canal to the
railway entrepreneurs connecting London to Birmingham and beyond, and to
south of the river. In the early twenty-first century over £6 billion in public
money had been invested in extending the channel tunnel rail link (CTRL), the
East London line and Docklands Light Railway station upgrades to Stratford.
Prior to this, over £3.5 billion had already been spent in extending the Jubilee
Underground Line (JLE) from central to south and east London, in so doing,
effectively saving the ailing Canary Wharf property development, connecting the
Millennium Festival Dome at Greenwich peninsula, and fuelling a two-thirds
increase in the number of visitor attractions and accommodation provision in the
new JLE corridor between 1993 and 2000 (Evans and Shaw, 2001).

A fundamental difference between then and today, therefore, is that the
contemporary 'urban cultural renaissance' (Evans, 2001) has been pre-
dominately publicly funded by the state (i.e. taxpayers), albeit for substantial
private benefit to commercial developers, landlords/holders and investors.
Notwithstanding the massive state investment to develop and stage the
London 2012 Olympics – nearly £10 billion – and ongoing investment by the
London Legacy Development Corporation,[1] the government's HM Treasury
has pledged an additional £141 million of government funding towards the
Olympicopolis project, which they predict will deliver over 3,000 jobs,
attract 1.5 million additional visitors to London and generate £2.8 billion
of economic value to Stratford. In the words of the then Chancellor,
George Osborne: 'this will secure the legacy of our wonderful Olympic
Games, as well as creating thousands of jobs and boosting London's
economy by an estimated £95m each year' (Murphy, 2014, 6).

The Great Exhibition of 1851 and subsequent exhibitions had in contrast been
financed by private subscription, whilst entrepreneurs and industrialists had
developed much of the infrastructure, and until this first 'industrial turn', supported much cultural provision for workers and urban settlements where they
operated. So the claim that the success of *Albertopolis* and the legacy of cultural
institutions illustrate the strength of Victorian policies on cultural democracy
and the importance of state support for the arts (Roth, 2015) is debatable.[2]
Indeed, whilst Prince Albert through his presidency of the Royal Society of Arts
promoted the Great Exhibition, Queen Victoria on her accession had stopped
the annual grant to the patent theatres, an early example of a cut in state arts
funding (Pick, 1997).

In the previous century, the government had already signalled its support of national museums and galleries in the 1750s with the purchase of Soane's paintings for the nation, whilst the Royal Family had supported the arts for several centuries, before municipal and philanthropic (individual and industrial) provision had laid the foundations for a range of cultural amenities and opportunities 'for all'. The eighteenth century had seen integration of the arts (music, poetry, dramatic ritual) with commercial tasks, with many examples of employers who felt that their duties to their employees did not end with work, but should include a rich cultural environment. Best known perhaps was the Welsh textiles industrialist, Robert Owen, with his model society at New Lanark, Scotland in which every child was taught to read, write and sing; or John Strutt in Derbyshire who gave his workers time off to receive free musical tuition (so successful that the best players were poached and offered work elsewhere as music teachers). As Ruskin proclaimed: 'Life without industry is guilt, and industry without art is brutality' (1870 in Pick, 1997, 2). Birmingham also, whose population like London had dramatically increased (threefold from 1800 to 1851), was able to offer its workers plays, pantos, waxworks, panoramas, firework displays, concerts, and circus shows – enjoyed across social boundaries, whilst pleasure gardens in London and elsewhere provided a rich cultural diversity for Victorian's leisure time. Up and until the period to the Great Exhibition, art and industry – 'skill and hard work' – were neither exclusive nor in opposition, and: 'it would be wrong to think of music, literature and the visual arts as mere embellishments of commercial activity ... for long periods the arts were themselves an integral part of the wider commercial world' (Pick, 1997, 5).

Art and industry

In the post-1851 era, the Victorian factory system also advanced, making fundamental changes to the ways in which the working population lived. Carlyle among others had begun to use the word 'industry' in a new, perjorative way – no longer referring to 'hard work and diligence', but to more organised forms of mechanical reproduction transforming our way of life, captured in Carlyle's term 'the industrial revolution', signifying not just the changing nature of work and economy but social and cultural relationships and values. This contrasted for example with Wedgwood's employees who worked a shift, not piece-work system, with both men and women trained in a range of recognised art and crafts skills (his pottery bore the distinctive stamp of the individual designers who worked with him), but with few of the production line efficiencies that were to be adopted in the mechanised industrial revolution that the Great Exhibition had both celebrated and promoted.

This was reflected in the categorisation of the 13,000 exhibits on display into raw materials, machinery, manufactures and 'fine art', which arguably marked a further shift in the sub-division of art with fine art equated to the high skills applied to industrial products, as Pick maintains: 'the Great

Exhibition hastened the creation of the two distinct categories of fine art – one "design", forward looking, and the other, "crafts" concerned with the skills of the past' (Pick and Anderton, 2013). Indeed, the former director, Roy Strong, had proposed to suffix the V&A, with the 'National Museum of Decorative Art & Design'. As the V&A's first director, Henry Cole, concluded after the 1851 Exhibition: 'the history of the world records no event comparable in its promotion of human industry' (in Pick, 1997, 7). However, one of the key visions for the event was that of 'unity' (another key term used by the Exhibition's proponents was 'civilisation', directly equated with industrial development): 'as if the Fine Arts, the new factory systems, science and commerce were still united industriously pursuing common goals' (Pick, 1997, 7). This had been a founding aim of Prince Albert and Henry Cole on the formation of the original 'Museum of Manufactures', and the application of fine art to manufacturing, which was created to house objects purchased from the 1851 Exhibition, and its later manifestation as the Museum of Ornamental Art (then the South Kensington Museum), to today's V&A Museum – in this transition, effectively losing this art and science link.

Hard times

Shortly after the Great Exhibition, Charles Dickens published *Hard Times*, capturing the spirit-breaking mechanics of life in a newly created *Coketown*, where music, entertainment and recreation could no longer be a part of the working day, but a separate solace or sop – even a threat – to the new work ethic. This also cemented the divide between what today is termed the high and low/popular arts, between the entertaining leisure of pleasure gardens, showmen, music halls and popular publishing, and the worthy activities offered by civic and church authorities such as libraries, museums, galleries and improving 'lectures' – which meant that for the first time a real choice in how Victorians could spend what time they had left for leisure. The Exhibition event itself had exercised price and social discrimination – firstly open to the leisured classes, the 'great folks' who paid 5 shillings for admission in relative comfort, or on other days to the working classes who came in much greater numbers (as many as 70,000 daily), but paying only 1 shilling, with the 'working bees of the world's hives' being offered inferior facilities to view an exhibition supposedly glorifying their industriousness' (Pick and Anderton, 2013). The high arts-popular dialectic was also evident from observers such as Ruskin who 'dismissed the Crystal Palace as being neither a palace nor of crystal, but merely a glass envelope to exhibit the paltry arts of our fashionable luxury' (in Pick and Anderton, 2013, 135). Cultural production had been led by an expanding consumption market which drove the crafts and design manufacturing industries, as John Store Smith observed: 'the middle class family now possesses carpets and hangings … and not a few of our London middle-class tradesmen possess a better stock of family plate and linen than many a country squire' (Store Smith, 1972 in Pick and Anderton, 2013, 125).

The event had also generated what today would be a case of arts, or rather Olympics sponsorship – the drinks company Schweppes had paid £5,500 for the franchise and sold over 1 million bottles of their soft drinks. Coca-Cola, one of the main franchisees of the modern Olympics, contributes £64 million every four years. During the 17 days of the London 2012 Games, Coca-Cola served 18 million of its sugary products (Evans, 2019). Another Olympics parallel is the impact from this hallmark event on established arts providers and merchants who suffered from their trade being diverted to Hyde Park for the 1851 season, as the Exhibition soaked up both public support and spare capital – a complaint also aimed at the London 2012 Olympics where the government had diverted significant Lottery funding from designated 'Good Causes' and other parts of the country, to the capital-hungry Stratford enterprise in east London (Evans, 2016b).

The imperial Great Exhibitions also further cemented the dual cultural hegemony that had been reinforced as the nineteenth century progressed with English (and French) cultural production starting to dominate publishing, theatre and crafts, as early cultural globalisation was fuelled by the expanding Empires and industrialisation (Sassoon, 2006). The World's Fairs had originated in the French tradition of national exhibitions, a tradition that culminated with the French imperial Industrial Exposition of 1844 held in Paris, following on from a series of great exhibitions which had begun in the seventeenth century with exhibitions of works of art (predating the first Venice Biennale in 1895). These were held biannually from 1667 to 1793, and from 1793 to 1802 they were annual, before reverting to a biannual pattern under the French Empire. Along with the art exhibitions were exhibitions of French manufactured goods, which although not international in scope were the more direct ancestors of the universal exhibitions (Daniels, 2013). As Greenhalgh observed: 'the importance of these for Government at the time was evident; they were no mere trade fairs or festival celebrations, they were outward manifestations of a nation attempting to flex economic, national, military, and cultural muscles' (Greenhalgh, 1988, 6).

The Great Exhibition in London had also been preceded by two smaller exhibitions which were staged by the Royal Society of Arts in 1844 and 1849: 'wedding high art with mechanical skill' (Pick and Anderton, 2013, 135). The 1851 Great Exhibition was also an explicit advert for the British export industry, with the majority of exhibits coming from the Empire and predominantly Britain's manufacturing cities, for example Sheffield had 300 exhibits, from railway springs, vices, anvils to newly designed fenders and kettles. As Herbert Read observed in *Art and Industry*:

> Those splendid institutions in Trafalgar Square and South Kensington, now treasure-houses which attract pilgrims of beauty from every corner in the world, were first conceived as aids to the manufacturer in his struggle with foreign competitors. The National Gallery and the Victoria & Albert Museum in London, prototypes of similar institutions all over the world,

were not founded as Temples of Beauty but as cheap and accessible schools of design. (Read, 1932 in Pick and Anderton, 2013, 138)

The surplus generated from the event it was hoped, would help to set up museums in the leading industrial cities, but the balance was only sufficient to purchase the South Kensington Estate. The resentment and lack of support for the London 2012 Olympic event from the regions that was evident from the national population attitude surveys conducted by government (notably in Scotland – Evans, 2016b), was also present in 1851, with London capturing the legacy and financial benefits. Provincial industrialists responded to the London event with estates purchased and used for 'pleasure parks', such as Adderley Park in Birmingham (1856), the Arboretum in Nottingham (1852) built in the style of Crystal Palace, the Manchester Exhibition at Old Trafford Park (1857), and Kelvingrove, which housed the 1888 Glasgow International Exhibition, and which in turn raised funds for the Kelvingrove art gallery and museum.

Olympicoplis and masterplanning

Albertopolis was an idea developed by Prince Albert via the Royal Society of Arts, whilst *Olymicopolis* has been coined to reflect the London Mayor's Olympic legacy vision in 2013,[3] which clearly referenced the Victorian era: 'The idea behind Olympicopolis is simple and draws on the extraordinary foresight of our Victorian ancestors. We want to use Queen Elizabeth Olympic Park as a catalyst for the industries and technologies in which London now leads the world in order to create thousands of new jobs'. So the continuity between industry and the arts is evident here, with manufacturing industry now replaced by the creative, high-tech and 'knowledge' industries represented by a roll call of education and cultural institutions, including University College London, London College of Fashion (University of the Arts London), new satellite venues of Sadlers Wells Dance Theatre, V&A Museum and relocated Archives, and BBC3, joining a new outpost of Loughborough University already based in the former Olympic Press & Broadcasting Centre rebranded *Here East* (Figure 3.1), which also houses the broadcaster BT Sport and innovation centre, Plexal.

> East Bank is a new £1.1 billion powerhouse of culture, education, innovation and growth being built on the Queen Elizabeth Olympic Park. Spread across three sites – UCL East (UCL's new campus), Stratford Waterfront (BBC, the V&A, Sadler's Wells and UAL's London College of Fashion) and Here East (the V&A's new collection and Research Centre, and an existing space for UCL). It will open in 2021 with the Stratford Waterfront site opening from 2022. A brand new destination for London with world class culture and education at its heart. (Construction site hoarding, Olympic Park, 2019)

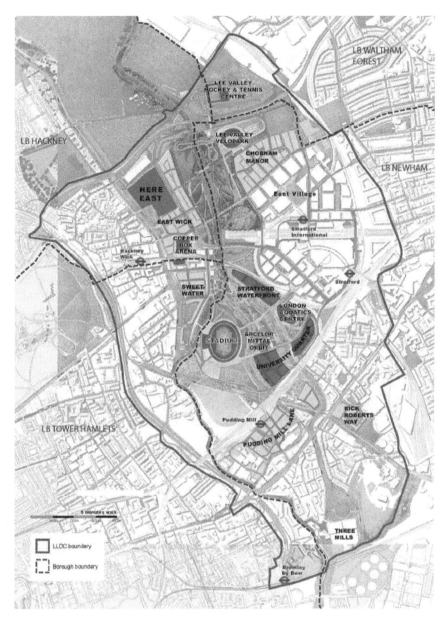

Figure 3.1 Olympic Park development zones, showing proposed Stratford Waterfront
and Olympicopolis quarter

Source: author, and see Evans, 2015.

Thus, in the eyes of the Mayor's legacy development corporation: 'creating a focus for investment and growth – emulating the legacy left in South Kensington by the Great Exhibition, we will promote the Mayor's vision for *Olympicopolis*, comprising cultural facilities, education and research institutions and workspaces, to stimulate job creation and economic growth across east London' (LLDC, 2014, 18).

A summary of the proposed plans for outposts of these institutions at the time of writing includes (and see Murphy, 2014, 6):

> A new V&A museum and exhibition venue for 'blockbuster' events of 20,000 m^2, to also be available for other institutions. Creating space for some 2.5million V&A treasures which cannot be shown in the main museum. (A proposal for a separate Smithsonian Institution with 3,700 m^2 exhibition gallery space has been shelved, instead collaboration with the V&A is planned).
>
> Sadler's Wells Dance theatre with 550 seats which will allow a wider range of new contemporary and popular dance, including for the English National Opera and Young Vic, who may also use it. A choreography school is also planned, allowing London to compete with the Brussels school, and a New York-style hip-hop academy
>
> University College London (UCL) campus to the south of Accelor Mittal Orbit of 50,000 m^2 for 4,000 students, including a design school, with a focus on robotics, smart cities, culture and conservation. A second phase could see it double in size: "UCL East will be another glittering jewel in the world class constellation of intellectual and cultural riches taking shape in the Queen Elizabeth Olympic Park". (Johnson, 2013)
>
> University of the Arts London (UAL) campus opposite the Aquatics centre, bring together all six of the university's campuses of the London College of Fashion (6,500 students), on one major site, developing synergies with Sadler's Wells' costume department and the V&A, including V&A Archives collection at nearby Here East.

These plans are provisional, and in some respects speculative, since few of the prospective organisations have secured all of the funding which will in several cases be reliant on the sale of properties elsewhere, and a new (Labour Party) Mayor has been in post since May 2016, replacing the Conservative, Boris Johnson. The total capital cost of the *Olympicopolis* development is put at £1.3 billion so the government contribution is a little over 10% of this target, and a major fundraising effort will therefore be required. This is being led by a new body, the Foundation for Future London ('The Olympicopolis Charity') that has taken over responsibility for the development from the Mayor's London Legacy Development Corporation (LLDC) with a remit to ensure that local communities and the broader public realise the social and economic benefits accruing from the

Figure 3.2 Panoramic view of Stratford Waterfront site under construction facing 'Stratford International Quarter'
Source: author, 2019.

Figure 3.3 Stratford Waterfront design facing the Olympic Stadium, showing London College of Fashion, V&A Museum, Sadler's Wells Theatre and BBC3
Source: Allies and Morrison/LLDC, 2019.

new Cultural and Education District, now known as 'East Bank' (with reference to London's South Bank cultural quarter), to be created in the heart of Queen Elizabeth Olympic Park. This body had itself emerged from the former Olympic Park Legacy Company and prior to this, the Olympic Development Agency which developed the sports facilities on the Olympic site. In contrast, the Royal Commission for the Exhibition of 1851 was established in 1850 by Queen Victoria to organise The Great Exhibition with Prince Albert appointed as President, and still acts as landlord for much of the *Albertopolis* estate today.

The reality is however, that fewer new homes will be built in the Olympic Park area than originally planned in 2004, in part as a result of the *Olympicopolis* project. The masterplan for the Olympic site gave permission for 10,000 homes (mainly one/two bedroom apartments), but in the revised plan in 2010 this had been reduced to 8,000, with family housing at the centre of the plan, inspired by London's great estates such as Grosvenor and Portland (Geoghegan, 2014). By 2012 a further 1,000 planned homes had been cut from this lower target to accommodate the new cultural hub. The Mayor's rationale for this trade-off is that it would lead to more homes being built in the wider east London area in the future; however, capital receipts from land sales for housing in the Olympic Park zone are required for the Mayor's Legacy Corporation (LLDC) to repay loans and Lottery funding used to finance the site and Park redevelopment. The bland and highly cost-engineered housing emerging in and around the Olympic Park[4] (including the converted Athlete's Village housing) owes little to the Georgian and Regency styles of the eighteenth- and nineteenth-century estates in Belgravia and Soho that the masterplanners envisaged, and this provides another *Back to the Future* example of how history and the cultural past is appropriated and interpreted to provide a rhetorical image of progress and benefits (Evans, 2015).

This is also reflected in the *Olymicopolis* vision, in the words of the new Foundation:

> these new facilities will strengthen the Park's offer for national and inter-national visitors, but also create a home for skilled artists, designers, tea-chers, engineers, scientists, architects and craftspeople – and the global companies that need this talent. These people will live and work throughout east London, but the Park will be the fulcrum of growth and a new symbol of London as a global powerhouse of creativity, learning and development

– or to put it more succinctly: 'we are in east London, of east London, and for east London'.[5] This is an indication of both the deferred gratification and place branding that risks undermining social sustainability. Affordability of the new housing is a barrier, since for actual property purchase, the value of a one-bed apartment would require borrowing of more than five times the average earnings of a Newham borough resident, while 'affordable' rent can represent 80% of market rates under current government guidelines.

Creative quarter

East London has historically and still today contains a very high proportion of London (and the UK's) practising artists and designers – from crafts/ designer-making to digital media – with clusters from Clerkenwell on the city fringe, through Hackney to Stratford. This historic association with place also reflects the industries that occupied these poorer parts of the city as London's 'cultural workshop' (Foord, 1999), including the Lee Valley that traverses the Olympic site, and where textiles, armoury/metalworks, food manufacturing/confectionery and early electronics and plastics were developed and made for home consumption and export. Like the semi-rural Kensington, the area also served as a market garden as well as the source of clean drinking water to a growing London population and as processor of most of its waste via waterways, sewers and pumping mills with the world's largest mill wheels at Three Mills, Bow. This Grade I listed mill building co-hosts an established cluster of creative practice, including London's largest film and TV studios and ancillary services, including 9 filming stages and 12 theatre spaces, the largest with the same floor size as the Royal Albert Hall arena in South Kensington, making it one of the only indoor venues suitable for large scale ballet, theatre and opera rehearsals. Located just outside the LLDC boundary to the south of the Olympic Park, this historic building and site frequently suffers from flooding, since the hydrological engineering undertaken to protect the Park and venues from flood risk, has effectively pushed this risk immediately outside to these adjoining areas.

The point here also, is that this history and legacy of crafts-based design and innovation, industrial heritage and the contemporary concentration of artists and new designers is not reflected or represented in the *Olympicopolis* vision or cultural plans, but rather a Guggenheim-style import of established cultural institutions without a vernacular reference. This existing cultural quarter had already been recognised in successive cultural and creative policy initiatives prior to the Olympics, including the former Mayor's Creative London strategy which designated Stratford and Hackney Wick (either side of the Olympic Park) as one of the city's ten 'Creative Hubs' (LDA, 2003). More than a quarter of the UK's artists' studio buildings were located in the five Olympic host boroughs (Greenwich, Hackney, Newham, Tower Hamlets, and Waltham Forest) prior to the Olympic redevelopment, but much of this has been sacrificed – 10,000 square feet of studio space lost in the build up to 2012 with only small-scale and fragmented new provision in otherwise soulless new developments (NFA, 2008). Stratford, where the *Olympicopolis* Waterfront development is to be located, had also been the focus of regional arts and economic development strategies prior to the Olympic project, with the creation of Stratford's cultural quarter, the extension of the Theatre Royal Stratford East and new arthouse cinema, and University of East London campus. So the presumption that the area was a cultural wasteland in need of a cultural regeneration makeover, is perhaps patronising and ignores several hundred years of arts and industrial creativity and innovation. Indeed, the Labour Mayor who has inherited the *Olympicopolis* project, has designated the Hackney Wick & Fish Island quarter overlooking the Olympic stadium and divided from the Olympic Park by the Lee Valley

Navigation canal, as one of his Creative Enterprise Zones. Unfortunately, before this 2–3 year initiative had started in 2019, affordable workspace, cultural facilities and local businesses have been displaced or priced out of a market dominated by commercial residential development, ironically promoted and granted planning permission by the Mayor's own legacy corporation (LLDC).

Fun palace

Close to the Zaha Hadid-designed Aquatic Centre where the *Olympicopolis* and University quarter are to be located at Mill Meads, another visionary structure was to be developed in the early 1960s – Cedric Price's *Fun Palace*, conceived in response to Joan Littlewood's brief, from her base at the nearby Theatre Royal Stratford East. An idea which, although embracing notions of heterotopia and possibilities of new technology, also descended from the Victorian and earlier Pleasure Gardens, Piers and People's Palaces.

The Fun Palace popularised as a 'laboratory of fun' and 'a university of the streets' was based on a design concept that was prescient in many ways – temporary and flexible, with: 'no permanent structures.no concrete stadia stained and cracking, no legacy of noble architecture, quickly dating' (Littlewood, 1964, 433). Price's vision was for a 'new kind of active and dynamic architecture which would permit multiple uses and which would constantly adapt to change ... thinking of the Fun Palace in terms of process, as events in time rather than objects in space' (Matthews, 2005, 79). The building would have no single entry point and divide into activity zones.

Price and Littlewood had assembled a multi-disciplinary team from architecture, art, theatre, technology, and even Situationists, with cybernetics and game theory driving the facility's day to day behaviour and performative strategies which would be stimulated through feedback from users. Price's seminal design (strongly influencing the Pompidou Centre, Paris; and in part realised in Price's Inter-Action Centre, north London), although adopted at the time by the Civic Trust, was never realised, the victim of London's reorganisation into 33 boroughs with the London County Council transferring the open spaces to a new benign Lea Valley Parks Authority. The Fun Palace presented both a challenge to, and break from, the hegemonic academy and museum which in Hooper-Greenhill's view discloses, 'the disciplinary practices ... as a clearly political institution committed to enhance and implement structures of authority and power' (Hooper-Greenhill, 1992), but from which the *Olympicopolis* project might draw inspiration, realising perhaps the earlier idea of 'museums without walls', and a genuinely open cultural democratic and innovative experience and facility for east London, rather than the new facadism (Evans, 2015) associated with the contemporary-designed impervious museum, university and cultural centre.

Archives

One of the rationales for museum outposts in the Olympic Park is the opportunity to increase gallery capacity, with an estimated 90% of the UK's art in storage (*The Observer*, 29 November 2015), this – together with new audience/access goals – has justified similar extensions of museums and galleries both in the UK (e.g. Tate) and abroad, as an act of cultural diplomacy and income generation (Ghose, 2013). Most notorious is the US Guggenheim franchise that rejuvenated Bilbao (Plaza, 2006), with further Guggenheims planned for Helsinki and Abu Dhabi (Rosenbaum, 2014). Major institutions have also taken the opportunity to reinforce their cultural brand and provide exhibition space for their accumulating collections at home and in new (art) markets such as the Louvre, Abu Dhabi. It is no coincidence that institutions planned for the *Olympicopolis* are also active in these Middle Eastern development projects, notably UCL and US institutions such as New York University and the Smithsonian. Post-Bilbao, however, a longer list of never-realised Guggenheim proposals for outposts in Tokyo, Taichung, Hong Kong, Rio, Salzburg, Singapore and Vilnius indicates the controversial and costly nature of these ventures, however, the Victorian progenitors of *Albertopolis* could have never imagined the extent of cultural globalisation and imperialism through their legacy, and in their name. As well as museum satellites, relocated university campuses combining faculties of art and design have also been central elements of major regeneration projects in cities such as Barcelona (Pobra Fabra University of Art & Design at Poblenou, post-Olymics former textile industrial neighbourhood – Figure 3.4); and Helsinki

Figure 3.4 University Pobra Fabra (upf) buildings in Poblenou, Barcelona, 2019
Source: author, 2019.

(University of Art & Design and Conservatoire in the Arabianranta ceramics factory district), whilst the city extension to Copenhagen at Orestad included a relocated Technical University and broadcasting corporation, although tellingly, failing to attract the desired artists and 'buzz' to this sterile new built environment (Evans, 2009).

Bilbao's economic success is built largely on tourism (the dominant visitor group to the Guggenheim) and payback via tourist hotel taxes (Plaza, 2006), and an international visiting art loan collection, rather than on national or regional cultural development (Evans, 2003). Expenditure cuts in the Basque region also reveal an inequitable distribution of resources, with arguably its most famous modern artist, the late Eduardo Chillida, whose sculpture park in Hernani – a location chosen by the sculptor himself – was closed in 2010 because of a funding 'shortage'. So there are lessons for any supposed cultural regeneration project such as *Olympicopolis*, that seeks to emulate this 'creative city' themed venture (Evans, 2009a).

The issue of expanding showcase facilities for art and museum collections is, however, a particular challenge for institutions and national cultural policy, with annual storage costs of £465,000 and £650,000 for the Tate and V&A respectively. Despite reductions in national and local cultural spending else-where (including real terms cuts to core grants, including the V&A), the government has pledged £150m for the British Museum, V&A and Science Museums to replace out of date storage at Blythe House in west London. However, a counter to the high storage costs and the creation of new outposts is to expand loan and outreach/ touring of collections to other cities and regions and existing venues. A reverse of this is seen in the return of 400,000 objects from the National Media Museum (NMM) in Bradford to the V&A, as part of the Royal Photographic Society (RPS) collection which is to be added to the V&A's existing collection of 500,000 photographs. The NMM had been in financial difficulty, leading to a focus on science & technology and the culture of light and sound,[6] but the director of the RPS voiced his: 'concern there would no longer be a single institution acting as a national museum of photography' (*Guardian*, 2 February 2016, p. 9), which the NMM had been created to do. The V&A itself had earlier aspirations to develop an outpost for its South Asian and other collections in Bradford, considering both Saltaire, and a converted Lister Silk Mills at Manningham which was estimated to cost £60m in 1995:

> the move was presumed to be a welcome gesture toward the large com-munity from the Indian sub-continent resident in the city since its migration to serve in the textile mills, now cleaned and swept to house imported collections and displays. Most of the collections proposed to be transferred were in fact Hindu and Jain, predominantly of human form deity figure representations and potentially highly offensive to Bradford's main ethnic minority of Pakistani, Bangladeshi and Punjabi origin.
> (Evans, 2001, 243)

The Olympic borough of Newham also has one of the most ethnically diverse populations in Britain, predominantly non-white European, with 32% declared to be Muslims and the largest groups from the Indian sub-continent (India, Bangladesh, Pakistan) and Africa, as well as more recent East European settlers. The neighbouring boroughs of Hackney and Tower Hamlets also contain high levels of non-European diversity, so what implications does this have for the historic collections and curation of the V&A and Smithsonian; is a hip-hop academy at Sadlers Wells *East* an anachronistic token; and what relevance will the design, engineering and technological specialisms of UCL (currently with no department or school of design) and the Loughborough University extension, have for east Londoners in the shadow of *Olympicopolis*? Will the opportunities from the creative and digital industries continue to bypass a lower and differently skilled workforce as they have to date in London's Tech City and Digital Shoreditch hub (Foord, 2012)? None of these fundamental cultural considerations so far feature in the *Olympicopolis* vision, masterplans or individual institutional statements, conceived as an explicit elite import by the former Mayor, Boris Johnson, and opportunistic expansion by these institutions (although the final configuration may well change). In this sense, the opposite of cultural democracy, but a clear statement of placemaking which seeks to extend London's tourism offer and urban sprawl, not unlike the *Albertopolis* experiment.

Conclusion

A fundamental issue in the location of state-funded cultural and educational institutions is who benefits, and how any major development contributes to cultural planning for the region and nation. Prince Albert's Victorian aim was that these new cultural institutions would be useful to the public and provide educational access to the masses. The extent to which the latest cultural and educational facilities and programmes, as privileged inheritors of the London 2012 mega-event, will attract and provide genuine access to residents of Newham and adjoining host boroughs is, however, questionable, given the profile of visitors, as well as students and staff, many of whom hold high cultural capital (Evans, 2016a). For example, those from least deprived neighbourhoods are twice as likely to attend museums as those from the most deprived (DCMS, 2010), whilst institutions such as UCL admit some of the lowest proportions of students from state schools. Arts participation as measured by the Arts Council found that Newham had the lowest rate in the country at 20% against a national average of 44%, with the highest rates (60% to 66%) in the country recorded in six central and west London boroughs – including South Kensington (ACE, 2010). In the case of the V&A, 45% of visitors identified themselves as already working, teaching or studying in the creative industries (V&A, 2014, 11) – not surprising given its past and present educational role – so the scope for those outside of this milieu may be limited in practice (Evans, 2016a).

With new museum facilities on their doorstep, proximity and access in the geographic sense may release latent demand, provided the exhibitions and programmes are of sufficient interest and relevance. However, since the 'Olympic' borough of Newham scores the lowest on officially recognised cultural and physical activity in England, the challenge for *Olympicopolis* and the Olympic legacy as a whole, is the extent to which it is able to transform, engage and reflect the cultural assets, history and aspirations of past and present residents and industry, including the significant presence of artists and designers surrounding the Stratford Waterfront site. This has not so far been revealed in the masterplanning and development proposals, nor how synergies will be manifested between these distinct institutions, organisational cultures and brands – proximity alone will not guarantee this, nor 'trickle down' effects in either a cultural or economic sense (Evans, 2001). Success measured through tourism and overseas students will not be sufficient to match Prince Albert and his fellow Victorian's goal of 'maintaining Britain's leading position in world affairs and giving working people the necessary tools for self-improvement and responsible citizenship' (Girouard, 1981), under the prevailing regime for higher education and the arts, and given the evidence of major cultural and education regeneration schemes elsewhere (Evans, 2016c), *Olympicopolis* may well **be in** east London, but risks failing to be either **of** or **for** east London and its rich cultural production roots.

Notes

1 Over £500 million in planning, development and post-Games transformation of the Olympic Park is estimated to have been expended between 2012 and 2016, most of this falling in the three years 2014–17 after the Park had opened.
2 *Culture and Democracy* was an explicit subject for consideration and discussion at a two-day event (14–15 May 2015) hosted jointly by the V&A Museum and Chelsea College of Art & Design, part of the University of the Arts London whose sister college, the London College of Fashion, is scheduled to relocate to Stratford as part of the *Olympicopolis* development in 2022. Entitled *Victorian Futures* this gathering and speakers (including the author) looked at comparisons between these two eras, starting with the Reform Act of 1832, the Great Exhibition of 1851 and *Albertopolis* legacy, and state-sponsored access to culture and education – and the aspirations and sentiments surrounding the *Olympicopolis* project.
3 The incumbent Mayor when London bid for and was awarded the London 2012 Olympic Games was Ken Livingstone (Labour Party), whose rationale for the project was primarily regeneration and affordable new housing. *Olympicopolis* and the cultural/education hub was not therefore part of the Olympic bid or approved masterplan which was agreed by host boroughs.
4 The masterplanning of the *Olympicopolis* site has been awarded to architecture firm, Allies & Morrison and a consortium of design and engineering firms, many of whom who were also part of the Olympic Park masterplanning team.
5 Foundation for the Future of London, Appointment of Director, 2015.
6 The NMM is considering changing its name to Science Museum North (it is already owned by the Trustees of the Science Museum) and has abandoned Bradford's International Film Festival, leading to fears that Bradford could lose its status as the world's first UNESCO City of Film.

References

ACE (2010) *Active People Survey.* London: Arts Council of England. www.artscoun cil.org.uk/participating-and-attending/active-lives-survey#section-4.

Bergmans, J. (ed.) (2010) 'Shaping West London'. www.myearlscourt.com/userfiles/up loads/main/FINALshapingWestLondon-lowres.pdf.

Civic Trust (1964) *A Lee Valley Regional Park: An Essay in the Use of Neglected Land for Recreation and Leisure.* London: Civic Trust.

Daniels, M. (2013) *Paris National and International Exhibitions from 1798 to 1900: A Finding-List of British Library Holdings.* London: British Library.

DCMS (2010) *Taking Part - Statistical Release. Adult and Child Report 2009/10.* London.

Evans, G.L. (2001) *Cultural Planning: An Urban Renaissance?* London: Routledge.

Evans, G.L. (2003) 'Hard branding the culture city: From Prado to Prada', *International Journal of Urban and Regional Research*, 27(2), 417–440.

Evans, G.L. (2005) 'Measure for measure: Evaluating the evidence of culture's contribution to regeneration', *Urban Studies*, 42(5/6), 959–984.

Evans, G.L. (2009a) 'Creative cities, creative spaces and urban policy', *Urban Studies*, 46(5–6), 1003–1040.

Evans, G.L. (2009b) 'From Cultural Quarters to Creative Clusters: Creative Spaces in the New City Economy'. In M. Legner (ed.) *The Sustainability and Development of Cultural Quarters: International Perspectives*, Stockholm: Institute of Urban History, 32–59.

Evans, G.L. (2010) 'Cities of culture and the regeneration games', *Journal of Tourism, Sport and Creative Industries*, 6, 5–18.

Evans, G.L. (2014) 'Rethinking Place Branding and Place Making through Creative and Cultural Quarters'. In M. Kavaratzis, G. Warnaby and G.J. Ashworth (eds) *Rethinking Place Branding: Critical Accounts.* Vienna: Springer, 135–158.

Evans, G.L. (2015) 'Designing legacy and the legacy of design: London 2012 and the Regeneration Games', *Architectural Review Quarterly*, 18(4), 353–353.

Evans, G.L. (2016a) 'Participation and provision in arts & culture: Bridging the divide', *Cultural Trends*, 25(1), 1–19.

Evans, G.L. (2016b) 'London 2012'. In J. Gold and M. Gold (eds) *Olympic Cities: City Agendas, Planning and the Worlds Games, 1896–2016.* London: Routledge, 378–399.

Evans, G.L. (2016c) 'Creative Cities: An International Perspective'. In G. Richards and J. Hannigan (eds) *Handbook of New Urban Studies.* London: Sage, 311–329.

Evans, G.L. (2019) 'Design of Contemporary Mega Events'. In A. Massey (ed.) *Blackwell Companion to Contemporary Design.* Oxford: Blackwell.

Evans, G.L. and Shaw, S. (2001) 'Urban leisure and transport: Regeneration effects', *Journal of Leisure Property*, 1(4), 350–372.

Foord, J. (1999) 'Creative Hackney: Reflections on hidden art', *Rising East*, 3, 69–94.

Foord, J. (2012) 'The new boomtown? Creative city to tech city in East London', *Cities*, 33, 51–60.

Geoghegan, J. (2014) 'Shifting legacy: Why Olympic Park plans are changing', *Planning Resource*, www.planningresource.co.uk/article/1305473/shifting-legacy-why-o lympic-park-plans-changing.

Ghose, S. (2013) 'Museums and cultural diplomacy projects in Qatar and the Middle East'. Paper presented at Institute of Cultural Diplomacy Conference, Berlin, 17–21 December.

Girouard, M. (1981) *Alfred Waterhouse and the Natural History Museum*. London: Nat Hist Museum.

Gold, J. and Gold, M. (2016) 'Olympic Futures and Urban Imaginings: From Albertopolis to Olympicopolis'. In G. Richards and J. Hannigan (eds) *The Sage Handbook of New Urban Studies*. New York: Sage, 514–534.

Greenhalgh, P. (1988) *Ephemeral Vistas: The Expositions Universelles, Great Exhibitions and World's Fairs, 1851–1939*. Manchester: Manchester University Press.

Hooper-Greenhill, E. (1992) *Museums and the Shaping of Knowledge*. London: Routledge.

Johnson, B., Mayor of London (2013) http://queenelizabetholympicpark.co.uk/the-park/attractions/olympicopolis.

LDA (London Development Agency) (2003) *Creative London: Vision and Plan*. London.

Littlewood, J. (1964) 'A laboratory of fun', *New Scientist*, 14 May, 432–433.

LLDC (2014) *10 Year Plan*. DRAFT V2.4 NA. London: Greater London Authority.

Matthews, S. (2005) 'The fun palace: Cedric Price's experiment in architecture and technology', *Technoetic Arts*, 3(32), 73–91.

Murphy, J. (2014) 'Plans for Olympic Park will secure legacy of the 2012 Games, says Osborne', *Evening Standard*, 2 December, London.

NFA (2008) *Summary Report: Artists' Studio Provision in the Host Boroughs: A Review of the Potential Impacts of London's Olympic Project*. London: National Federation of Artists' Studio Providers, December.

Pick, J. (1997) 'The arts industry'. Gresham College Lecture, London, 14 April.

Pick, J. and Anderton, M. (2013) *Building Jerusalem: Art, Industry and the British Millennium*. London: Routledge.

Plaza, B. (2006) 'The return on investment of the Guggenheim Museum Bilbao', *International Journal of Urban and Regional Research*, 30(2), 452–467.

Read, H. (1932) *Art and Industry*. London: Faber & Faber.

Rosenbaum, L. (2014) 'Forum: Should we be cynical about international museum franchises?', *Apollo*, 22 December, 1–2.

Roth, M. (2015) 'Victorian futures', 14–15 May,London: Chelsea College of Art.

Ruskin, J. (1870) *Lectures on Art, No.3: The Relation of Art to Morals*, Section 95. Oxford.

Sassoon, D. (2006) *The Culture of the Europeans from 1800 to the Present*. London: Harper Collins.

Store Smith, J. (1972) 'Social Aspects'. In A. Briggs (ed.) *Victorian People: A Reassessment of Persons and Themes, 1851–1867*. Chicago: University of Chicago Press.

V&A (2014) *Victoria and Albert Museum Annual Report and Accounts, 2013–2014*. London.

4 A World Fair for the future

Revisiting the legacy of the Expo '98 urban model

Patricia Aelbrecht

Introduction

Modern-day Expos, at least in Western countries, have had a problematic reception and history, not least in terms of their legacies. Lisbon's Expo in 1998 has been an exception to this chequered past and an exception to subsequent European World Fairs. The feeling of well-being cultivated in the celebrations of science, technology, culture, nation states and icons of national pride of World's Fairs/Expos has often been short-lived (Rydell, 1993). Grand plans and buildings were constructed to express these ideologies of progress. Money was never spared. Because these narratives of celebration rarely envisioned concrete urban plans for the future, most of them fell rapidly in decline. Most Expo sites stayed undeveloped, if not abandoned, and burdened with massive debts (ibid.). Many became relics of an event that promised to bring a glorious future to the hosting country, reminding us of the limited long-term benefits (and ongoing costs) of expo sites. Montreal Expo 1967, Knoxville Expo 1982, New Orleans Expo 1984 and Seville Expo 1992 are good examples. Because of these perceived failures, for some countries such as the USA, the once popular fair is no longer conceived as a guarantee to success or attractive to city developments (Wilson and Huntoon, 2001; Linden and Creighton, 2000).

In this uncertain climate, the Lisbon Expo of 1998 marked a change in attitude towards the urban and architectural design of World Expos: from re-used iconic buildings to the use of the urban plan as a trigger for urban redevelopment. Unlike most previous fairs, where an abrupt shift from celebration to decline occurred, the Lisbon Expo continually celebrates its existence. By designing a new neighbourhood in Lisbon in the aftermaths of the Expo, I argue that the history of World Fairs was rewritten. Hence, drawing on the Lisbon case in this chapter I will demonstrate that the Lisbon Expo represents a shift in attitude towards the design of World's Fairs urban plans (see earlier exposition on which this chapter expands; Aelbrecht, 2014).

The Lisbon Expo plan was the first World Fair to effectively adopt an urban and architectural plan for the future. Ideologies of nation states so prominent in previous Expos did not disappear; however, they were placed more at the background. By embracing a new model, Lisbon intended to regenerate a post-industrial site, to improve the city's relationship with the river and increase Lisbon's competitiveness within the European context. Ten years onwards the Lisbon Expo site has been acknowledged by the public as a thriving neighbourhood and financial district, and has received some scholarly attention.[1] Interestingly, Parque Expo, the state-funded development company created to design the Expo site, was invited to provide consultancy services to Expo Shanghai and to other cities in the world. Despite this rising interest in Expo '98, little research has been done on the urban plan as a new Expo model. Most of the focus has been placed on the planning lessons than on its role as an Expo (Swyngedouw et al., 2002; Carrière and Demazière, 2002).

This chapter critically analyses the afterlife of the Lisbon Expo plan in two ways: first, by placing the Lisbon urban model within the history of design of World Fairs; and second, by analysing the history of the reception of its urban plan and its legacies and lessons for planning and urban design. Methodologically, both parts are based on a thorough archival research in both the archives of Parque Expo in Lisbon and the Bureau International des Expositions (BIE) in Paris, and on oral historical accounts with the protagonists of the urban plan before, during and after the Expo event. Furthermore, in order to highlight the key elements of the urban plan, an in-depth reading of its planning and design has been undertaken. Not only did the Expo '98 create an important new urban model for future World Fairs, but it has also contributed to debates on urban regeneration and placemaking.

The changing roles and models of World Fairs

Because World Fairs have always been celebrations of progress and national pride, it requires its organisers to imagine not only forms of celebrating the present and the past but also to design and construct urban and architectural models that communicated this. Over time and geography, these ideas and models changed. If during the nineteenth century World Fairs were above all displays of economic activity and products, during the twentieth century they had predominantly educational purposes to demonstrate technological advances, and artistic novelties on a worldwide scale (Rydell, 1993). And although financially World Fairs were always a serious burden, creating great gaps in the city's economy, many countries kept aspiring to host them. As a result, the beginning of the twentieth century saw an uncontrolled multiplication of Expos with very similar themes that were progressively emptied of their informative and cultural content. The new expo themes increasingly strengthened their trade component as fairs. It is in this historical moment that we have to see the creation of the Bureau International des Expositions (BIE) in 1928. Their aim was to control the Expo's time of occurrence and to discipline their organisation, function and theme. One of the improvements they made was the making of a preliminary enquiry with a focus on the spatial and economic guidelines (BIE, 1988). From that moment on every candidate country had to comply as much as possible either when wanting to submit a candidature or when applying to get recognition for an exposition. Implicit in this enquiry was a belief that only Expos that would have a feasible economic model to pay themselves and have a conscious after-use in mind could be the most viable candidates.

For the BIE, the Expos that marked the history of the twentieth century were the ones that had more visitors or a stronger physical impact on the fair site, such as the Paris Expo 1889, the Chicago Expo 1893, the Brussels Expo 1958 and the Montreal Expo 1967. From those, only the ones that left more enduring and memorable physical testimonies, such as monuments, buildings or public spaces, would become models for Expos to follow (Vincent LosCertales, personal communication, 10 January 2012). Paris and Brussels fit perfect within these new ideas. Both became for the BIE the two most important Expo models (ibid.). It is no surprise than that the Paris Expo is seen as the first Expo model. It inaugurated the era of thematic exhibitions with larger cultural contents and the building of significant event heritage such as the Eiffel Tower and the Champ de Mars. Implicit in its design was already an after-use in mind that was to build permanent event heritage. Because the Expo was so centrally planned, most of the built structures became part of the city's urban plan and gave birth to a tourist industry. The second Expo model, Brussels, is very different. Created after the Second World War, the primacy of the economy was dissolved to some extent in the apogee of architecture. This was rendered visible in the increased size and variety of exhibition pavilions, caused by the increasing number of participants and progressive diversification of national messages. Thanks to the development of concrete for building and new typologies, this was a time in which the modernist spirit embraced great architectural experiments.

After the Brussels's Expo and the busy years of post-war reconstruction, stories of failures followed and the fairs' legitimacy and rhetoric of progress were questioned. This is what happened with the Knoxville Expo 1982, the New Orleans Expo 1984 and the Seville Expo 1992. By 1988, these consecutive failures led to a new disciplinary effort from the part of the BIE, which resulted in the creation of a new category of recognised Expos, alongside the universal Expos (Parque Expo, 1999) These would be smaller in size, shorter in duration, and more economical with long-term aims for a post-Expo use. World Fairs were now expected to leave a different kind of testimony: not monuments but legacies for the future.

It is in this changing context that the Lisbon Expo of 1998 brings a new attitude to the making of World Expos: from re-used iconic buildings to the use of the urban plan as catalysts of urban redevelopment. With it, I argue that a new era and third Expo model was brought forward in the urban and architectural design of World Expos.

The Expo '98: a new urban model for World Fairs

The Expo '98 brought a new reflection to the traditional formula of Expos. This was visible already from its inception in its candidature (Portugal, 1991). More than only emphasising the re-use of land or iconic buildings as was the case in Paris and Brussels, its candidature envisioned a clear strategic plan with long-term aims for post-Expo use. The BIE saw that this was a step in the right direction (Vincent LosCertales, personal communication, 10 January 2012). In addition, the Lisbon Expo was the first to follow the new format of Expos introduced by the BIE in 1988 to make Expos more economic for the hosting countries. With only 25 hectares and only taking three months, it was smaller in size and shorter in duration.[2] These three factors – post-use, size and duration – had considerable weight in the decision of the BIE. For the candidature of the Expo '98, there was only another candidate Toronto, which despite having a more developed proposal than Lisbon, as it was the second time it competed, its approach was not more than a real estate project (ibid.).

As opposed to Toronto (Oliver, Chapter 10), the Lisbon Expo plan was not yet formalised; however, its objectives were clear at the international, national and regional level. There were four main reasons that influenced the BIE in selecting Lisbon instead of Toronto. First, the Lisbon Expo's idea was triggered to promote the image of Lisbon and Portugal within a new global context, while at the same time it intended to act as a means to regenerate an area of the city – the oriental area of Lisbon – that could contribute more decisively to transform Lisbon as a city of the twenty-first century (Portugal, 1991). Second, the strength of the Expo '98's candidature was also explained by its strong political support and the location and theme chosen (Vincent LosCertales, personal communication, 10 January 2012). Its candidature was presented to the BIE in 1989 as an initiative of the Portuguese government, and thus as a truly national project (Portugal, 1991). The government formed a working group that included various ministries, namely Foreign Affairs, Commerce and Tourism, Transport and Culture, and representatives of the city halls of Lisbon and Loures, and consultants of various technical and architectural domains, to work on the proposal's concept and theme of the candidature (ibid.).

Thirdly, the BIE also considered the selected location very appropriate for the event. It was perceived as an area of opportunity according to the 1992 strategic plan of Lisbon (Vincent LosCertales, personal communication, 10 January 2012). It had great landscape value, excellent accessibilities, enough space available for an event of this dimensions, and relatively little urban occupation in adjacent areas. It stretches alongside Lisbon's main river, the Tagus River, located in the periphery of Lisbon only five kilometres from Lisbon's main tourist centre, and under the city's main international airport. In addition, it had the necessary transport infrastructure for holding an event with international dimensions. It was not only well connected with the transport network and airports; it had the possibility to further expand its infrastructure with the construction of new metro and tramlines (Portugal, 1991). The location had around 300 hectares of uninhabited land available, all property of the Portuguese state. The site was only partially occupied by old and derelict industrial buildings, which included a gas factory, a refining plant, a slaughterhouse, a few fuel storage tanks and storage containers from the harbour of Lisbon, a military depot and waste and sewage treatment facilities. Besides that, there was not any conflict of interest that could stop the project (Heeren, 1991). Hence, the selection of this location was seen by the organisers of the Lisbon's Expo as a great opportunity to regenerate an old industrial area and re-establish the urban balance in Lisbon by developing the periphery but also, because it was empty, it could allow great freedom of urban intervention (Manuel Salgado, personal communication, 12 April 2002).

The fourth reason was the theme. The Expo theme, 'The Oceans, a Heritage for the Future', coincided with the five hundred years of Portuguese discoveries, more in particular with the arrival of Vasco da Gama in India and the 'Year of the Ocean' designated by the UN (Portugal, 1991). At the same time such celebratory themes made sure that the memories of dereliction of the post-industrial landscape were replaced with memories of a past glorious empire. Undeniably, Lisbon's Expo '98 candidature demonstrated to the BIE that Lisbon had a clear vision for the future.

Once Lisbon's ambitious candidature was selected by the BIE as the hosting country for the Expo '98, the Portuguese government did not wait long with its planning. Immediately they formed a state-funded legislative body, Parque Expo SA, which incorporated the functions of a development company to guarantee the successful continuation of the project and realisation of the Expo. According to its organisers, this company had to complete the Expo event within four years because it avoided the need for a public inquiry and could not be subject to normal legislation or supervision from the City Hall (ibid.).

Parque Expo formed its own team of planners and architects (led by the architect and urban planner Vassalo Rosa) to plan and execute the masterplan and work out a financial model for the whole event. Expo Vancouver 86, Expo Brisbane 88 and Expo Seville 92 and the 92 Olympic city Barcelona were selected as urban models (Mega Ferreira, 1994). Out of them they took several important lessons for their urban model. From Expo Vancouver and Brisbane, they learned that the use of temporary buildings with modular designs can be easily sold, and constructed, deconstructed and reassembled at new sites to accommodate new needs. Ironically enough, from Seville they learned what should not be done. An Expo site cannot be developed as mono-functional if it wants to create any after-life. And from Barcelona, they concluded that the quality of the urban design plays an important role for a successful urban renewal (Manuel Salgado, personal communication, 12 April 2002). Out of these lessons they were able to formulate a plan consisting of three strategies (see Table 4.1): (1) at the planning level, that is the broad urban context; (2) design level, that is its public spaces and architecture; and (3) economic level, with a robust financial plan (BIE, 1992). Underlying these strategies was the initial goal set in the candidature to incorporate a post-Expo, in other words, to design an urban plan that could encompass two phases in the

Expo development. A first phase was designed to guarantee the successful realisation of the actual Expo and its goals; and a second phase to revise and extend
the initial urban plan of the Expo event in order to construct a neighbourhood
(Figure 4.1) (Joao Vassalo Rosa, personal communication, 13 April 2010).

Hence, at the planning level, one of the first objectives was to ensure that
the plan fitted the 1992 approved strategic plan for Lisbon that defined the
directions of urban development. The second objective, following the model
of the Olympics in Barcelona, was to think of the project primarily as the
creation of a new centre in Lisbon, and only secondarily as an Expo (Manuel

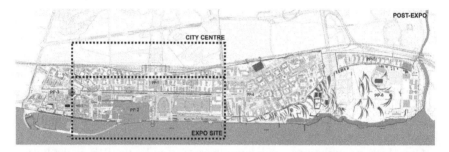

Figure 4.1 The two phases of the urban plan: the Expo and Post-Expo Plan of Lisbon
      Expo '98
Source: author, reprinted with permission from Parque Expo S.A, Lisbon.

Table 4.1 Strategies for planning, designing and financing the Expo' 98 project

Strategies of the Expo '98 Project		
(1) Planning Level	*(2) Design Level*	*(3) Development, Management and Financial level*
2 in 1 plan: Expo and Post-Expo.1st objective: plan Integrated in the 1992 strategic plan of Lisbon	Architecture: with re-use in mind; provision of both temporary and permanent structures.	Developing/managing model: creation of an private company 'Parque Expo' with access to public capital which was given the duty of design-
2nd objective: first: the creation of a center; second: an expo.	Urban design: with permanence and functionality in mind; designing public spaces with double function: for event and post-event.	ing, developing, construct- ing and dismantling the World Exhibition, but also of buying, developing and selling land in the whole
Planning principles:		zone!
- inclusion of Mixed-use (housing, services and commerce)		Financial model: pay the development with the
- provision of economic anchors		selling of land and pavi- lions to private investors
- improvement of strategic infrastructure.		and developers after the closure of the event.

(Source: author, 2011, reprinted with permission from Parque Expo S.A, Lisbon).

Salgado, personal communication, 12 April 2002). These objectives clearly emphasised the importance of a coherent town-planning framework in which two principles were employed (Parque Expo, 1999).

The first was to improve the transport infrastructure to increase accessibility. This included the expansion of the international airport; the building of new national and international roads, in particular to Spain; a second bridge to link the centre with southern riverbank; and the creation of more public transport links. All these projects were already included in the strategic plan because they were seen as necessary to the growth and survival of the city (ibid.). The Expo was thus seen an opportunity to implement them. The second principle underlying the basis of the plan, to create a new centre, was to help in structuring the economic and social fabric (Joao Vassalo Rosa, personal communication, 13 April 2010). This implied a mixed-use plan and the provision of post-event economic anchors of development. Accordingly, the future centre of the new neighbourhood balanced a mix of urban facilities, namely commercial business leisure and cultural activities, whilst the rest of the plan, namely the two areas surrounding the Expo site in the north and south surroundings, would be filled mainly with residential areas (Portugal, 1991). The anchors provided included an intermodal station with trains, buses and metro, a Lisbon exhibition centre, an Oceanarium, a multifunctional pavilion, a variety of public spaces and parks, and other relevant amenities such as a hospital and a university. The inclusion of mixed uses and in particular of housing was a lesson taken from the failure of Seville (Joao Vassalo Rosa, personal communication, 13 April 2010).

At the design level, the main aim of Parque Expo was to guarantee the transition and extension of the memory and use of the Expo event into the new neighbourhood. This implied a strong design rationale for its architecture and public space. For the architecture, they envisioned the re-use of buildings through the provision of permanent and temporary constructions, continuing the tradition of previous Expos (see Figure 4.2) (Portugal, 1991).

The temporary constructions were explicitly meant to allow enough flexibility to fulfil the different needs of the participant countries and quick dismantling after the Expo closure. These included pavilions with modular structures (the module basis was of 256 square metres, 16x16 metres) and other installations for restaurants, kiosks and some information pavilions. Some of these pavilions of modular structure were conceived with a double function in mind. This was a lesson taken from Brisbane and Vancouver (ibid.).

The permanent structures, on the contrary, served to preserve the memory of the event. They included public spaces and various iconic buildings such as the Portuguese pavilion, which was converted after the Expo event to an exhibition space, and other thematic pavilions such as the case of the pavilion of 'knowledge of the seas', which was adapted into a museum of science, or the Atlantico pavilion which became an important concert venue.

Figure 4.2 Temporary Information. Pavilion converted into a bar (top), Portugal
    pavilion (middle), Atlantico pavilion (bottom)
Source: author.

There is no doubt that the architecture was an important factor to guarantee the post-Expo use. This was already a known fact from previous Expo
events such as the Paris model. In the Lisbon model during the development
of the project it became clear that the success of the urban plan depended

more on the effectiveness of the urban design to transform the Expo into a neighbourhood (Joao Vassalo Rosa, personal communication, 13 April 2010). Therefore it can be argued that the public spaces were designed to become the permanent framework of the future neighbourhood. The public spaces had implicit in their design a double function. On the one hand, they followed the strict requirements of Expo's plans, namely to offer great comfort and accessibility for the expected 9 million visitors and have a festive and ephemeral character; while on the other, they designed a plan that made it possible to be used immediately after the closure of the event. As such, it was necessary to provide not only a great variety of public spaces that would keep the memory of the event but also to achieve some clarity and unity to not to create a permanent exhibition (ibid.). Hence for the purpose of the event it created a diverse and dense landscape of public spaces, which incorporated references to different themes with different temporal, functional, cultural and typological origins from medieval, classic, to modern. The result was a variety of public spaces in terms of form, enclosure – covered, enclosed but open to the sky or simply open – and materials – Portuguese traditional stone, wood or grass (see Figure 4.3) (Fernandes, 2005).

As explained by Vassalo Rosa, the project leader, for the purpose of the post-use of the public spaces, three fundamental aspects were taken into account: legibility of the urban spaces, a physical relationship with the river and a positive integration of the surrounding and existing urban fabric (Joao Vassalo Rosa, personal communication, 13 April 2010).

In order to ensure a good sense of legibility among the public spaces, the designers organised the public space along four axes: (1) a public axis perpendicular to the river that aggregates the main public activities (station, shopping centre, main square 'Rossio dos Olivais'); (2) a main accessibility axis (the Avenue D. Joao II) and only heavy traffic road that links the PN with the city and adjacent areas; (3) a leisure axis fully pedestrianised that stretches along the whole riverfront; and (4) a secondary accessibility axis with conditioned traffic (a boulevard with trees, the *Alameda dos Oceanos*) that works as the spine of the neighbourhood connecting the three neighbourhood areas (the southern residential area, the central public area and the north residential area). The relationship with the river was reinforced by transforming the riverfront into a ludic area fully pedestrianised and by guaranteeing a gradation of density construction from high to low from west to east, to the river. To integrate the plan with the surrounding, the main public buildings were located in the peripheries of the site to improve the relation with them (ibid.).

Parallel to the planning and urban design of the urban plan, the Parque Expo also devised a financial plan, which could guarantee the successful realisation of the event and completion of the urban development (Castro et al., 1997). The initial intention was to have zero costs. They expected that in 20 years they would pay back the event's development with the selling of land and pavilions to private investors and developers. However, as usually is the case, in reality they had more costs with the whole development than they predicted. But at least the realisation of the Expo was mostly paid (Aquilino Machado, personal communication, 28 December 2011).

Figure 4.3 The three most emblematic public spaces of the Expo '98 plan: the main
square 'Rossio dos Olivias' (top), the riverfront (middle), the Boulevard
Alameda dos Oceanos (bottom)
Source: author.

As shown, the Expo '98 marks a radical transformation in the philosophy and
mode of operation of World Fairs. It was the first to combine a clear strategy in
terms of town-planning, urban design and architecture with a bold financial
model (Swyngedouw, 2002). Because it was the first of the type it became soon

recognised as a third model in the design of World Expos, an Expo as catalyst of urban renewal (Vincent LosCertales, personal communication, January 10, 2012). The BIE strongly advised subsequent Expos to use it as a base for urban development, and furthermore, to visit the site to experience it at first hand. However since its inception some doubts have been raised about its effectiveness, as we will see in the next section.

The reception of the model and its legacies

After 20 years we can see that the Lisbon Expo continues to celebrate its existence. Today it is a thriving residential neighbourhood and successful commercial leisure and business centre (Miguel Menezes, personal communication, April 9, 2010). This success is often presented in terms of numbers: 1,247 million square metres of housing, 626 million of offices, 190 million of commerce and 364 million of other collective functions, a total of 19,000 inhabitants (which is estimated to reach 30,000), a floating population of workers of 50,000 during weekdays, and 250,000 visitors per week (Parque Expo, 2008). As the president of neighbourhood association said, 'it has almost the population of a city, some cities in Portugal do not have even this amount of population' (Miguel Menezes, personal communication, 9 April 2010).

Several reports and surveys made by the Parque Expo about the Expo Lisbon reveal that residents, workers and visitors are in general very satisfied with the urban development, in particular with the variety and quality of design of the public spaces and public art (Parque Expo, 2008). Some suggest that the new created neighbourhood, now called Park of the Nations, offers the public spaces that Lisbon does not have. The few people that dislike it are often those nostalgic for the traditional city and have great prejudice against new and modern developments (ibid.).

The Expo '98 success went beyond everyone's expectations, even for its mentors and designers (Mega Ferreira, 2008). Vassalo Rosa, the project leader of the plan, recognised that other similar developments take at least 10 years to build and another 20 to become a lively neighbourhood. Ten to 20 years is normally the time needed for a masterplanned neighbourhood to take roots and become a community (Joao Vassalo Rosa, personal communication, 13 April 2010). However, although the plan has become a success, its recognition as an urban model has been slow. If Shanghai has attentively followed its steps, the same was not true of Hannover (which adopted only its financial model), Zaragoza and Aichi, and other posterior Expos (Aquilino Machado, personal communication, 28 December 2011). The reception of the model needs thus further scrutiny.

Several explanations can be given why the Expo '98 has not been fully embraced as a successful Expo model. The first is that the Expo '98 was never a financial success. Although it paid off most of the event, an audit found in 1997 that the Expo '98 had a loss of 0.09 million euros (Castro et al., 1997). This was just known two years after the event, which was the only moment the accounting was made public. Although this was not at all expected, we cannot forget that all World Fairs have been 'financial failures, though some are more creative in their accounting than others' (Rydell, 1993).

The second is related to its neoliberal planning approach, namely its search for growth, competitiveness and a regime of exception outside the statutory planning policies, which caused intended and unintended socio-spatial outcomes (Swynge-douw et al., 2002). One very visible spatial outcome is the separation of the new neighbourhood from the surrounding urban fabric. This is seen as a failure of the urban planning to articulate it with its adjacent residential neighbourhoods at the west (Carrière and Demazière, 2002). Instead of working out the relationship between the new and old neighbourhoods, it can be interpreted that the plan has accentuated their division by placing the railway line in between them, despite the creation of nine passages under it, and leaving all zones in between full of un-definitions. As a result, the railway line is perceived as a symbolic barrier for the inhabitants of both sides. Although it remains unclear whether this spatial out-come was intended, it is well known by now from the outset of the project that this in-between zone was difficult to integrate because of the negative connotation of social housing of the neighbourhoods in the west (ibid.; Fernandes, 2005).

The most criticised social outcome, however, is the fact that the Park of the Nations has become a homogeneously middle- and upper-class income neigh-bourhood. For some critics, this was an expected effect of the financial model adopted from the outset to develop a self-sustained Expo, in other words of 'zero costs' (Aquilino Machado, personal communication, 28 December 2011). For them the plan instead of aiming to solve the needs of the area, it wanted to obtain the maximum profit from the market estate through the increase of land values and a property boom. This became even more clear in the post-Expo stage, where much emphasis was placed on making this neighbourhood a new centre in Lisbon, turning this area into one of the most expensive areas in Lisbon, with housing only for the affluent. This led to some critics to say that it was becoming a kind of luxurious and solitary ghetto (Graca Dias, 2007).

Not all its outcomes have been perceived as negative, in particular in dealing with its urban design and architecture. The director of the BIE considered Expo '98 as the most beautiful event ever, praising the high quality of its public spaces and pavilions (Publico, 1998). Since then, the acknowledgements in relation to its urban plan have not stopped. Many of its pavilions and the public spaces have won architecture prizes both nationally and internationally.[3] At the national level, according to Mega Ferreira, one of the Expo's mentors, it established a new pattern of urban quality for Lisbon and Portugal in general (Graca Dias, 2007). Many cities, in particular middle size ones, now wish to have public spaces, urban furniture and parks like the Expo '98. This sudden interest in public space led to the creation of an urban regeneration programme 'Polis' in 28 cities in Portugal, 10 of which were assigned to Parque Expo (Ministerio do Ambiente do Ordenamento do Territorio e do Desenvolvimento Regional 2008). The Parque Expo was then a proclaimed urban consultancy company until its demise in 2012, selling advice to cities all over the world such as Chicomba in Angola, Recife in Brasil, city of Praia in Cape Verde, Cairo in Egypt, just to mention a few, and of course to international exhibitions such as Shanghai, Hannover and Zaragoza.[4] Among these Expos, it can be argued that Shanghai followed more closely the Lisbon model. From the beginning of its candidature its organisers asked advice from Parque Expo and visited Lisbon several times (Vincent LosCertales, personal communication, 10 January 2012). In the Expos of Hanover and Zaragoza, the Parque Expo had a minor role, influencing only their financial model and building the Portuguese pavilion at both.

Like Expo '98, the planning of Shanghai Expo 2010 also begun with 'after use', 'permanent' and 'functional' thinking in mind to minimise the costs and the wasteful use of land sources, and to build the infrastructure that the city did not have. As such, its strategy also had a dual role, which was formalised in a 'two in one' plan: to organise and build an Expo while fulfilling the requirements of the city's masterplan (Leung, 2008). As a matter of fact the Expo 2010 was seen as the implementation of the strategic plan of the city. The result was a selection of a site that could help to revitalise two inner city post-industrial riverbanks and the inclusion of cultural amenities as after uses. However, unlike the Lisbon Expo, housing was not included in the plan. Despite the recognition of the importance of including it, this decision was justified by Shanghai officials that it followed the city's masterplan to have a dominant cultural focus (Vincent LosCertales, personal communication, 10 January 2012). The future will say whether this was a good decision.

More importantly, the perceived success of the organisation and planning of the Lisbon Expo '98 has brought the rise of a more comprehensive and strategic type of planning in Portugal, with the underlying idea that planning needs to be thought carefully at different scales and focus on both short and long terms. This is a remarkable achievement in a country where 'ad hoc' planning has been often the rule.

Parallel to its urban design and planning achievements, the Expo '98 plan also gained international momentum in several conferences. From 1998 to 2005, ten symposiums were organised by the BIE to discuss the role of 'International exhibitions as catalysts of development' (1998), the 'Legacy of International exhibitions' (2000), the 'long-lasting effects of ephemeral events', just to mention a few. The Parque Expo also organised in 2008 together with Portuguese Order of Architects a conference on the 10 years of 'Expo '98 city imagined/ city', inviting the architects involved and Portuguese scholars to discuss the project. Since the Shanghai Expo in 2010, a cycle of conferences on 'Best Urban Practices' has been regularly taking place in the BIE (BIE Urban Best Practices Area, 2012). More recently, in 2011, the Global City Conference in Abu Dhabi had a panel about 'How to Maximize Benefits from Mega Events' and in 2013 and 2014 the 'International Megaevents and Cities Conferences' in London and Rio respectively.

In all these conferences it has been increasingly recognised that 'Expos can contribute to create better cities' and can leave larger legacies than other megaevents like sporting events (LosCertales, 2011; Kang, 2011). Two reasons have

66   *Patricia Aelbrecht*

been often brought forward. The first is that Expos are inherently placemaking and place-marketing enterprises because they exist and communicate through the medium of buildings, objects and displays. The second is that Expos can use their themes to pursue ideas, visions, meanings and practices and pull them together to spur urban development and regeneration. In Expo Lisbon the idea of celebrating the five hundred years of discoveries effectively supported its post-use. It replaced memories of dereliction and disuse of the eastern part of the city by national pride and hope, and it created a thriving community (Jose Moreno, personal communication, 15 April 2010). This recognition has been paralleled by wider public acceptance that hosting mega-events can actually provide the basis for high quality urban plans and design. Despite some of its economic drawbacks, there is no doubt that the Expo '98 was an opportunity to upgrade the Portuguese planning system and to modernise, internationalise and boost Lisbon's image and economy. The use of mega-events as urban catalysts had been already experienced in Portugal though in a smaller scale with the designation of Lisbon as a European Capital of Culture in 1994, but it was only with the Expo '98 that Portugal had the opportunity to fully test it (Metaxas et al., 2011).

Although success can be evaluated in many ways, two lessons are particularly relevant for the planning and designing of future Expos, and urban regeneration projects. The first is to select a location clearly integrated in the strategic plan of a city. This implies clear objectives at the international, national and regional levels. With the Lisbon case, it was seen that the selected location not only had the necessary resources and attractiveness for holding an event of international dimensions – accessibilities, availability of space, landscape value and allow great freedom for urban intervention – but also it was considered an area of opportunity to regenerate a post-industrial wasteland, rebalance the city's growth and local economy and raise the city's image. The location has thus an important weight in achieving all these objectives.

The second is to think from the beginning in the post-use. As seen with Expo '98, this implies a coherent Town Planning framework, and a clear strategy for long-term aims. The plan must include a fine grain mixed-use plan of housing, services and commerce, to guarantee population presence and to be economically viable. The architecture has to be conceived with an idea of re-use and the urban design with an idea of permanence. In Expo '98, many buildings were either temporary to be quickly dismantled or permanent to be re-used. The public spaces were designed from the outset with a definite double function, which enabled them to act as both as event spaces and ordinary public spaces. Of course the success of these strategies, as was seen with Expo '98, also depends on the financial model and on the administrative capacity and continuity in carrying out the post-use.

Acknowledgements

The author is grateful to the Secretary General of BIE Vincent LosCertales, the librarian from the archives of BIE Mrs Sandrine Toiron and the geographer

Aquilino Machado from Parque Expo for providing the necessary information for this chapter. I also would like to thank the architectural historian Wes Aelbrecht for his valuable comments.

Interviews

Vincent LosCertales (Secretary General of BIE), personal communication, 10 January 2012.

Aquilino Machado (Human Geographer at Parque Expo), personal communication, 28 December 2011.

Manuel Salgado (Architect), personal communication in Newspaper Publico, 12 April 2002.

Joao Vassalo Rosa (Masterplanner Expo '98), personal communication, 13 April 2010.

Miguel Menezes, personal communication, 9 April 2010.

Jose Moreno (President of Neighbourhood Association of the PN), personal communication, 15 April 2010.

Notes

1 Since 1998 that many conferences have been organised to discuss the Expo '98.
2 In 1988, the BIE decided to introduce a new category of Expos smaller in size – with a maximum 25 hectares – and duration – between three weeks and three months, to add to the usual category that has the duration between six weeks and six months; and to substitute the labels of 'Universal' and 'International' for 'Registered' and 'Recognised' (meaning officially recognised by the hosting country).
3 The prizes include 2004 Prize Publituris for the 'Best Congress Space' for the Atlantico pavilion; 2003 Prize Order of Engineers 'As one of the most Remarkable National Works' for the Urban Park and Gare do Oriente station; 2001 Gold medal from the International Committee and International Association of Sports and Leisure Equipment; 1999 Prize for the best Urban Project in the Iberian Peninsula; 1998 several Prizes Valmor for the Portugal pavilion, Acquarium 'Oceanario de Lisboa' and Atlantico pavilion (a distinguished Portuguese Prize for Architecture), among many others.
4 The end of Park Expo in 2012 was more politically than economically motivated. Although Portugal had been living since 2009 in great economic recession, Parque Expo was thriving as an urban consultancy both nationally and internationally. Its demise can be explained by a change of national political power from a Socialist (PS) to a Conservative party (PSD), and therefore from its advocators to its opponents, respectively.

References

Aelbrecht, P. (2014) 'World Fair for the Future: A Study of the Legacy of the Expo '98 Urban Model'. In L. Hollengreen, C. Pearce, R. Rouse and B. Schweizer (eds) *Meet Me at the Fair*. Pittsburgh, PA: ETC Press, 485–502.

BIE (1988) *Preliminary Enquiry for BIE Registration or Recognition of International Exhibitions* (Version Ammendment 1928). Paris: Bureau International des Expositions.

BIE (2012) *Urban Best Practices Area.* Available at: www.bie-paris.org/site/en/Shanghai %202010/upba/135-urban-best-practices-area-ubpa.html (accessed 10 January 2012).

BIE (2012) *Global City 2011 Conference: How to Maximize Benefits from Mega Events.* Available at: www.bie-paris.org/site/en/articles/general-news/398-globa l-city-2011-conference.html, (accessed 10 January 2012).

Carrière, J.P. and Demazière, C. (2002) 'Urban planning and flagship development projects: Lessons from Expo 98, Lisbon', *Planning Practice and Research*, 17(1), 69–79.

Castro, A., Lucas, J. and Ferreira, Matias V. (1997) 'A "Engenharia" Financeira e as Variacoes Orcamentais Da Expo '98', *Sociologia - Problemas e Praticas*, 24, 211–230.

Fernandes, J.M. (2005) *7 Anos De Lisboa: 1997–2004 (arquitectura, Património, Urbanismo, Polémicas)*, Cidade De Lisboa. Lisboa, Livros Horizonte.

Graca Dias, M. (2007) 'Parque Das Nacoes'. Parque Das Nações: Noticias, Opinião, Fotografia. Available at: http://parquedasnacoes.blogspot.com.

Heeren, H. (1991) "Expo '98: An Ambitious Goal," *The Anglo-Portuguese News*, Lisbon, 2 May.

Kang, S.J. (2011) 'How to maximize benefits from mega events'. Presented at the Global City 2011 Conference, Abu Dhabi.

Leung, L. (2008) 'World Exposition (EXPO) and sustainable world city development: A case study of Shanghai EXPO 2010'. *MSc thesis, Urban Planning, The Centre of Urban Planning & Environmental Management, The University of Hong Kong*, 50–67.

Linden, G. and Creighton, P. (2000) 'Expo Article'. *Expo Exchange*. Washington D.C: Urban land Institute.

LosCertales, V. (2011) 'How to maximize benefits from mega events'. Presented at the Global City 2011 Conference, Abu Dhabi.

Mega Ferreira, A. (1994). Correspondence between Mega Ferreira (mentor Expo '98) and Vincent LosCertales, Secretary General of BIE, 20 January 1994, BIE archive, Lisbon.

Mega Ferreira, A. (2008) 'Context of Expo '98', in Seminar of 10 years of Expo' 98: City imagined/ city built, 7–8 November 2008, Portugal Pavilion, Park of the Nations, Lisbon (DVD format).

Ferreira, A. (2008) 'Contexto da Expo '98', Seminário 10 anos da Expo' 98: Cidade imaginada/ cidade concretizada, 7–8 Novembro 2008, Pavilhão de Portugal, Parque das Nações, Lisboa (formato DVD)].

Metaxas, T., Bati, A., Filippopoulos, D., Drakos, K. and Tzellou, V. (2011) 'Strategic place marketing and place branding: 15 years of mega-events in Lisbon', *Munich Personal RePEc Archive (MPRA) Paper No. 41004*, 1–27.

Ministerio do Ambiente, do Ordenamento do Territorio e do Desenvolvimento Regional (2008) *Portugal Politica De Cidades Polis XXI 2207–2013.*

Parque Expo (1999) *Documentos Para a História Da Expo '98: 1989–1992*, Parque Expo '98. Lisbon: Parque Expo S.A.

Parque Expo (2008) *Percepcao Da Qualidade De Vida Do Parque Das Nacoes.* Lisbon: Parque Expo S.A.

Portugal (1991) 'Portugal's Reply to Preliminary Enquiry for BIE Registration or Recognition of International Exhibitions (7 October, 1991)'. In *Documentos Para a História Da Expo '98: 1989–1992*, Parque Expo '98. Lisbon: Parque Expo S.A.

Publico (1998) *Expo '98 De Alto Nivel Conceptual e Estetico: Ole Simpson Deu Nota Elevada a Exposicao Mundial De Lisboa.* Lisbon: Publico.

Rydell, R.W. (1993) *World of Fairs: The Century-of-Progress Expositions.* Chicago: University of Chicago Press.

Swyngedouw, E., Moulaert, F. and Rodriguez, A. (2002) 'Neoliberal urbanization in Europe: Large-scale urban development projects and the new urban policy'. *Antipode*, 34(3), 542–577.

Wilson, M.I. and Huntoon, L. (2001) 'World's Fairs and Urban Development: Lisbon and Expo '98'. In *International Urban Planning Settings: Lessons of Success, International Review of Comparative Public Policy*, 12. Oxford: JAI, Elsevier Science.

5 The regional scale of contemporary mega-events

The Milan Expo 2015, the post-event and the challenges for public policies and spatial planning

Stefano Di Vita

Introduction

In a phase of growing disaffection with mega-events – that is evidenced by increasingly frequent withdrawals of city candidatures (in particular in Western countries) and their growing unsustainability (real or perceived) – Olympics and Expos seem more and more able to develop transcalar relationships with their spatial and socio-economic contexts: local, urban, regional, macro-regional and global (Di Vita and Morandi, 2018). Against this backdrop, and taking into account the regional scale of contemporary urban space (Soja, 2000; Scott, 2001; Hall and Pain, 2006; Brenner, 2014), this chapter analyses the case of the Milan Expo 2015 and ongoing post-Expo phase by focusing specifically on their connections to the Milan urban region: that is, a post-metropolitan space that extends from the Milan Municipality and Metropolitan City to the wider urbanised area of the surrounding provinces[1] (Balducci, Fedeli and Curci, 2017).

The localisation of the exhibition venue, the endowment of road and rail infrastructures, the development of green and blue networks, as well as the articulation of collateral initiatives and related placemaking processes have extended to an area that is larger than the Milan urban core. However, the capability of the 2015 'Worlds Fair' to interpret the regionalisation of contemporary urban space appears as the unintentional product of an implicit and unaware urban agenda, as it has been totally unplanned and external to any kind of wide strategic vision for the city and its surroundings. Referring to this interpretation, this chapter reflects on the current and potential capability of the ongoing post-Expo process and projects to consolidate and exploit the regional dimension of its spatial and infrastructural connections, as well as of the socio-economic networks that is able to intercept.

Within this lack of, and need for, an explicit strategic vision supporting spatial planning in the Milan urban region, the Expo 2015 and related post-event activities seem able to confirm that mega-events should not be considered as extraordinary phenomena, but rather as complicated episodes of ordinary urban change processes (Di Vita and Morandi, 2018). This new approach could be an important legacy provided by the Milan World's Fair to the hosting urban region, as well as to the ongoing Italian bid to host the 2026 Winter Olympics.

The intrinsic contradictions of mega-events and the relevance of the Milan case study

According to their large diffusion throughout world cities, their capability to synthesise the complexity of usually fragmented urban change processes, the long duration from their bid to their legacies, as well as their changing role in relation to different phases of world urban dynamics, mega-events can be considered as privileged reflection scenario on contemporary urban phenomena, also in relation to global geo-economic and geopolitical trends (Di Vita and Morandi, 2018).

Since the 1990s, as the promotion of city brands has grown as a priority of post-industrial urban policies, mega-events have become privileged tools of urban marketing and repositioning for host cities in world urban networks (Clark, 2008; Page and Connell, 2012; Muñoz, 2015; Gruneau and Horne, 2016) promoting their touristic and media attractiveness (Hall, 1992; Cashman and Hughes, 1999; Chalkley and Essex, 1999; Roche, 2000). Nevertheless, the world crisis – breaking out in 2008, first as a financial and economic crisis, and still ongoing as a social and political crisis (e.g. austerity) – now demands a deep reflection on the goals, tools and mechanisms of urban change processes: on the one hand, in order to upgrade growth dependent urban agendas by the last expansive cycle of the real estate market (Rydin, 2013; Knieling and Othengrafen, 2016); on the other, in order to update them to the regional scale of contemporary urban space.

In this context, the organisation of mega-events, and the exploitation of their material and immaterial legacies from the perspective of post-metropolitan spaces, could be an opportunity to reduce their intrinsic spatial and socio-economic unsustainability, which has affected their international reputation; for instance, the post-event abandonment of specific venues and infrastructures, or their negative impacts in terms of public debt and corruption, and the related social conflicts (Surborg, Van Wynsberghe and Wyly, 2008; Hayes and Karamichas, 2011; Poynter and MacRury, 2012; Gaffney, 2013; Broudehoux and Sánchez, 2015; Müller, 2015).

Against the backdrop of well-known spatial and socio-economic disasters, which have been led by global events such as the Olympics and Expos,[2] several cities have recently withdrawn their bids to host mega-events[3] because of political change or contrary public polls, petitions or referendums. Indeed, mega-event processes are often contradictory, and their outcomes cannot be taken for granted: their results and legacies frequently differ according to the cultural, political and socio-economic features of the hosting cities and countries, and they can change in relation to time variables (i.e. short-term or long-term) and space variables (i.e. local, urban or regional scale).

Figure 5.1 Italian pavilion at Milan Expo 2015
Source: editor.

Within this context, the Milan Expo 2015 and its post-event stage represent an important case study. On the one hand, according to their temporal dimension, the event bid and projects were promoted in 2006, before the outbreak of the global crisis, whereas their following organisation, implementation, celebration and post-event planning phases have been directly affected by the economic downturn, thus requiring different approaches and solutions from the past. On the other hand, according to their spatial dimension, the Expo and post-Expo spatial and infrastructural projects have involved a wide physical space, that extends to the scale of the urban region, whilst the networks of connected initiatives and involved actors are transcalar (from the local scale, to the national and international one)[4] (Di Vita and Morandi, 2018).

Whether mega-events are potential keys for reading contemporary urban phenomena, these specificities of and innovations in the Milan Expo and post-Expo stimulate a deep reflection about the necessary updating of both the event and post-event planning (Getz, 2008; Wilson, 2009; Gold, Gold, 2010; Kassens-Noor, 2016) in the frame of post-crisis urban agendas, policies and plans. Furthermore, this reflection cannot ignore the changes of the related process in time, and the transcalarity of the connected urban dynamics and networks in space.

Transcalarity of the territorial relationships fostered by the Milan Expo 2015

As it is quite usual in the development of big projects which are promoted on the occasion of mega-events, lights and shadows have characterised the process and outcomes of the Milan Expo 2015. According to the Candidature Dossier,[5] the organisation of the 2015 World's Fair, based on the theme 'Feeding the Planet, Energy for Life', provided Milan with temporary venues to host the exhibition in a former huge greenfield[6] site that was located between the municipal areas of Milan and Rho.[7]

The Expo site was placed in the surroundings of the new city fairground (that opened in 2005), the related railway and metro stations (that were respectively integrated within a new interchange node), and one of the most important motorway gate to the city, within the northwest sector of the Milan urban region's core: that is, along the most international access to the city, on the way to the Malpensa international airport, as well as to Switzerland and France, by directly connecting the exhibition area to several metropolitan city's districts and country's regions. At the same time, the Expo 2015 provided Milan with new public spaces (i.e. the renovation of the former city dockyard) and infrastructures (i.e. the new metro lines M4 and M5, and the new regional motorways Brebemi, Pedemontana and Teem), even though several interventions were not completed on time,[8] and others were postponed after the actual event finished, because of delays, lack of time and a decrease in economic resources.

After gaining the event, the implementation of dedicated works was quite difficult because of the financial crisis impacted on the necessary funds to finance the project,[9] the complexity of the governance process, as well as the availability of land where the exposition was to be located.[10] Despite these problems, which effectively penalised the event organisation itself, the Milan Expo 2015 has been a catalyst for resources, which have supported the ongoing phase of urban change within a process of growing internationalisation,[11] city repositioning and branding, both in terms of business and tourism.[12] The exposition itself was successful in relation to the safety of the site construction and use, its accessibility, and its capability to attract several participant countries and more visitors than expected during the exhibition semester[13] (Di Vita and Morandi, 2018), from 1 May to 31 October.

One of the innovations provided by the Expo 2015 concerns the spatial dimension of the event that extends to the scale of the urban region, not only according to the development of new infrastructures but also to the suburban location of the exhibition area, that is representative of a broaden perception and size of contemporary urban dynamics and phenomena. Furthermore, despite the BIE requirements for the localisation of its expositions in a completely fenced-in precinct, the placement of the Expo site in an enclave isolated by infrastructural barriers on each side, and the lack of relationships of the bid masterplan with its surrounding context, an unconventional and innovative vision was promoted on the occasion of the 2009 conceptual masterplan.[14] On the one hand, it aimed at representing the event theme (related to food and nutrition) spatially and democratically by supposing to provide participant countries with similar strips of land to be cultivated on the basis of their specific agricultural practices. On the other, through the two orthogonal main boulevards recalling the matrix of Roman settlements (that is, the Cardo and Decumano), it aimed at emphasising the orientation of surrounding urban tissues[15] along the Milan northwest infrastructural bundle of roads and railways (Di Vita and Morandi, 2018).

This solution was partially due to the need for experimenting with new spatial event-based projects, which were inspired by the same economic downturn and decrease of available economic resources. Even though it was partially modified through its integration with the issue of digital innovation and the consequent reintroduction of traditional pavilions,[16] the Expo 'planetary garden' also challenged the growing relations between cities and agriculture, which in Milan are particularly and traditionally strong.[17]

Despite the partial decrease in its potential for spatial innovation, the democratic approach of the Milan Expo 2015 remained, for instance, in the so-called thematic clusters. They were pavilions, alternative to the national ones, which were planned to host together those countries not able to afford their independent and autonomous participation in the event. Therefore they were collective pavilions,[18] which were designed through the collaboration of university academics and students coming from several universities worldwide under the coordination of the Politecnico di Milano (Collina, 2015), thus favouring university expertise in international cooperation. Similarly, the Expo masterplan contributed to making both the exhibition project and site as a node of transcalar networks (local and supra-local) through the destination of the former farmhouse named Cascina Triulza into the 'pavilion of the third sector', hosting social events and activities by not-for-profit organisations. These networks were not only temporary but were also able to exploit their potential after the event's conclusion, with this pavilion – managed by the Foundation Triulza[19] – working as 'Lab-Hub for Social Innovation' without interruption since its inception in 2013.

According to the Candidature Dossier, the Expo site was to be integrated with the Water Way project – originally promoted as navigable canal to connect the exhibition area to the ancient dockyard in the city centre (the Darsena). However, in the face of decreasing resources and the increased awareness of technical difficulties, as well as the growing sensitivity around the spatial expression of the event at the scale of the urban region, the 2009 conceptual masterplan maintained the proposal of this new infrastructure according to its hydraulic function,[20] but they combined it with landscape and leisure provision. Despite its incomplete implementation,[21] the project was adapted into a wider landscape plan able to connect the existing metropolitan parks in the northwest sector of the Milan urban region, whose potential could be still exploited in the post-event phase.

Besides the spatial and infrastructural projects, the organisation and management of the Milan Expo 2015 also made a contribution to the event's transcalarity. As it is usual for mega-events promoted by the CIO[22] (Summer and Winter Olympics) and the BIE[23] (Expos/World's Fairs), the Milan universal exhibition sought to reconcile 'exceptional' supra-national standardised regulations to 'ordinary' local policies and plans.

Whilst the 2006–2007 event bid was successful – thanks to an unprecedented cooperation between the National Government, the Regional Government, the Provincial and Municipal Administrations,[24] and the Milan Chamber of Commerce and Trade Fair Foundation – the establishment of the official Expo governance arrangements after the event was awarded by the BIE in March 2008, was as complicated as the definition of the agreement about the acquisition of the Expo areas themselves. Despite the persisting conflicts between the National Government, the Regional Government and the Milan Municipal Administration,[25] the official governance for the event was approved by a National Decree in October 2008, leading to:

- the Expo 2015 SpA management company,[26] tasked with the planning and building of the exhibition area, and the organisation and management of the event itself;
- the so-called Tavolo Lombardia,[27] aimed at improving the regional and urban accessibility to both the city and the exposition site (Basso and Di Vita, 2018).

Together with the short time from candidature to celebration and the immovable deadline of the Expo opening to visitors, the specific event planning and governance were established and strengthened according to a para-emergency approach. In particular, the Milan Expo 2015 provided a specific process of intentional emergency building,[28] thus confirming theories on a progressive 'normalisation' of the 'state of exceptions', and this para-emergency approach led to negative effects on the development of the event's material and immaterial projects (Basso, 2017). The establishment of exceptional policy measures, such as special procedures, planning tools and governance arrangements (promoted by specific national and regional laws),[29] was often criticised because of the fragmentation of actors and confusion of rules, the frequent derogations from ordinary procedures and legislations, and the related inefficiencies and episodes of corruption[30] (Basso and Di Vita, 2018). Nevertheless, this complexity has not affected the capability of experimenting with unprecedented transcalar cooperation (public-public or public-private). On the contrary, Milan World's Fair has involved a huge system of other (official or otherwise) programmes and actors, which has positively contributed to the organisation and management of collateral initiatives, and which have fostered beneficial effects in terms of territorial governance.[31] In some cases they have contributed to the exploitation of the event theme at the scale of the urban region, by merging and enhancing local relationships with national and international ones (Di Vita, 2017). For example, the E015 Digital Ecosystem,[32] the Expo Working Groups,[33] Expoincittà,[34] Explora,[35] the Territorial Coalitions for Expo,[36] Expo and Territories,[37] Laboratory Expo,[38] and Women for Expo,[39] as well as the Urban Food Policy Pact and the Milan Food Policy[40] (Basso and Di Vita, 2018).

This articulated system of initiatives could be considered as part of the event's immaterial legacies, even though they are as yet, difficult to assess, especially in the short term. This is an open challenge that could apply through the post-event re-use of the Expo site, as well as the development of a wide and long-term agenda for the urban region. At the moment, they evidence the transcalar territorial articulation of the Expo 2015 and its connected placemaking processes, which have been enabled by the re-activation of several built and open spaces fostered by the universal exhibition and its collateral initiatives: from the Expo site to the Darsena, passing through all those places involved by the above mentioned spatial and infrastructural projects and cultural programmes (Bruzzese and Di Vita, 2016).

Transcalarity of the territorial connections aimed by the Milan post-Expo

During the exhibition semester, the Expo area worked as a transcalar platform between local and global flows of people, goods and information, as well as a new centrality at the scale of the urban region. Also thanks to improved transport connections and the low cost of evening entry tickets to the Expo, the site was perceived as a new extension of the urban environment. Unfortunately, despite general plans[41] aimed at the real estate redevelopment of the exposition area, a specific legacy plan for the post-event re-use of the site was only approved in 2017.[42] The specification of the main strategies and functions became necessary after the failure of the 2014 public competition for selecting the real estate buyer and developer of the area.[43] A change in the post-Expo governance was therefore inevitable, leading to the direct involvement of the National Government in the structure of the post-event dedicated delivery vehicle.[44]

This change, implemented by the Renzi Government, was functional to the allocation of new public investment in the area,[45] which was originally excluded, but then provided to support the development of new public facilities. In order to overcome the traditional assembly of urban spaces, which had been undermined by the crisis (Bolocan Goldstein, 2015), these included the new Human Technopole research centre on life sciences and biotech, and the new scientific campus of the Università degli Studi di Milano. Together with the new Galeazzi private hospital and the proposal for an innovation district (hosting private firms operating in the field of technology),[46] these public facilities have been gradually and fragmentally promoted in order to integrate the original real estate development project, which mixed residential and productive functions, and to make both the site and its context (urban, regional and national) more attractive for investors. The goal has been to capitalise on Milan's efforts for the Expo organisation and celebration, as well as the event successes, in order to promote both the international consolidation of the local knowledge economy system that confirms the Milan urban region as the cultural and economic capital of the country, both nationally and worldwide (Bolocan Goldstein, 2015).

According to its peri-urban, but very accessible location, and to the new and articulated functional mix approved by the 2017 post-Expo masterplan, the post-event scientific and technological park (now called Mind)[47] has the potential to elevate the site as central to the urban region. In doing so, it could be able to intercept and exploit local and supra-local networks, both material and immaterial: from transport to actors, such as local and national public institutions and companies, as well as local and international enterprises and associations. In particular, in relation to the specialisation of its planned public and private functions, this large urban transformation could lead to the configuration of a transcalar node for the biomedical sector, with potential benefits to both the spatial and socio-economic spheres.[48]

In order to consolidate its role of centrality at the scale of the urban region, and to enhance its capability to intercept transcalar material and immaterial networks, the development of spatial, infrastructural and functional connections will be strategic, thus challenging the traditional fields of the urban policy, planning and design. Whilst urban design and masterplanning of the post-event site development was recently assigned to the private Australian company Lend Lease[49] (also active in the London 2012 Olympic Village, Evans, 2010), weaknesses remain with the relationships with the ongoing planning system of the urban region itself. Indeed, according to an implicit extension of the Expo para-emergency approach,[50] current plans – municipal, metropolitan and regional – tend to not interfere with the redevelopment of the Expo site in order to not further slow down its configuration and implementation.

Together with the gradual innovation in its functional mix, the post-event process has recently experimented with new dedicated procedures – for instance, by entrusting to Lend Lease both the technical advice for the executive masterplan and its partial implementation. Nevertheless, as the Milan Expo 2015 and post-Expo have been mainly disadvantaged by political and institutional conflicts (in particular, between the city, the region and the state), which have partially threaten their organisations, the process is still promoted from the Arexpo sectoral point of view, thus limiting a wider and longer-term strategic vision (Pasqui, 2018). As the ongoing post-event scenario confirms, the ordinary local public administrations of the Milan urban region risk being detached from planning procedures for years because the post-Expo legal framework is disproportionately imbalanced by its independence from ordinary policy and planning tools and its development imperatives (Basso and Di Vita, 2018). On the other hand, the development of an explicit urban agenda could avoid risks of unplanned and incomplete implementation of current proposals, such as those which occurred during the first metamorphosis of the city from the 1980s to the 2008 global crisis (Armondi and Di Vita, 2018).

This agenda could support the long-term exploitation of the Expo 2015 cultural contribution to global ethical issues which connect to its theme reflected in the Urban Food Policy Pact,[51] the Milan Food Policy and other initiatives promoted on the occasion of the universal exhibition. Similarly, it could also enhance a capacity-building process in event planning and management, as well as inter-institutional or public-private networking activities. This process and these activities make an important contribution to the articulation of the event legacies, which could be exploited through a systematic and organic approach, rather than a sectoral or para-emergency one (Basso and Di Vita, 2018).

Legacies of the Milan Expo and post-Expo projects and processes

Is the Expo indebted to Milan or is Milan indebted to the Expo (Pasqui, 2015)? For sure, Milan has been able to introduce several innovations in mega-event planning and management (e.g. theme, settlement, networking, opening to different users). At the same time, the Expo 2015 and post-Expo to date has led to positive effects on the urban economy and environment, even though several districts of the urban region still suffer from the never-ending condition of urban inequality and segregation of some neighbourhoods (Ranci and Cucca, 2016) within a growing process of 'poor metropolitanization' (Centro Studi PIM, 2016).

The Milan Expo and post-Expo legacies reciprocally intercept material and immaterial issues. In general terms, the Milan exhibition and the current post-event exploitation of venues, infrastructures and collateral initiatives represent an innovative discontinuity from the past event editions approved by the BIE. Indeed, they have challenged the traditional model of the Expo and post-Expo enclaves by exploiting (not always intentionally and consciously) their potentially transcalar relationships and connections (Bolocan Goldstein, 2015), both physical and intangible: from those at the local scale to those at the international level, with a city now extended into the wider region.

This challenge has been met through the localisation of the exhibition area and the future innovation district in a peri-urban place that is physically and culturally, locally and globally well connected, as it had already happened in previous Expo editions (i.e. the ones of Lisbon 1998, Zaragoza 2008 or Shanghai 2010) (Di Vita and Morandi, 2018). This implicit goal has also been mainly achieved through the Milan Expo and post-Expo integration with smaller events and initiatives, which have spread at the urban, regional, national and international levels, and which in many cases have been maintained and renovated even after 2015, also in connection to the main cultural and economic assets of the city and its region (i.e. design, fashion, food, music, publishing). Accordingly, this discontinuity has been working in relation to the spatial and temporal dimension of both the city and the Expo, by representing one of the main event and post-event legacies, and demanding its further strengthening.

On the one hand, the spatial dimension has changed not only in relation to the Expo and post-Expo site masterplans of (what remained of) the planetary garden (2009) and of the Mind innovation district (2017) – for instance, by respectively reinterpreting the event theme of food and nutrition, and the post-event theme of health and predictive medicine. It has changed in relation to their correspondence to the regional scale of contemporary urban space, for instance by locating in a peri-urban and very connected place, and taking the shape of new centrality of the urban region and node between local and supra-local flows of people, information and goods. It has also changed according to the urban and regional spread of collateral events and related exhibition spaces, whether officially recognised or not. On the other hand, the temporal dimension has changed according to the integration and exploitation of such an extraordinary exhibition in a still ongoing process of urban festivalisation, whose origins can be identified before the Expo, in by-now consolidated events (i.e. the Milan Design Week and Fashion Week).

This process is frequently criticised because of the congestion, gentrification and some ephemeral outcomes it provides, even though it is not possible to ignore that it contributes to the ongoing Milan cultural and economic development, both according to its direct effects and to its potential in terms of city branding (Camera di Commercio di Milano, 2016). Besides, despite its original problems and weaknesses in terms of planning and governance, the post-Expo process itself has potential to experiment with new approaches, procedures and contents within the current urban metamorphosis. Even though it is not yet possible to assess it completely, the recent reconfiguration of goals, governance and plans concerning the post-event re-use of the Expo site has inverted the usual order of the Milan urban transformation projects, from spatial development to function selection, into the opposite one, from functional programme to space solution (Bolocan Goldstein, 2015). This inversion could partially avoid the risks of the development of new urban voids in a still weak post-crisis phase for the real-estate market. Nonetheless, this change has not corresponded yet to the development of new visions and plans for the city and its urban region that could also avoid the risks of conflicts with other existing urban functions, spaces and projects.

As the knowledge economy encompasses both local spaces and multiscalar networks, material (infrastructural, spatial) and immaterial (cognitive, financial, organisational, relational), these potentials of innovation foster the reconfiguration of the post-Expo redevelopment project into a knowledge hub, able to exploit its transcalar features. This could be an innovative and timely challenge for urban policies and planning, which demand new functional and spatial assets, as well as new strategic and spatial planning approaches, procedures and contents. This challenge could exploit the Milan Expo's discontinuty within the post-event phase if the post-Expo strategies, plans and projects for the re-use of the exhibition area will be able to face the whole Milan urban region and overcome the current enclave effect (Bolocan Goldstein, 2015), firstly by improving the physical connections with its immediate spatial surroundings, and secondly by enhancing its functional relationships with existing and planned centralities and activities in the Milan urban core and its region, going beyond the current administrative fragmentation (no longer corresponding to the ongoing urban dynamics), and supporting the regional polycentrism (historically evoked, but never achieved). Similarly, the 'Expo in città' network of collateral events could be usefully integrated into the ongoing regeneration processes of the urban peripheries in order to exploit city branding by avoiding the risks of 'festivalization' of the urban space, and stimulating social inclusion (Morandi, 2018). Thus, this challenge demands further innovation in terms of both the territorial governance and agenda that should be explicit and shared.

Conclusion

Despite the growing unsustainability of and disaffection with mega-events – which are mainly related to their disruption and diversion of ordinary urban processes, plans, projects and economic resources – Olympics and Expos could be able not only to implicitily interpret, but also to explicitily exploit the potential of the regional scale of contemporary urban space. This is the intermediate level between local and supra-local flows that it is necessary to deal with in order to better enhance the transcalar relationships between mega-events and their spatial and socio-economic contexts – local, urban, regional, macro-regional and global.

The Milan case proves that mega-events cannot be considered anymore as 'exceptions' but as recurrent episodes of wider urban change processes, according to their long processes and broadening spaces (Di Vita and Morandi, 2018). Also, in order to reduce their negative externalities (i.e. high costs in a context of decreasing availability of economic resources, territorial congestion, inequalities and unsustainability), the Milan case shows that mega-events need to deal with transcalar networks of urban activities, functions and spaces in the frame of the knowledge economy (Bolocan Goldstein, 2015).

Whilst, in a globalising urban world, rising tensions between cities and states, determined by growing urban spaces and networks, call for updated tools of planning and systems of governance (Rydin, 2013; Knieling and Othengrafen, 2016), and the overhaul of traditional scales of public authorities becomes necessary (Dierwechter, 2017), wide urban regions are more and more crucial in their duality which connects the international and the sub-national (Taylor, 2013; Herrschel and Newman, 2017).

Against the backdrop of the Milan Expo 2015 and post-Expo outcomes and legacies, the withdrawal of the Rome candidature to the 2020 and 2024 Summer Olympics, as well as the ongoing worldwide reactions to globalisation and related socio-economic criticalities (Fainstein, 2010; Harvey, 2012), Italy has been making another contribution to the debate about mega-event and urban planning and governance. Nevertheless, it has been making it in a creative way, within its traditional inner political conflicts, and without a clear and shared strategy. On the occasion of the ongoing bidding for the 2026 Winter Olympics, within the preliminary national selection process of the Italian candidate, the Italian National Olympic Committee (CONI) has tried to experiment with an innovative solution by promoting a macro-regional candidature to involve all the three competitors: Turin and the Piedmont Alps, Milan and the Lombardy Alps, and Cortina d'Ampezzo and the Veneto Alps.

Despite the risks in terms of planning and governance, this candidature could have been challenging and timely for both the enrolled cities and regions, and the International Olympic Committee (IOC): not only because of the main aim of re-using existing venues and infrastructures, but mainly because it could have experimented with a macro-regional mega-event, that could have involved one of the most dynamic world city-regions (Balducci, Fedeli and Curci, 2017). Unfortunately, at the end of September 2018, because of transcalar conflicts between political parties, and in-between their city, regional and national representations, Turin refused to share this candidature, that was officially presented by the CONI to the IOC as the 'Milan and Cortina' bid to the 2026 Winter Olympic Games. Milan-Cortina won the bid to host the 2026 Winter Olympics, despite Turin's withdrawal, beating Stockholm, whose bid was judged to lack public support (see Olson, Chapter 8).

Even though the ongoing candidature is spatially reduced, in comparison with the original proposal, the expectation for a territorial project, and not only for a mega-event one, remains. This project should be innovative not only in terms of spatial scale but also in terms of goals and contents, approaches and methods, as well as planning and governance. In this regard, an interesting example is provided by the German IBA editions of the Emscher Park (1989–1999) and Parkstad (2013–2020), which offer several suggestions for long-term urban agendas about post-metropolitan spaces on the occasion of hosting temporary mega-events (Di Vita and Morandi, 2018).

Notes

1 Whilst the Milan Municipality covers an area extending for 182 km^2 and hosting around 1.4 million inhabitants and the Milan Metropolitan city covers an area extending for 1,575 km^2 and hosting around 3.2 million inabitants, the Milan urban region includes the surrounding provinces of Varese, Como, Lecco, Monza-Brianza, Bergamo, Lodi and Pavia in Lombardy, and Novara in Piedmont, hosting around 7.5 million inhabitants (OECD, 2006).

2 For instance, Athens 2004 and Rio de Janeiro 2016, just to mention the most famous and recent problematic cases (Petsimeris, 2012; Broudehoux and Sánchez, 2015).

3 For instance, in the case of Summer Olympics, Rome withdrew from the bids to the 2020 and 2024 Games; Boston, Budapest and Hamburg from the bid to the 2024 Games; Amsterdam, Shanghai and Vienna from the bid to the 2028 Games. In the case of Winter Olympics, Oslo withdrew from the bid to the 2022 Games; Auckland and Queenstown, Barcelona, Boston, Dresden, Graubunden and Quebec City from the bid to the 2026 Games (Di Vita and Morandi, 2018).

4 See the following paragraph.

5 This was developed in 2006–7 by the Milan Expo Bidding Committee and approved in March 2008 by the Bureau International des Expositions (BIE).
6 That extends for approximately 1,050 million m^2.
7 In particular, the Expo area lies within the boundaries of the Milan municipality (85%) and the Rho municipality (15%).
8 For instance, only the metro M5 and the motorways Brebemi and Teem were concluded on time for the event celebration, whereas the metro M4 and the motorway Pedemontana are still under contruction.
9 In parallel to the impact of the world crisis on the Milan real estate market, resulting in the interruption of several redevelopment projects, dedicated funds were seriously reduced from an initial budget of 3.227 billion euros (in 2007) to 1.446 (in 2012), shared by the National Government (833 million euros), the regional and local public authorities (477 million euros), and the private sponsors (136 million euros) (Di Vita and Morandi, 2018).
10 On the total of the areas involved by the Accordo di Programma (around 1,050,000 m^2), originally their main owners were private: from the Milan Trade Fair Foundation (520,000 m^2), to the real estate company Belgioiosa Srl (260,000m^2). Whilst no real alternatives for the Expo localisation were discussed, several political fights affected their acquisition and, accordingly, the development and implementation of the event and post-event plans and works. The planning agreement was approved in late 2011 and works started at the beginning of 2012 only (Di Vita and Morandi, 2018).
11 In Milan, the main Italian financial and economic hub (OECD, 2006), as well as the main core of the Italian knowledge-based, creative, digital and sharing economy (Camera di Commercio di Milano, 2016), 17.7% of regular jobs are taken by foreigners, 15% of the enterprises are run by migrants, and university students total 200,000–7% of them foreign students (Di Vita and Morandi, 2018).
12 Besides the strengthening of the demand for the location of up-market brands, the number of tourists increased from 5.6 million (in 2010) to 7.3 million (in 2015) and 7.4 (in 2016), and the rate of leisure tourism (culture, events, shopping) increased by 50%, more than business tourism (Camera di Commercio di Milano, 2016).
13 Around 140 participant countries, and 21.5 million real visitors in comparison with the expected 20 million.
14 That is, the preliminary version of the new masterplan, following the Expo assignment to Milan, proposed by a committee of international designers such as Stefano Boeri (Italy), Richard Burdett (UK), Joan Busquets (Spain), Jaques Herzog (Switzerland) and William McDonough (US).
15 Which have been connected through a couple of pedestrian bridges overpassing the infrastructural barriers surrounding the exhibition area.
16 Officially, in order to balance this event innovative vision with more pragmatic solutions and, consequently, to make the exposition more attractive for international investors, pavilions of participant countries were reintroduced.
17 For instance, in its urban region, Milan hosts one of the widest and most important agricultural parks (the Southern Agricultural Park) dedicated to both food production and leisure, as well as a deeply-rooted agribusiness system (Assolombarda, 2017).
18 These clusters articulated into themes related to food (*Cereals and Tubers; Cocoa; Coffee; Fruit and Legumes; Rice; Spices*) or to geographical areas (*Arid Zones; Bio-Mediterranean; Islands*).
19 Specifically established by 67 associations (website: www.fondazionetriulza.org/en/).
20 To take the water to the Expo site's perimetral canal, and then to disperse it.
21 Only the north sector (from the Naviglio Villoresi to the Expo site) and central sector (around the Expo site) were completed on time for the event opening, whereas the south sector (from the Expo site to the Naviglio Grande) was stopped because of technical and environmental reasons, and the related protests by groups

of citizens and associations, with the only exception of the rehabilitation of the former Darsena in the city centre (one of the most successful urban spaces upgraded on the occasion of the Expo outside the perimeters of the exhibition area).

22 The Comité International Olympique.
23 The Bureau International des Expositions.
24 Despite, during the bidding phase, their different political orientation: National Government and Provincial Administration to the left, and Regional Government and Municipal Administration to the right.
25 Despite, during the organising phase, their similar political orientation to the right.
26 Formed by the Ministry of Economy and Finances of the Italian Government (40%), the Lombardy Regional Government (20%), the Milan Municipal Administration (20%), the former Milan Provincial Administration (10%), and the Milan Chamber of Commerce (10%).
27 Directed by the Lombardy Regional Government.
28 According to its preventive declaration of 'major event' in 2007, before the event official assignment to Milan.
29 This model transferred the National Civil Protection system – introduced in order to tackle 'natural emergencies' – to atypical (but intentional and planned) 'administrative emergencies' due to ineffective/complex government activities/issues (Basso and Di Vita, 2018).
30 For instance, some anomalies were found in selection criterions to assign contracts (Basso and Di Vita, 2018).
31 For instance, shown in 2016–2017, on the occasion of the post-Brexit Milan candidature to the relocation of the European Medicine Agency (EMA) headquarter.
32 Promoted by Expo 2015 SpA with the Milan Chamber of Commerce and national or local associations of industry and commerce sectors, with technical and scientific coordination by the Politecnico di Milano's Cefriel (www.e015.regione.lombardia.it/PE015/).
33 Promoted by Promos (a Milan Chamber of Commerce agency) (www.tavoliexpo.it/).
34 Promoted by Milan Municipality and Milan Chamber of Commerce (http://it.expoincitta.com/).
35 Promoted by Lombardy Regional Government with Expo 2015 SpA, Milan Chamber of Commerce and Unioncamere Lombardia (www.wonderfulexpo2015.it/).
36 Promoted by provincial or sub-provincial pacts, agreements or associations within the Lombardy regional area.
37 Coordinated by the Italian Presidency of the Council of Ministers (www.expo2015.org/archive/it/progetti/expo-e-territori.html).
38 Promoted by Expo 2015 SpA and Fondazione Feltrinelli (Website: www.fondazionefeltrinelli.it/laboratorio-expo/).
39 Promoted by Expo 2015 SpA, Fondazione Mondadori and the Italian Minister for Foreign Affairs (www.we.expo2015.org/it/).
40 Both promoted by the Milan Municipality and Fondazione Cariplo in cooperation with other cities, local actors and stakeholders (www.comune.milano.it/wps/portal/ist/st/food_policy_milano/Milan+Food+Policy).
41 Besides the 2006–2007 Expo Candidature Dossier, the reference is to the 2011 Expo Agreement and to the 2013 first post-event masterplan for the Expo site, just defining area regimes and plot ratios, but not specific strategic functions.
42 By the second post-event masterplan for the Expo area.
43 Indeed, also because of the financial and economic crisis, no private operators candidated to this public call.
44 That is, Arexpo Spa, established in 2011 by the Lombardy Regional Government (34.67%), the Milan Municipality (34.67%), the Milan Trade Fair Foundation (27.66%), the former Milan Provincial Administration (2%) and the Rho Municipality (1%), and modified in 2016 through the involvement of the Ministry of

84   *Stefano Di Vita*

Economy and Finances of the Italian Government (39.28%) with the Lombardy Regional Government (21.05%), the Milan Municipality (21.05%), the Milan Trade Fair Foundation (about 16.80%) and, with minor quotas, the new Milan Metropolitan City (1.21%) and the Rho Municipality (0.61%).

45 Beginning with 150 million per year, for a total amount of 10 years, allocated by the Italian Government at the end of 2015.

46 According to the idea suggested by Assolombarda (the Lombardy association of industrialists) in 2014.

47 That stands for Milan Innovation Distric (Website: www.mindmilano.it/).

48 According to the 2017 masterplan for the re-use of the Expo site, the Human Technopole will host 1,500 scientists and researchers, the Università degli Studi di Milano scientific campus will attract about 20,000 users a day, whereas the Galeazzi Hospital will bring around 17,000 users a day (adding to future residents and to workers in national and international enterprises relocating in the area). In particular, the Human Technopole, coordinated by the Italian Institute of Techonology in collaboration with some Milan universities, aims at being a research hub by providing multi-disciplinary research activities on the fields of Medical genomics, Neurogenomics, Agri-food and nutrition genomics, Data science, Computational life sciences, Nano science and technology, and Analysis, decision and society (Bolocan Goldstein, 2015), thus reinterpreting and exploiting the Expo 2015 theme ('Feeding the planet, energy for life').

49 The company that won the second public competition, promoted by Arexpo in 2017.

50 See the previous paragraph.

51 Signed by 113 worldwide cities and delivered to the UN General Secretary, Ban Ki-Moon, on 16 October 2015.

References

Armondi, S. and Di Vita, S. (eds) (2018) *Milan: Productions, Spatial Patterns and Urban Change*. London and New York: Routledge.

Assolombarda (2017) *Milano Scoreboard 2017*. Milano: Assolombarda. [Online: www.osservatoriomilanoscoreboard.it/en].

Balducci, A., Fedeli, V. and Curci, F. (eds) (2017) *Post-Metropolitan Territories: Looking for a New Urbanity*. London and New York: Routledge.

Basso, M. (2017) *Grandi eventi e politiche urbane. Governare «routine eccezionali»: un confronto internazionale*. Milan: Guerini e Associati.

Basso, M. and Di Vita, S. (2018) 'The Planning and Governance of the Expo 2015 and the Post-event. The Growth of a New Awareness: Overcoming the State of Exception'. In S. Di Vita and C. Morandi (eds) *Mega-Events and Legacies in Post-Metropolitan Spaces: Expos and Urban Agendas*. Basingstoke: Palgrave Macmillan, 39–63.

Bolocan Goldstein, M. (2015) 'Post-Expo geographical scenarios', *Urbanistica*, 155, 118–122.

Brenner, N. (ed.) (2014) *Implosions / Explosions: Towards a Study of Planetary Urbanization*. Berlin: Jovis Verlag.

Broudehoux, A.M., and Sánchez, F. (2015) 'The Politics of Mega-Event Planning in Rio de Janeiro: Contesting the Olympic City of Exception'. In V. Viehoff, and G. Poynter (eds), *Mega-Event Cities: Urban Legacies of Global Sport Events*. Farnham and Burlington, VT: Ashgate.

Bruzzese, A. and Di Vita, S. (2016) 'Learning from (Milan) Expo', *Territorio*, 77, 95–105.

Camera di Commercio di Milano (2016) *Milano produttiva 2016*. Milan: Bruno Mondadori.

Cashman, R. and Hughes, A. (eds) (1999), *Staging the Olympics: The Event and its Impact*. Sydney: University of New South Wales Press.

Centro Studi PIM (2016) 'Spazialità metropolitane. Economia, società e territorio', *Argomenti e Contributi*, 15, Special Issue.

Chalkley, B. and Essex, S. (1999) 'Urban development through hosting international events: A history of the Olympic Games', *Planning Perspectives*, 14(4), 369–394.

Clark, G. (2008) *Local Development Benefits from Staging Major Events*. Paris: OECD.

Collina, L. (ed.) (2015) 'Building the Expo', Domus, Special Issue.

Di Vita, S. (2017) 'Planning and governing large events in Italy: From Milan to Rome', *Archivio di Studi Urbani e Regionali*, 119, 119–138.

Di Vita, S. and Morandi, C. (2018) *Mega-events and Legacies in Post-Metropolitan Spaces: Expos and Urban Agendas*. Basingstoke: Palgrave Macmillan.

Dierwechter, Y. (2017) *Urban Sustainability through Smart Growth*. Cham: Springer.

Evans, G.L. (2010) 'London 2012'. In J. Gold and M. Gold (eds) *Olympic Cities: City Agendas, Planning and the World's Games, 1896–2012*. London: Routledge, 359–389.

Fainstein, S.S. (2010) *The Just City*. Ithaca: Cornell University Press.

Gaffney, C. (2013) 'Between discourse and reality: The un-sustainability of mega-event planning', *Sustainability*, 5, 3926–3940.

Getz, D. (2008) *Event Studies: Theory, Research and Policy for Planned Events*. London and New York: Routledge.

Gold, J.R. and Gold, M.M. (eds) (2010) *Olympic Cities: City Agendas, Planning and the World's Games, 1896–2012*. London: Routledge.

Gruneau, R. and Horne, J. (eds) (2016) *Mega-Events and Globalization: Capital and Spectacle in a Changing World Order*. London and New York: Routledge.

Hall, C.M. (1992) *Hallmark Tourist Events: Impacts, Management and Planning*. London: Belhaven.

Hall, P. and Pain, K. (eds) (2006) *The Polycentric Metropolis: Learning from Mega-City Regions in Europe*. London: Earthscan.

Harvey, D. (2012) *Rebel Cities: From the Right to the City to the Urban Revolution*. New York: Verso Books.

Hayes, G. and Karamichas, J. (eds) (2011) *Olympic Games, Mega-Events and Civil Societies*. Basingstoke: Palgrave Macmillan.

Herrschel, T. and Newman, P. (2017) *Cities as International Actors. Urban and Regional Governance: Beyond the Nation State*. Basingstock: Palgrave Macmillan.

Kassens-Noor, E. (2016) 'From ephemeral planning to permanent urbanism: An urban planning theory of mega-events', *Urban Planning* 1(1), 41–54.

Knieling, J. and Othengrafen, F. (eds) (2016) *Cities in Crisis*. London and New York: Routledge.

Morandi, C. (2018) 'From the Post-Expo 2015 to an Urban Agenda for Milan'. In S. Di Vita and C. Morandi (eds) *Mega-Events and Legacies in Post-Metropolitan Spaces: Expos and Urban Agendas*. Basingstoke: Palgrave Macmillan, 65–78.

Müller, M. (2015) 'The mega-event syndrome: Why so much goes wrong in mega-event planning and what to do about it', *Journal of the American Planning Association* 81(1), 6–17.

Muñoz, F. (2015) 'Urbanalisation and City Mega-Events. From 'Copy & Paste' Urbanism to Urban Creativity'. In V. Viehoff, and G. Poynter (eds), *Mega-Event Cities: Urban Legacies of Global Sport Events*. Farnham and Burlington, VT: Ashgate.

OECD (2006) *OECD Territorial Reviews: Milan, Italy.* Paris: OECD Publishing.

Page, S.G. and Connell, J. (eds) (2012) *The Routledge Handbook of Events.* London and New York: Routledge.

Pasqui, G. (2018a) 'Expo 2015 and Milan: Intertwined stories', *Urbanistica,* 155, 106–109.

Pasqui, G. (2018b) 'The last cycle of Milan urban policies and the prospects for a new urban agenda'. In S. Armondi and S. Di Vita (eds) *Milan: Productions, Spatial Patterns and Urban Change.* London and New York: Routledge, 133–144.

Petsimeris, P. (2012) 'Producing space for cosmopolis: Urban development in Olympic cities in Europe – lessons from Barcelona, Athens and London'. Paper presented at the Annual Meeting of the IGU Urban Geographic Commission 'Transformations of the Urban', Dortmund (Germany), 21–27 August.

Poynter, G. and MacRury, I. (eds) (2009) *Olympic Cities: 2012 and the Remaking of London.* Farnham and Burlington, VT: Ashgate.

Ranci, C. and Cucca, R. (eds) (2016) *Unequal Cities: The Challenge of Post-Industrial Transition in Times of Austerity.* London and New York: Routledge.

Roche, M. (2000) *Mega Events and Modernity.* London and New York: Routledge.

Rydin, Y. (2013) *The Future of Planning: Beyond Growth Dependence.* Bristol: University of Bristol Policy Press.

Scott, A.J. (ed.) (2001) *Global City-Regions: Trends, Theory, Policy.* Oxford: Oxford University Press.

Soja, E.W. (2000) *Postmetropolis: Critical Studies of Cities and Regions.* Oxford: Basil Blackwell.

Surborg, B., Van Wynsberghe, R. and Wyly, E. (2008) 'Mapping the Olympic growth machine: Transnational urbanism and the growth machine diaspora', *City: Analysis of Urban Trends, Culture, Theory, Policy, Action,* 12(3), 341–355.

Taylor, P. (2013) *Extraordinary Cities: Millennia of Moral Syndromes, World-System and City/State Relations.* Cheltenham: Edward Elgar.

Viehoff, V. and Poynter, G. (eds) (2015) *Mega-event Cities: Urban Legacies of Global Sport Events.* Farnham and Burlington, VT: Ashgate.

Wilson, M. (2009) 'Event Engineering: Urban Planning for Olympics and World's Fairs'. In S.D. Brunn (ed.), *Engineering Earth: The Impacts of Mega-Engineering Projects.* Dordrecht: Springer Science+Business Media, 1045–1056.

6 Fighting Faust

Resisting exclusion in Rio de Janeiro's pre-Olympic urban image-construction programme

Anne-Marie Broudehoux

In 2009, Rio de Janeiro was selected as host of the 2016 Summer Olympics, just a few years after Brazil had been chosen to hold the 2014 Fédération Internationale de Football Association (FIFA) World Cup, with Rio hosting the finals. As one of the rare cities in recent history to receive the world's two top sporting mega-events, especially within a two-year span, Rio de Janeiro would embark on a massive urban image-construction programme, to prepare for this unprecedented 'double whammy'.

This chapter centres upon the transformation of Rio de Janeiro in the years leading to the hosting of the two mega-events, with a special focus on its socio-spatial implications. Based on almost ten years of empirical research in Rio de Janeiro, it details various seductive urban image-construction strategies developed to sell both the body and the soul of Brazil's tourism capital, in order to lure foreign investors and visitors. It also explores the dark underside of event-led urban redevelopment and its lasting consequences upon vulnerable members of society. The chapter further describes various means of resistance to exclusion, invisibilisation and silencing, as they were deployed in the months leading to the city's two mega-events, and discusses the mitigated impacts of these various strategies.

Striking a Faustian bargain in making the Olympic city

It is somewhat a cliché to state that sporting mega-events have as much to do with image as they have to do with sport. Mega-events represent great image-construction endeavours for athletes, corporations, politicians, cities and nations alike, and their organisation is dominated by image management and planning. Host cities especially benefit from these exceptional moments for the production and consumption of images, which constitute unique opportunities to impress a new reality upon their landscape, through the accelerated implementation of large urban projects and the projection of illusory urban representations.

In their attempt to build a seductive place image that will attract inward capital and tourists, host cities deploy a vast range of persuasion techniques to embellish local reality, at times resorting to various forms of manipulation to conceal flaws and downplay shortcomings. Critics describe such deceptions as inherent outcomes of the Faustian bargain that event cities have struck in their desire to outdo their predecessors and leave a mark in mega-event history. If Julier (2005) talks of 'creative repackaging', Greene (2003) describes host cities as 'staged cities', promoted as models of success and prosperity to obscure grim urban realities and divert attention from growing inequality. Rojek (2013) strongly condemns mega-events' hypocritical façade, which are easily co-opted by the entities that manage, operate and design them. He calls greedy, manipulative politicians and their hidden economic interests 'backstage puppet masters', who appropriate these events to reap short-term benefits, political and financial.

Metaphors abound to describe the culture of covert deceit that characterises the spectacular, albeit superficial, makeovers cities undertake to look their best for the event. David Harvey (1988) talked of carnival masks, while I have used the Potemkin village analogy in my writing (Broudehoux, 2004; 2017). Carlos Vainer[1] underlines the dark underside of event-led urban redevelopment by taking the Faustian reference a step further. For him, if the Faustian legend aptly mirrors the mechanisms of image construction, it is one of its reinterpretations, found in Oscar Wilde's novel, *The Picture of Dorian Gray*, that best illustrates the vain and self-indulgent transformation of overambitious cities. The narrative of a carefully constructed façade of youth and beauty, that conceals the dark, twisted picture of its corrupted soul, echoes some of the ways in which cities engage in costly cosmetic urban beautification while concealing the hardship, injustice and corruption that lay behind this superficial image.

Rio de Janeiro's mythical image as 'Cidade Maravilhosa'

Endowed with a unique topography, a spectacular shoreline and a rich urban culture, Rio de Janeiro has historically enjoyed a great reputation as Brazil's prime tourism destination. Consequently, the city has long been concerned with the production and dissemination of a positive urban image. As one of the most visited cities in the Southern Hemisphere, Rio de Janeiro has learned to capitalise upon its image to attract attention and opportunities. It was the French poet Jeanne Catulle Mendes, author of *Rio: La ville merveilleuse* (1912), who coined what would become the city's most enduring slogan: *Cidade Maravilhosa*, the Marvellous City. The phrase was immortalised in multiple songs, including André Filho's 1935 homonymous carnival march, consecrated as the city's official anthem in the 1960s. Various films, novels and other cultural products contributed to the diffusion of images and representations of the city that would establish *Cidade Maravilhosa* as a brand and consolidate Rio's claim to be the most beautiful city in the world (Ramos Machado, 2004).

Since the 1970s, stereotypical elements of the city's image, from its exuberant tropical nature and rich cultural dynamism to its proverbial bohemian lifestyle, had dominated official representations of the city, conveying a sense of exotic effervescence and laid-back cosmopolitanism. In defining its competitive advantage, the city capitalised upon its unique natural assets, including beaches, lagoons, waterfalls, mountains and tropical forest, as well as upon its rich cultural traditions in terms of music, architecture, carnival and gastronomy. Successive image-construction campaigns led by Riotur, the city's tourism bureau – namely *Rio Incomparavel* in 1997 and *Rio Maravilha* in 2002 – overemphasised the 'sea, sex and sand' stereotype long attached to the city's brand. They clearly strove to maintain a consensual representation of the city as a light-hearted, easy-going tropical paradise of carefree excitement and leisure, in the face of rising drug-related violence and criminality, widespread poverty, and rampant social inequality and environmental degradation (Broudehoux, 2000).

As local conditions deteriorated at the turn of the millennium, it became increasingly difficult to conceal the fact that those idyllic tourist representations reflected a mere fragment of local reality, that of beach neighbourhoods of the southern littoral such as Ipanema, Copacabana and Barra da Tijuca. In contrast, the vast majority of *carioca* inhabited an entirely different universe, namely Rio's poorly serviced, substandard informal settlements known as *favelas*. Local political and economic elites, image makers and city marketers thus devised a number of strategies in order maintain appearances without having to challenge the socio-economic system upon which this inequality was based. Ranging from psychological blindfold, to blissful denial, to revanchist attacks, and passive concealment, these strategies would be amplified with the coming of mega-events.

Rio de Janeiro's sporting mega-Events and urban image construction

Rio de Janeiro's incursion into the realm of mega-events dates back to 1992, with the United Nation's Conference on Environment and Development (UNCED). Over the next decades, the city would more firmly embrace mega-events as a core promotional strategy, hosting, among others, the 2007 Pan American Games, the 2010 World Urban Forum, the 2011 Military World Games, the 2013 World Youth Day, the 2014 FIFA World Cup, the celebration of its 450th anniversary in 2015 and the 2016 Olympic Games. Hosting mega-events was pursued as an 'aggregator of value' (Gaffney, 2016) that could help position Rio among great world cities and as a unique opportunity to stimulate global interest. To use state governor Sergio Cabral's own terminology, these events were part of the 'trophies' the city had been collecting to buttress its stature, consolidate the local brand, and elevate its position in the global hierarchy (Gaffney, 2016). Other accolades include the admittance, in 2011, of Corcovado mountain, upon whose summit sits the famous Cristo Redentor statue, among the seven contemporary Wonders of the World, and UNESCO's designation of the city's overall landscape as part of World Heritage in 2012 (Gaffney, 2016).

In the years preceding its two recent sporting mega-events, Rio de Janeiro thus embarked on a vast, multi-faceted urban image-construction programme.

However, the presence of the favela in the urban landscape would prove to be one of the principal image 'problem' the city had to face, especially due to its association with poverty, crime, and under-development. An overwhelming proportion of image-construction strategies devised by the city thus focused on attenuating the 'favela problems', especially by toning down the visual ubiquity of poverty in the city's landscape. Consequently, Olympic and World Cup preparations were both marked by a desire to limit the visibility of favelas, and strove to divert attention from the poverty, violence and social inequality that were tearing the city apart.

Ironically, these initiatives had to work against the foreign community's growing fascination with the favela, whose powerful, adrenaline-rush appeal made it a sought-out attraction, elevated to the status of icon (Zeiderman, 2006). In recent decades, the favela had acquired a sort of cult status and become an object of fetish in the global geographical imaginary, where it came to occupy a unique position as both a trendy trademark and a fashionable commodity (Freire-Medeiros, 2008).[2] The favela's glamorisation in the global mass media, especially as an exotic stage set for African American pop stars' music videos, such as Michael Jackson's Spike Lee-directed 'They don't care about us' (1996), contributed to international popularisation. The favela also became a fashionable site for international art projects, such as Dutch artists Haas and Hahn's 2010 *favela painting* project at Santa Marta, or French artist J.R.'s 2008 *Women are Heroes* installation at Providência.

Needless to say, such fetishisation did not go down well with local elites and authorities, who widely condemned the over-visibilisation of the favela it promoted that threatened to tarnish Rio's international image. The filming of Michael Jackson's video was widely opposed by city authorities, who argued that its display of local poverty would damage the local tourism industry and ruin Rio's chances to host the 2004 Olympics (Schemo, 1996). They similarly condemned the distopic image of Rio de Janeiro portrayed in Brazilian 'reality' movies and so-called *slumsploitation* films, as a lawless city devoid of morality and hope (Gilligan, 2006; Jaguaribe, 2004).

In response, mega-event promoters and local elites developed a series of strategies that would help restore their own vision of the Marvellous City. The following section details various symbolic erasure strategies devised in order to minimise the appearance of poverty in the landscape. They range from media-based, promotional strategies that project highly controlled representations of the city; more aggressive interventions to remake the city's physical landscape, to camouflage strategies and façadist beautification that seek to conceal or soften visible traces of poverty.

Seduction, propaganda, and place-image control

The Rio de Janeiro's pre-Olympic rebranding began with a series of propaganda initiatives circulated on a variety of media platforms, that sought to project an idealised albeit partial representation of reality, from which poverty and the associated notions of crime and decay were excluded. Rio's winning Olympic candidacy file, submitted to the IOC in 2007, was a great exercise in image control, that carefully avoided urban realities that could negatively affect global perceptions. It would later serve as a template for Olympic propaganda material.

Of the candidacy file's 174 photographs, an overwhelming proportion (45%) depicted the city's littoral South Zone (Zona Sul), home to Rio's wealthiest residents and host to only two Olympic competitions. The entire file contains a single image of a favela, a surprising fact given the omnipresence of these informal settlements, home to a quarter of the city's population. In panoramic views of the city, favelas are airbrushed, cropped out, digitally erased or washed out. Event venues located in Rio's poor Zona Norte are only pictured in close-up shots, to avoid revealing the poor communities that surround them. The famous Maracanã Stadium is invariably shown from the same angle, thereby dodging the sight of nearby Mangueira, a favela known for its traditional, prize-winning samba school and carnival champion.

Drawing upon enduring clichés and seductive assets, the bid document focused on the natural beauty of the city's scenery, juxtaposing images of its curvaceous landscape with the sculpted bodies of local *carioca* engaged in a variety of sporting activities. Such aestheticised representation played a triple role, acting as a sensual titillation for potential visitors while naturalising Rio's vocation as Olympic host and reassuring potential visitors by diverting attention from more sensitive urban issues. The use of such suggestive compositions resonates with the notion of 'geoporn', introduced by Chris Gaffney (2016) in the context of Olympic Rio de Janeiro, to describe the specific ways in which geographic imaginaries are mobilised to stir desire and manufacture consensus about the event-city. Based on a definition of pornography as 'the sensational depiction of acts so as to arouse a quick, intense emotional reaction', Gaffney points to the use of erotically loaded images of Rio's urban landscapes in the marketing of mega-events, which sensually portray the city's playgrounds of beaches, samba, football and carnival to stimulate consumer fetishes. He describes the use of representational techniques of possession and domination and the consensual narrative portrayed in these geopornographic images as extending the privileged masculine gaze to fuel the mega-event spectacle. Such representation simultaneously disguises the uneven power relations that make the image possible while masking the violence, domination, perversity and exploitation that are inscribed into the landscape (Gaffney, 2016).

Once Rio de Janeiro had secured its host status for both the 2014 FIFA World Cup and the 2016 Olympic Games, local elites' wish to negate the existence of favelas in visual representations of the city intensified. In 2011, major newspapers in Rio de Janeiro ran a full-page Petrobras advertisement, showing an idealised birds-eye view of the city in which all favelas had been replaced by lush vegetation. In April 2013, a little over a year before the 2014 World Cup, Rio de Janeiro's favelas also disappeared from Google Maps.

Since 2009, Google had been pressured by City Hall and Riotur, who lodged a formal complaint against the company's mapping service for giving favelas more visibility and prominence than formal neighbourhoods. Google finally agreed to replace the word favela by the euphemism *morro* or hill on maps of the city, a decision that was widely contested by citizens groups for contributing to the symbolic erasure of these territories from the virtual landscape.

Yet another revealing propaganda moment that sought to control representations of the favela was at Rio de Janeiro's Olympic Opening Ceremonies, held on 5 August 2016. Media around the world praised Brazil's openness in addressing so transparently, in this Olympic extravaganza, some of the most problematic aspects of its history, from colonialisation and slavery to the constitution of one of the most unequal societies in the world. However, if the favela was omnipresent throughout much of the ceremonies, the hardship and suffering that underscore its existence, from economic exploitation and discrimination, to marginalisation and state abandonment, were entirely overshadowed by its aestheticised representation as a joyful, rainbow-coloured urban playground. This caricatured favela, at once deproblematised and depoliticised, served as a mere backdrop for festive dance choreographies and other performances. The real favela, scathing, raw, and unsparing, was pushed into the background, as an inconvenient, egregious reality that should not be openly discussed in front of foreign guests.

The bulldozer approach to image construction

As the city prepared to host the world's most prestigious sporting events, not only did the urban poor suffer symbolic erasure from official and media representations, but they were also subjected to concerted campaigns of physical expulsion from the city's panorama. A major strategy used to reclaim Rio de Janeiro's grandiose image in preparation for the two mega-events was slum clearance. Perhaps the most common global response to the excessive visibility of an embarrassing urban poverty is the forced evictions of vulnerable city residents, with their displacement to less visible sites and the demolition of their squatter settlements. Unlawful eviction practices have become such a pervasive feature of sporting mega-events that Vale and Gray (2013) turned them into an Olympic discipline: the displacement decathlon.

While such removals were justified by the construction of event-related infrastructure and venues, many were obviously related to image construction and real estate speculation. The hegemonic rhetorical association between urban decay and crime helped justify the violent dislocation of the poor, concealing the economic motivations of slum clearance, as investors continue to view the less fortunate and their physical manifestations as liabilities to land valuation. This process of 'creative destruction' (Schumpeter 1942), re-labelled 'accumulation by dispossession' by Harvey (2004), allows capital to expand into new territories, with the transfer of high-value urban land from the urban poor to upper-income groups.

Speculators benefit from the potential rise in value of the land freed by squatters, while municipalities benefit from new tax revenues.

Since it has become politically difficult for local and national governments to justify forced evictions and massive demolitions, an alternative way to displace the poor without resorting to slum clearance is to combine several small-scale urban interventions to effectively reduce the size of a settlement. In pre-event Rio de Janeiro, the construction of cable cars, access roads, elevators and sanitation systems contributed to the gradual erosion of many favelas, especially those located in key tourist sectors, such as Providência, a centenary favela in the heart of Rio's port district. Displaced residents were generally rehoused on the far periphery, away from job opportunities and basic services. The long commute, added housing fees and transportation costs often resulted in the further impoverishment of these families. Massive displacements to the urban fringe also exacerbated socio-spatial segregation.

This dispossession was often carried out in a brutal, opaque and disrespectful way, without proper advance warning or in absentia. Local authorities resorted to a host of coercive tactics to facilitate speedy slum eviction, to convince people to sign away their homes and to wear out the resolve of the most stubborn residents. If legal persuasion strategies failed, authorities resorted to less licit approaches, using violence and terror tactics to remove people from coveted territories. Denounced as 'strategies of war and persecution' (ANCOP, 2011, 8), intimidation tactics included infrastructure denial, public service cuts, misappropriation and destruction of property, home invasions without court orders and the marking of houses for demolition without explanation. Some strategies bordered on state terrorism, as bulldozers showed up without notice, partially demolished people's homes with their contents inside, and left neighbourhoods in rubbles, as a breeding ground for vermin. One particularly heartless strategy, which could be termed *disperse and rule*, consisted of scattering displaced individuals from the same community over different urban sectors, so as to permanently sever solidarity bonds and prevent further legal recourses (Sylvestre and Oliveira, 2012).

Examples of violent dispossession include the 2010 razing of the Mêtro-Mangueira favela, near Maracanã Stadium, demolished to build an open-air parking lot. After being presented with a take-it-or-leave-it offer, residents who refused to leave were cut off from state services and left to suffer among the rubble of their departed neighbours' homes, in living conditions that exposed them to unbearable health hazards. Drug addicts moved into abandoned ruins, increasing local insecurity. The United Nations would criticise these evictions on human rights grounds, causing Rio's government to moderate its approach (Campbell-Dollaghan, 2013). However, in January 2014, a new wave of evictions was carried out with a rare violence at the same location, as special shock-troops prevented residents from blocking the destruction of the remaining homes. At the time of the Olympics in 2016, the site was still in rubble and could not be used for parking.

Rio de Janeiro's mega-events thus exacerbated the differential treatment given to favelas, worsened the state's lack of responsibility towards their residents and consolidated their status as territories of exception. While there are no official records of the number of event-related evictions throughout Rio de Janeiro, the *Popular Committee for the World Cup and the Olympics* estimates them to be close to 100,000 (AMPVA, 2016). This is tremendous, given the massive housing deficit suffered by the Brazilian poor. Days before the 2016 event, Brazilian sociologist Carlos Vainer (2016) accused the city and state governments of the crime of urbanicide, stating that the Games had caused the worst expulsions of the poor the city has ever known, beating the record set during the Lacerte dictatorship of the 1970s, when close to 60,000 people were expelled.[3] Not only did evictions destroy large portions of the urban fabric, but 49 days before the Olympic opening ceremonies, the state of Rio de Janeiro declared a 'state of calamity', implying it was nearly bankrupt and that all available state resources would be redirected to finishing Olympic preparations. Innumerable public services were cut and thousands of state employees, from civil servants to university professors, stopped receiving their salaries, a situation that would last for months, in some cases years.

Concealment in the construction of exclusive place images

Another strategy used in pre-Olympic Rio de Janeiro to make territories of poverty less visually offensive to foreign visitors was visual concealment. Billboards, screen walls and other visual filters were erected near tourist attractions and along major roadways, especially those linking event sites to the city centre and the airport, in order to block the view of slums that could not be demolished. Shortly after Rio was awarded the 2016 Olympics in 2009, mayor Eduardo Paes erected a series of 'acoustic barriers' along the freeway connecting the airport to downtown. Few residents of Maré, a long-established favela bordering this main road, were fooled by claims that these half-inch thick acrylic screens were meant to protect them against harmful highway noise. The barrier was decried not only as a blatant attempt at concealing their existence but also as a mode of containment, blocking access to the roadway where many earned a living selling snacks to motorists stuck in traffic jams. Soon after its erection, the barrier was heavily vandalised. It was repaired in the months leading to the Games and decorated with Rio 2016 brand-identity decals.

Other types of visual filters used to block the view of poor neighbourhoods included the construction of large infrastructure, such as the elevator to the favela of Cantagalo in Rio de Janeiro's chic Ipanema beach neighbourhood. Erected in 2010, this disproportionately large structure spans the entire width of the dead-end street in whose axis it is located, entirely blocking the view of the favela from the world-famous beach.

Beautification as means of camouflage

Yet another approach commonly used in pre-Olympic Rio de Janeiro to mini-mise outward manifestations of poverty in the urban environment combined various tactics of beautification and urban camouflage to tone down percep-tions of decay, with a visual discourse that is both neutralising and pacifying. In this case, slums were neither hidden nor destroyed, but embellished so as to become visually acceptable. Aestheticisation often took the form of faça-dist projects that beautify the most visible portion of a neighbourhood, or landscaping interventions near the point of contact with the formal city, that softened the interface between two separate worlds. One example of a costly infrastructure project erected as an event-led camouflage strategy is the Niemeyer footbridge in Rocinha. This signature arch, designed by Brazil's most famous architect Oscar Niemeyer, distracts from the view of Latin-America's largest squatter settlement, especially as seen from one of the main access roads to Barra da Tijuca, the elite district where most Olympic competitions took place.

Another beautification initiative developed in Rio de Janeiro in preparation for its two sporting events consisted in painting some strategically located favelas in a cheerful palette. Originally initiated as 'social' projects by foreign artists or private sponsors such as the AkzoNobel international paint con-glomerate, these interventions transformed poor communities into abstract paintings or playful assemblage of brightly coloured blocks, highly reminis-cent of naive representations of the favela popularised in tourist art. These promotional projects generally affected only the most visible façade of favela buildings and local residents rarely had a say in the colour or pattern painted on their own house, the overall ensemble being predetermined by its sponsor. A great example of such façadist interventions was found in Santa Marta, one of Rio's most visited favela, of Michael Jackson fame (above).

In spite of the reductive character of such representation, which objectified the favela, reduced to a mere object of visual consumption, this approach was adopted in 2010 by the state and imposed upon existing communities in var-ious new housing projects, such as the Program for Accelerated Growth (PAC) in Rocinha's Rua 4 project. The patronising and infantilising nature of such interventions contributed to the symbolic disqualification of the poor and perpetuated their subaltern position in contemporary society. By masking the conditions of exclusion and exploitation from which these settlements were born and by concealing traces of the discrimination and abandonment long inscribed on their walls, such practices effectively anaesthetised the poli-tical power of the favela. The lyrics of 'Favela Amarela' (Yellow Favela), a popular 1960 samba song by Junior e Oldemar Magalhaes, underlines the deceit and hypocrisy of such an aestheticisation strategy. '*Favela amarela, ironia da vida. Pintem a favela, façam aquarela, da miséria colorida*' (Yellow favela, irony of life. They paint the favela as a watercolour of colourful misery) (author's translation).

Exclusion by design

A last strategy of erasure in the production of Rio de Janeiro's Olympic image relied upon an exclusive urban design approach which was engineered to create inhospitable spaces for the poor and other undesirable users. Akin to what Garnier (2008) calls a 'preventive architecture of fear', event-related public spaces were laid out in a way to limit their possible appropriation by the homeless and landscaped so as to eliminate dark corners, shady setbacks or opaque screens behind which indigents could find refuge. The festive redesign of Rio's urban spaces as playful and convivial leisure spaces for people 'of the right sort' (Harvey, 2001) also facilitated the planned gentrification of city districts. Rio de Janeiro's port area, a historically marginalised neighbourhood populated by poor Afro-Brazilians, was subjected to such a substitution process. Much of its population and small-scale industries were expelled from the sector, as it was sanitised, sterilised and re-appropriated by a 'more deserving' elite (Sánchez and Broudehoux, 2013).

Other intentionally exclusive spaces include the Olympic Park at Barra da Tijuca and areas surrounding other event venues, conceived according to a military-inspired defensive planning approach that limited their accessibility. The parameters established by the Rio 2016 Bid Book and the technical requirements of the IOC required Rio de Janeiro's Olympic Park to be 'geographically bounded site'. Located on a triangular peninsula stretching far into a lagoon, it was bordered by water on two-thirds of its periphery. Access to the Park was limited to the base of the triangle attached to the mainland, where the sites few, easily monitored entry points are located. Like other IOC-mandated Olympic Parks, it was protected by a multilayered safety perimeter and tightly controlled borders, and was isolated behind a *cordon sanitaire*, an unbuilt buffer zone that kept dangerous social elements at bay. Event sites were virtually closed off from public access during the event. A complex filtering system selectively determined admittance, based on wealth, status or social capital. Entry was granted to members of the press or the event organisation, athletes and their families, and event ticket holders.

Flusty (2001) rightly warns of the danger that these interdictory spaces, designed to systematically exclude those judged to be unsuitable, could be easily naturalised so as to become acceptable urban realities after the Games. They could also exacerbate a phenomenon that Soja called the 'splintering of neoliberal urban space' (2000, 299), with the creation of urban archipelagos of fortified enclosures. In a city such as Rio de Janeiro, already suffering from deep social inequality and fragmented by exclusive enclaves, such exclusionary Olympic image construction only exacerbated an already unsustainable situation.

Modes of resistance to event-led image construction

Various population groups have reacted to some of the image-construction initiatives adopted in pre-event Rio de Janeiro, devising a host of tactics to challenge ill-advised decision-makers, to contest discriminatory measures, to undermine top-down image-construction efforts and to hijack the event spectacle. Recriminations generally centred upon housing evictions, public service cuts, the privatisation of public land, restricted access to collective resources, and the tightening of the social control apparatus. The following sections detail a series of strategies of resistance adopted by local citizens in the years leading to the city's two mega-events.

Organised forms of collective resistance

In pre-event Rio de Janeiro, one of the most effective way to counter the mega-event spectacle was through organised forms of collective resistance and active engagement in social movements. Collective acts of civil disobedience included public demonstrations on city streets, the peaceful occupation of public spaces, and more violent, explosive actions that made the global headlines. In spite of the democratic deficit that surrounded mega-events preparations in Brazil, when citizens groups and organisations were systematically excluded from the general decision-making process and targeted by the state, a surprisingly robust, organised and active civil society emerged. This was exceptional, especially given the Brazilian state's growing authoritarianism, the country's recent history of dictatorship and the relative youth of its democratic institutions. One example of a civil society organisation that emerged in pre-event Rio de Janeiro was the *Fórum Comunitário do Porto* (Port Community Forum), a coalition of residents, scholars, activists and community leaders created in January 2011 to fight for the rights of residents of Rio's port area.

Across the country, social actors also developed a vast network of 'people's committees' (*comitês populares da Copa e das Olimpíadas*) to fight the World Cup and the Olympics. These committees were born out of an association created at the time of the 2007 Pan American Games in Rio to fight unlawful evictions. Activists, academics and legal aid workers banded together to help citizens groups develop resistance strategies, organise civil disobedience actions and fight relocation and exclusion in the courts. Over the years, this coalition coordinated civil society actions across the country and managed to collect an impressive amount of information on processes, expenditure and rights violations. The national network released two reports, in 2011 and 2014, documenting various abuses and irregularities (ANCOP, 2011, 2014).

Rio's *Comitê Popular* played a central role in the struggle for the survival of Vila Autodromo, a small fishing community located on the edge of the Olympic Park. The Comitê helped local residents gain visibility for their cause, hold on-site festive gatherings and solidarity events, and organise protest marches both in Barra da Tijuca and in the city centre. Members of the *Comitê* were extremely creative in devising resistance strategies, for example organising savvy social media opinion campaigns such as the 'Urbanize Now' celebrity video clips which were widely circulated on the web. The *Comitê* also managed to secure the mailing list of all major media outlets and made a point of keeping them informed of all new developments.

Other local groups and issue-based associations joined transnational resistance networks to give visibility to their struggle, at times managing to bring the issue into the international spotlight. For example, in their effort to gain a voice in the debate, street vendors in Brazil joined StreetNet International, an NGO originating from South Africa formed before the 2010 World Cup, which campaigns for the rights of the urban poor, including shanty town dwellers, migrant and refugee communities, and sex workers. In 2011, StreetNet International commissioned a study of informal traders in the 12 Brazilian host cities of the 2014 World Cup as a preliminary step to establishing its *World Class Cities for All* campaign in Brazil, which has since then helped raise awareness the plight of informal workers and street vendors around the world.

The most widespread strategy used by these coalitions was mass demonstrations. Street protests were common in Brazil in the run-up to the 2014 World Cup. In June 2013, over a two-week period that coincided with FIFA's Confederations Cup, Brazil was shaken by social conflicts on a scale rarely seen in recent history. Throughout the country, crowds in the tens of thousands, among which diverse sectors of civil society were represented, called for a radical transformation of Brazilian society and a deep reform of the exercise of political power (Badaró, 2013). Recriminations ranged from housing evictions and the rising cost of public transportation, to police brutality, public education, healthcare, and other pressing collective issues. Protests also testified to widespread frustrations about public exclusion from the multi-billion-dollar World Cup bonanza. So deep was public anger that even hitherto unpoliticised youth and members of the middle class joined the movement (Vainer, 2013).

In Rio de Janeiro, where mobilisation was the strongest, protests quickly focused upon Brazil's corrupt political system, driven by opportunism, impunity and prejudice. The excessive amount of public funds squandered on the hosting of sporting mega-events and the vast fortunes funnelled into a handful of engineering construction firms to build stadia too gigantic for local needs, figured prominently among grievances. The fact that an event that stood to be FIFA's most lucrative ever would be almost entirely financed by the Brazilian state infuriated protesters (Nunes 2014). They further denounced the handover of land forcibly taken from poor communities to private developers. The work accomplished by Rio's *Comitê Popular da Copa e das Olimpíadas* played a significant part in raising public awareness of the hardships posed by event-led image construction. The *Comitê* had been very vocal in condemning shady deals in the construction of World Cup stadia, unjustified evictions and controversial demolitions, especially near the Maracanã, all of which entered the public debate and were widely featured in slogans and on posters during the 2013 protests (CPCORJ, 2013, 2015).

Creative strategies of resistance

What came out of the crisis was an incredibly rich approach to collective resistance. Highly strategic, evocative urban sites were used for the expression of discontent: it was around major stadia, in front of emblematic infrastructure and near establishments of power that people came to voice their grievances. Demonstrators employed a creative narrative strategy that unsettled authority by mimicking the aestheticised discourse of state politicians. At once witty, humorous and theatrical in tone, slogans creatively merged social demands, mega-event criticism and contempt of Rio's city-branding initiatives, symbolically challenging the consensus that had hitherto prevailed around sporting mega-events: 'We want FIFA-standard public schools', 'Call me a stadium and invest in me!', 'How many schools are worth one Maracanã?' (Rosner, 2013).

Acts of resistance were largely borrowed from the realm of the spectacle, in their theatricality, dramatic language, exaggerated imagery and festive dimension. Rio being a city with a century-old carnival tradition and with a taste for the dramatic and spectacular, many protests were highly carnivalesque in mood, and drew their strength from carnival's subversive power (DaMatta, 1991). Literally using spectacle to fight spectacle, urban youth used deception and disguise to denounce the masquerade of capitalist greed that had travestied their city and its most basic values (Rosner, 2013). Many participants wore masks and costumes, dressing up as superheroes or as Anonymous' Guy Fawkes. They turned protests into artful performances of urban citizenship, using the city as a stage to reconquer contested urban territories and to reconfigure city spaces. The state's reply to the string of protests was a well-choreographed show of force, with the spectacular deployment of armed troops that turned the joyous street festival into a war zone, right in front of the cameras of the global media, which almost unanimously condemned the repression.

Playful acts of resistance

Other collective strategies of resistance to exclusive practices of urban image construction developed in pre-Olympic Rio included informal and apparently innocuous festive actions that took advantage of the global spotlight on the city. Often convened through social media from the initiative of various groups and individuals, these events' innovative, non-confrontational approach, and highly playful, friendly character helped draw participants while attracting sympathy and solidarity to their cause. For example, in early 2014 young people of colour from all over Rio de Janeiro converged on upscale shopping malls on weekends for a 'little outing' or *rolezinho*, to denounce exclusionary measures that limited access to urban spaces for marginalised people. Often victimised by security guards as potential criminals, these youth from the mostly black periphery asserted their right of access by 'taking a little walk', attracting hundreds, and sometimes thousands of participants to elite shopping centres. Just a few months before the World Cup, news of the swift and sometimes violent expulsion of these peaceful teens travelled the world and brought negative attention to the widespread segregation that plagued the city.

To similarly denounce widespread discrimination, on several weekends in 2014 and 2015, a series of picnics convened on Facebook encouraged people from the poor North Zone to congregate on the elite beach of Ipanema for a festive, family friendly excursion. Ironically called *faroferos*, these events adopted a deprecatory moniker commonly used by elite carioca to deride unsophisticated beach-goers who carry their own lunch (*farofa* is grilled manioc flour). These events were held to protest the police expulsion of underprivileged, black youth from public buses that connected the poor periphery to the littoral on weekends, on suspicion of criminal intent, as part of event-related security crackdowns. These mostly poor, black families thus symbolically reclaimed their right to the city's waterfront, too often monopolised by the white, rich elite.

A third example of playful acts of collective resistance organised in Rio de Janeiro to bring together diverse communities affected by World Cup-related projects and to denounce the exclusionary nature of the event was the *Copa dos excluidos* (Cup of the Excluded). This informal football tournament was organised in the summer of 2014 by the *Comitê Popular da Copa*. In a fun-filled, day-long gathering, families shared food, drinks, and played football in a highly convivial act of resistance, whose harmless, light-hearted and highly symbolic nature could only attract public sympathy for their cause.

City walls as support for the expression of dissent

Yet another form of resistance to event-led urban image construction in Rio de Janeiro was waged on the walls of the city. Artists, especially graffiti artists and muralists, were also extremely prolific in denouncing event-led abuses. Throughout the city, giant murals depicted the poor's exclusion from the mega-event festival and exposed the greed and corruption of government and FIFA leaders. Rarely aggressive in tone, the murals were poetic and evocative, for example featuring a skinny, tearful child with a football on his dinner plate, or satirical, representing businessmen playing football with a moneybag. For their part, graffiti generally bore a more accusatory tone, repeating *ad nauseam* the same slogans throughout the city: FIFA go home! World Cup for Whom?

The walls of vulnerable communities also became privileged sites for artistic expressions of dissent. In 2008, internationally renowned French artist J.R. had used the favela of Providência as a canvas for his photographic project, *Women are Heroes,* which celebrated the strength of underprivileged mothers around the world. In 2012, Mauricio Hora, a photographer and lifetime resident of the favela of Providência, borrowed from JR's approach to save over a dozen houses slated for demolition to make way for a controversial cable car (*plano inclinado*), built as part of the Porto Maravilha urban improvements. He pasted giant photographs of local residents on the façade of their homes and forced city authorities to revise the project. In the same favela, Portuguese artist Alessandro Farto, alias Vhils, chiselled away plaster on partially demolished homes to create vivid oversised portraits of displaced members of the community (Evans, 2015).

Discussion: the actual reach of Rio de Janeiro's resistance movement

As popular responses to event-led urban image construction suggest, in the form of collective resistance movements, symbolic forms of contestations, and other minor acts of subversion, a large portion of the Rio de Janeiro's population was not duped by the mega-events spectacle, but was willing to partake in various actions to fight dispossession, contest exclusionary policies and protect the common interest in the face of greed, corruption and power abuses. Popular protests unmasked the false promise of collective benefits to be yielded by hosting mega-events and made visible the destructive potential of the image-construction programmes those events fostered.

These resistance strategies also suggest that urban images are not just the product of top-down processes, but are also shaped by bottom-up, self-organising, citizen-activist movements. In their struggle against corporate-led urban image-construction practices, those excluded have developed empowering forms of mobilisation, proposed an alternative urban vision, and carved out their own public spheres. By publicly voicing their grievances, occupying the city's public spaces and showing solidarity for diverse causes, protesters forced sporting-event institutions and civic leaders alike to rethink their positions and to seek more sustainable approaches.

There is little evidence to suggest that these varied actions can effect major changes in terms of state policy and event-led project implementation. The sheer economic and political power of event organisers, sponsors and rights holders severely restrict the scope for bottom-up action and limit their measurable impacts. However ineffectual some of these resistance strategies may appear, recent amendments to official FIFA and IOC regulations suggest that grievances are being heard and that decision-makers are at least taking notice.

The above discussion has underlined some of the subtle new ways Rio's citizens have developed to appropriate the spectacle for their own purposes, using parody, masquerade and emerging technologies to successfully regain a voice on the urban stage. The emergence of new modes of communication has helped create a novel, alternative form of public sphere, predicated upon participatory exchanges that transcend localities and allow for more inclusive representation. If the impact of these weapons of the weak remains incidental, they have nonetheless achieved small moral victories which allowed members of Brazilian society to maintain the pride and dignity they are so often denied. The examples cited suggest that abusive urban image-construction initiatives has awakened the active participation of hitherto apolitical population groups to fight for their rights.

Regardless of their immediate influence, these diverse strategies represent important coping mechanisms the powerless and disenfranchised and afford a certain sense of control that may nurture an emboldening sense of entitlement. By allowing the poor to voice their frustrations and to criticise the regimes who condone such exclusionary urban visions, these resistance strategies have allowed people to question established power structures and to open the door to more radical actions. Even the most innocuous forms of resistance can register a cumulative effect, and slowly build a greater impact. Partaking in these protest movements helped create imagined communities of resistance and collectivities of interests that can empower the powerless, lay the groundwork for more concrete political actions and potentially lead to more efficient and better organised forms of opposition. They also enabled the expression of critical and dissenting views in the public realm, which can help open-up spaces within which new solidarity movements may be forged and political agendas refined. The broad public circulation of subversive messages may also mobilise potential followers and garner popular support, thereby contributing to the formation of a stronger civil society that will protect democratic institutions and basic human rights.

The political landscape of mega-event planning appears to be changing and may actually never be the same. At a time when the dominant media are abandoning their public responsibilities, grassroots groups and civil society organisations are finding alternative means to gain public visibility and voice. By refusing to be silenced, by taking to the streets in protest, by talking to the global media or partaking in events like *rolezinhos* or *farofaço*, they are reclaiming their right to participate in society, to represent themselves on their own terms and to claim their rightful place in their city's image.

Conclusion

This analysis of event-led urban image-construction practices and of the strategies developed by local citizens to minimise their negative impacts demonstrated some of the ways in which the hosting of mega-events may exacerbate local power disparities in ways that threaten both democracy and social justice. It revealed some of the darker aspects of the event-city, more bent on protecting the benefits and interests of its sponsors than ensuring the welfare of its own citizens. These transformations reinforce the exclusionary nature of the neoliberal city, where elites and middle-class citizens are increasingly granted privileged access to city spaces that are privatised for their benefit and enjoyment, while the poor and the marginal are targeted by new modes of exclusion and invisibilisation.

In the context of growing public lack of responsibility towards the poor, the chapter suggests that the visibility of urban poverty is becoming a highly political issue in mega-event hosting. Politics, Rancière (2006) writes, is the struggle of an unrecognised party for equal recognition in the established order. Aesthetics is bound up in this battle, Rancière argues, because the battle takes place over the image of society, what it is permissible to say or to show. Politics is thus aesthetics in that it 'makes visible what has been excluded from a perceptual field and in that it makes audible what used to be inaudible' (Rancière, 1995, 226). In this sense, the invisibilisation of the poor does not merely signify their visual concealment, but represents a form of disenfranchisement and silencing that denies their citizenship right as legitimate members of society. Don Mitchell (2003) talks of the right to be seen, the simple right to be present and visible in public space, as a fundamental right that allows the most economically deprived to exist as citizens and to participate in society. To invisibilise the poor is to attempt to silence them, to neutralise their voice and to deny them any political weight. To hide poverty is also to perpetuate it, to refuse to face the structural causes of social inequality and to sustain the myth that the free market is a fair system that can provide for all members of society.

Notes

1 Such a parallel between the vain and self-indulgent transformation of ambitious cities and Wilde's modern retelling of the myth of Narcissus was first drawn by Brazilian sociologist Carlos Vainer in a personal conversation in 2015.
2 Global attraction for the favela has been attributed, in part, to the global popularity of Brazilian 'reality' movies such as *City of God* (2002), and to the use of such neighbourhoods as a backdrop in mainstream Hollywood films, a trend branded *slumsploitation* (Gilligan, 2006; Jaguaribe, 2004).
3 Carlos Vainer (2016) *Being Urban in the Global South: Issues and Challenges.* Keynote address at the International conference: Rethinking Cities in the Global South: Urban Violence, Social Inequality and Spatial Justice, Centre for Urban Policy and Governance, 19–23 January. Online. Available at: https://www.youtube.com/watch?v=NMCyhcT26c4.

References

AMPVA (Associação de moradores e Pescadores da Vila Autodromo) (2016) *Plano Popular da Vila Autodromo: Plano de desenvolvimento urbano, economico, social e cultural.* Rio de Janeiro.

ANCOP (Articulação Nacional dos Comitês Populares da Copa) (2011) *Dossiê Megaeventos e Violações de Direitos Humanos no Brasil.* Rio de Janeiro: ETTERN/ Fundação Heinrich Böll.

ANCOP (Articulação Nacional dos Comitês Populares da Copa) (2014) *Dossiê Megaeventos e Violações de Direitos Humanos no Brasil.* Rio de Janeiro: ETTERN/ Fundação Heinrich Böll.

Badaró, M.B. (2013) 'A multidão nas ruas: construir a saída para a crise política' [The multitude on the streets: Building an exit for a political crisis]. Unpublished text. History Department, Federal Fluminense University.

Broudehoux, A.-M. (2000) 'Image Making, City Marketing, and the Aesthetization of Social Inequality in Rio de Janeiro'. In Nezar AlSayyad (ed.) *Consuming Tradition, Manufacturing Heritage: Global Norms and Urban Forms in the Age of Tourism.* London: Routledge, 273–297.

Broudehoux, A.-M. (2004) *The Making and Selling of Post-Mao Beijing.* London: Routledge.

Broudehoux, A.-M. (2017) *Mega-Events and Urban Image Construction: From Beijing to Rio de Janeiro*. London: Routledge.

Campbell-Dollaghan, K. (2013) 'Make way for the Olympics: The paramilitary clearance of Rio's slums', *Guardian*, 11 October. Available at: www.gizmodo.in/news/Ma ke-Way- For-the-Olympics-The-Paramilitary- Clearance-of-Rios-Slums/articleshow/ 23991312. cms (accessed 24 October 2016).

CPCORJ (Comitê Popular da Copa e Olimpíadas do Rio de Janeiro) (2013) 'Dossiê Megaeventos e Violações dos Direitos Humanos no Rio de Janeiro'. Available at: http s://comitepopulario.files.wordpress.com/2013/05/dossie_comitepopularcoparj_2013.pdf (accessed 7 June 2018).

CPCORJ (Comitê Popular da Copa e Olimpíadas do Rio de Janeiro) (2015) 'Megaeventos e Violações dos Direitos Humanos no Rio de Janeiro'. Available at: http:// rio.portalpopulardacopa.org.br/?page_id=2972 (accessed 7 June 2018).

DaMatta, R. (1991) *Carnivals, Rogues, and Heroes: An Interpretation of the Brazilian Dilemma*. Notre Dame, IN: University of Notre Dame Press.

Evans, G.L. (2015) 'Graffiti Art and the City: From Piece-Making to Place-Making'. In A. Ross (ed) *Handbook on Graffiti and Street Art*. London: Routledge, 164–178.

Flusty, S. (2001) 'The banality of interdiction: Surveillance, control and the displacement of diversity', *International Journal of Urban and Regional Research*, 25(3), 658–664.

Freire-Medeiros, B. (2008) 'And the Favela Went Global: The Invention of a Trademark and a Tourist Destination'. In M. Valença Marico, E. Nel and W. Leimgruber (eds) *The Global Challenge and Marginalisation*. New York: Nova Science, 33–52.

Gaffney, C. (2016) 'Geo-porn: Selling the city through mediated spectacle'. Urban Transformation Processes: The Role of Flagship Architecture as Urban Generator, American Association of Geographers Conference, San Francisco.

Garnier, J.-P. (2008) 'Scénographies pour un simulacre: l'espace public réenchanté', *Espaces et sociétés: le consommateur ambulant*, 134, 67–81.

Gilligan, M. (2006) 'Slumsploitation: The favela on film and TV', *Metamute*. Available at: www.metamute.org/en/Slumsploitation-Favela-on-Film-and-TV (accessed 8 June 2018).

Greene, S.J. (2003) 'Staged cities: Mega-events, slum clearance and global capital', *Yale Human Rights and Development Law Journal*, 6, 161–187.

Harvey, D. (1988) 'Voodoo cities', *New Statesman and Society*, 1, 33–35.

Harvey, D. (2001) *Spaces of Capital: Towards a Critical Geography*. New York: Routledge.

Harvey, D. (2004) 'The 'new' imperialism: Accumulation by dispossession', *The Socialist Register*, 40, 63–87.

Jaguaribe, B. (2004) 'Favelas and the aesthetics of realism: Representations in film and literature', *Journal of Latin American Cultural Studies*, 13(3), 327–342.

Julier, G. (2005) 'Urban designscapes and the Production of aesthetic consent', *Urban Studies*, 42, 869–887.

Mitchell, D. (2003) *The Right to the City: Social Justice and the Fight for Public Space*. New York: The Guilford Press.

Nunes, R. (2014) 'There will have been no World Cup', *Aljazeera*. Available at: www. alja zeera.com/indepth/opinion/2014/05/brazil-world-cup-protests-201452910299437439. html (accessed 12 June 2018).

Ramos Machado, T. (2004) *Para a 'Cidade Maravilhosa', um 'Plano Maravilha': uma análise crítica sobre produção da imagem turística e marketing urbano no Rio de Janeiro*. Rio de Janeiro: Universidade Federal do Rio de Janeiro.

Rancière, J. (1995) *On the Shores of Politics*, trans. L. Heron, London: Verso.

Rancière, J. (2006) *The Politics of Aesthetics*. London: Continuum.

Rojek, C. (2013) *Event Power: How Global Events Manage and Manipulate*. London: Sage.

Rosner, N. (2013) 'Tinker Research Reports, Summer 2013: Masking urban marginality', Center for Latin American Studies, 7 July. Available at: http://clas.berkeley.edu/research/problematizing-socio-spatial-development-margins-rio-de-janeiro (accessed 11 June 2018).

Sánchez, F. and Broudehoux, A.-M. (2013) 'Mega-events and urban regeneration in Rio de Janeiro: Planning in a state of emergency', *International Journal of Urban Sustainable Development*, 5(2), 132–163.

Schemo, D.J. (1996) 'Rio frets as Michael Jackson plans to film slum', *New York Times*, 2 November, 3.

Schumpeter, J. (1942) *Capitalism, Socialism, and Democracy*. New York: Harper & Row.

Scott, J.C. (1985) *Weapons of the Weak: Everyday Forms of Peasant Resistance*. New Haven, CT: Yale University Press.

Soja, E. (2000) *Postmetropolis: Critical Study of Cities and Regions*. Oxford: Blackwell.

Sylvestre, G. and de Oliveira, N. (2012) 'The revanchist logic of mega-Events: Community displacement in Rio de Janeiro's West End', *Visual Studies*, 27(2), 204–210.

Vainert, C.B. (2013) 'Mega-eventos, mega-negócios, mega-protestos' [Internet]. [cited 22 July 2013]. Available at: www.ettern.ippur.ufrj.br/ ultimas-noticias/196/mega-eventos-mega-negocios-mega-protestos.

Vainer, C.B. (2016) 'Being urban in the Global South: Issues and challenges'. Keynote address at the international conference: Rethinking Cities in the Global South: Urban Violence, Social Inequality and Spatial Justice, Centre for Urban Policy and Governance, 19–23 January. Online. Available at: www.youtube.com/watch?v= NMCyhcT26c4.

Vale, L.J. and Gray, A. (2013) 'The displacement decathlon: Olympican struggles for affordable housing from Atlanta to Rio de Janeiro'. *Places*, April. Available at: https://doi.org/10.22269/130415.

Zeiderman, A. (2006) *The Fetish and the Favela: Notes on Tourism and the Commodification of Place in Rio de Janeiro, Brazil*. Stanford, CA: Stanford University Press.

7 A new road and rail link from the mountains to the coast

The mixed legacy of Sochi's most expensive project

Sven Daniel Wolfe

Introduction: life after the games

It is nearly five months after the 2014 Winter Olympics and Saak Kar-apetyan,[1] who lives about 15km up from the Black Sea coast in the small village of Akhshtyr, needs to do the family shopping. He and his wife, Anna, climb into their Niva 4x4 and drive down the mountain. At first it is a bumpy dirt road, but soon it becomes graded and then concrete. A yellow pipe snakes alongside the road as they descend, giving villagers the option to connect to municipal gas for the first time. Once they descend into the valley, the road terminates at a high gravel platform guarded with fences and barbed wire. On top are the rails for the new *Lastochka* train, and parallel beyond them runs the New Krasnaya Polyana Highway – Krasnaya Polyana being the site of the mountain cluster of Olympic venues. Both road and rail were built for the Olympics, augmenting the original arterial road running from mountains to coast. Saak and Anna turn left to drive alongside the high tracks. They are heading down to the market on the coast in Adler but this is not a simple journey. The nearest onramp to the new highway is almost 10km south of their village – technically about two-thirds of the way to their destination. There is no southbound onramp, however, so it is only possible for them to travel north. In theory, they could take the new highway north, at the first opportunity cross the river, and then turn south again to use the original arterial road toward the coastal cluster of Olympic venues. Instead of this circuitous route, they pass the limited onramp and continue on what they call 'the old road', which rapidly decreases in quality. They weave around pot-holes and rockslides, rarely losing sight of the inaccessible new highway and the *Lastochka* train that, only once, whizzes by on its way to the resorts in the mountains.

The Sochi region received unprecedented investment during the run-up to the 2014 Olympics. Costing a record \$55 billion (approximately 1.5 trillion rubles), this seven-year period is better understood not merely as preparation for a sporting celebration but rather as an ambitious urban and regional development project with the world's most prestigious mega-event attached (Golubchikov, 2017; Golubchikov, 2014). Aside from building the competition venues, this preparatory project involved overhauling the region's transit infrastructure, a huge development push that included building or recon-structing over 360km of roads and 200km of railways (OlympStroy, 2013). Although construction work took place all over the Sochi region, the two clusters of Olympics venues – one on the coast and the other in the mountains about 45km away – can be considered the epicentres of development attention (see map – Figure 7.1).

The New Krasnaya Polyana Highway and the *Lastochka* train were built to link these two clusters, simultaneously fulfilling Olympic transport require-ments and improving upon the existing connection provided by the original arterial road. If anyone in Sochi were to benefit from improved transit infra-structure, surely it must be those, like the Karapetyans in Akhshtyr, who live in between these major sites of Olympic development. Instead, the results for locals living alongside this transit corridor are more mixed and spatially uneven. This chapter explores these mixed results and investigates the effects on some of the people who live between the Olympics clusters. It spotlights Sochi's most expensive transport infrastructure intervention and, in focusing on the legacy period after the Olympics, it examines the government's pro-mises of development and regeneration and explores the degrees to which

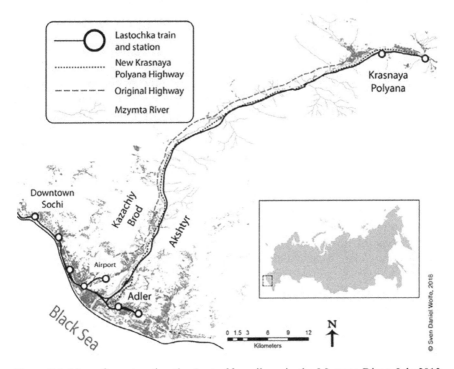

Figure 7.1 Map of constructing the *Lastochka* railway in the Mzymta River, July 2013
Source: author.

Figure 7.2 Constructing the Lastochka railway in the Mzymta River, July 2013
Source: author.

these promises were fulfilled. The chapter looks beyond issues of cost, corruption, and opaque ownership structures to explore the micro-level of what has happened to the people who are living in the aftermath of this Olympic development project.

Mega-events, urban regeneration and Sochi

Mega-events like the Olympics and the World Cup are about more than sport, and hosting them creates profound social, political, economic, infra-structural, and environmental impacts for the host nation, region and city (Horne and Manzenreiter, 2006; and Veal, 2007). One of the most common motivations for hosting is to leverage the increased attention and investment that accompanies the mega-event in order to undertake major urban devel-opment or regeneration projects in the host city (Coaffee, 2010; and Chalkley, 1998; Gold and Gold, 2016; Hiller, 2000; Poynter et al., 2015). Perhaps the most famous example of mega-event-led regeneration is the 1992 Summer Olympics, which helped transform industrial Barcelona into a world-class tourist destination, albeit at higher costs than promised and with accompanying gentrifications and population displacement (Baade and Matheson, 2016; Baade and Matheson, 1995; Baade and Matheson, 2007). Since then, the so-called 'Barcelona Model' has been deployed as a rationale for mega-event hosting worldwide, either implicitly or explicitly, in both emerging and established economies. Hence, English organisers attempted to catalyse an ambitious transformation of the relatively deprived areas of East London in the 2012 Summer Olympics, though this was not without gentrification processes and other exclusionary effects (Poynter et al., 2015; Poynter et al., 2013). Similarly, Brazilian elites used the World Cup and the Olympics in Rio de Janeiro to engage in radical stadium-led urban redevelopment, accelerating transformations of the city to cater to the international tourist class. At the same time, Rio's socio-spatial transformations unleashed gentrifications across the city's residential areas and exacerbated the exclusions of the marginalised and the poor (Gaffney, 2015; 2010) Sochi (2014) continues this pattern of planning rationales, as organisers married mega-event hosting to a wide-ranging programme of urban and regional development.

Alongside their local goals for urban development or regeneration, mega-event planners must also complete a variety of infrastructural projects in order to satisfy hosting requirements. These are strict, contractually regulated, and verified by periodic visits from the event owner (in the case of the Olympics, the International Olympic Committee). Among many other requirements, host cities must provide problem-free transport for a variety of client groups, ensuring efficiency, safety, throughput capacity, punctuality, and reliability (International Olympic Committee, 2016). Transport improvements are commonly cited as one of the positive long-term impacts of hosting and generally escape the controversy that tends to accompany other mega-event-led developments (Cashman, 2006; -Noor, 2013a; Preuss, 2004). Indeed, when executed in concert with the region's development goals, investments in transport can provide long-lasting benefits for the region and tend to escape the 'white elephant' curse of oversized infrastructure that is unneeded after the games (Bovy, 2010; -Noor, 2012).

Like other mega-events, hosting the Winter Olympics requires substantial investments into transport infrastructure like airports, roads, and railways in order to accommodate the size of the event as well as to allow for the unpredictability of winter weather. However, when compared to other mega-events, the Winter Games tend to be hosted by smaller cities. So, after massive upgrading, they are often left with oversized infrastructure. Further, because they are hosted in more rural areas, there is a higher risk of construction projects damaging the natural environment (Chappelet, 2008). At the same time, there is also the possibility that hosting could provide long-lasting enhancements to transport infrastructure, particularly in hard-to-reach mountainous areas (Essex and Chalkley, 2004). The primary challenge is to balance the short-term needs of the event – managing extremely high traffic for a limited time – with the longer-term needs of the host city, which usually does not need such high-capacity transport networks. It is therefore particularly risky for smaller cities, with their comparatively smaller overall needs, to host the Winter Olympics.

In this light, the Sochi 2014 provides a study in extremes. First is the issue of cost, though it is not unusual to see cost overruns for mega-events: since 1960 the Summer Olympics have run an average of 176% over budget, while the Winter Olympics have broken budgets by an average of 142% (Flyvbjerg et al., 2016) Nor is it surprising that transport construction projects tend to break budgets (Cantarelli et al., 2010; et al., 2004; 2003). Notwithstanding these tendencies, the Sochi Olympic road and rail project shatters records. The combined project cost between $8 and $10 billion (285 billion rubles), making it one of the world's most expensive construction projects, and the railway alone boasts the highest per-kilometre costs worldwide (Anti-Corruption Foundation, 2014; Müller, 2014). The project was majority funded by the federal government, managed by state-owned Russian Railways, and executed by contractors connected to influential politicians. Part of the reason for the project's exorbitant costs was the terrain: there were substantial engineering challenges involved in constructing the road and rail in and alongside the Mzymta River, as well as building 46 new bridges and drilling 12 new tunnels through the Caucasus mountains (Sochi 2014 Organizing Committee, 2015). Another factor was a profiteering phenomenon in mega-event development where unscrupulous contractors delay construction in the context of the fixed event deadline in order to secure higher rents (Baade and Matheson, 2015; Baade and Matheson, 2015). On top of this, Russia's issues with corruption and neopatrimonial rent distribution also exacerbated the costs, though it is difficult to know the extent of this problem due to the opacity of the relationships in question (Wolfe and Müller, 2018).

Financial burdens aside, however, there also are questions of usage. Operations during the event went smoothly, and both road and rail managed the high demands of Olympic passenger transit between the clusters. 38 *Lastochka* trains regularly sped – as the Russian name suggests, like a flock of swallows – between the mountains and the coast, and 963 buses ran between venues on 15 routes with wait times between two and five minutes (Sochi 2014 Organizing Committee, 2015). Spectators travelled for free by presenting their visitor's badge (a security feature that accompanied ticket purchase) and Sochi's normally bottlenecked streets were clear for the duration of the Games. This traffic-free situation was not only a result of upgrading city roads and highways, however, but rather brought about by instituting a new traffic management regime. Authorities temporarily removed crosswalks, shut off traffic lights, established dedicated Olympic travel lanes, and required residents to apply for permits to drive during the event (Petrova and Myazina, 2013). Similar traffic reduction strategies have been employed effectively not only in Russia, but also by organisers in many host cities, including London, Athens and Sydney. Inconveniences like these are often standard fare for host city residents, and typically their complaints are assuaged by the knowledge that the event is temporary and that the long-term benefits should be worth the short-term pain.

Transport infrastructure functioned smoothly during the Olympics, but what was the situation for residents after the games left? This chapter is an attempt to address this question, as well as to help alleviate the lack of studies centring on the post-event period. It relies on documents and reports from the Russian Federal Government, the Sochi 2014 Organizing Committee, Olympstroy (the Russian state-run Olympic delivery agency), and the International Olympic Committee, as well as speeches and press releases from politicians and businesspeople involved in the production and delivery of the Games. It also uses materials from organisations and media not directly involved with the Olympics, such as the Anti-Corruption Foundation, the World Wildlife Fund, Vedomosti and Novaya Gazeta, as well as academic literature on mega-events in general and Sochi in particular. Finally, the chapter draws on fieldwork in Sochi 2007–2017 including regular episodic interviews with 22 residents in villages along the Mzymta River.

What's in it for Sochi?

There were numerous motivations for hosting the Winter Olympics in Sochi, set out in the Russian bid to the International Olympic Committee and the Russian federal government's guiding document to develop Sochi (Russian Federal Government, 2006; Sochi 2014 Organising Committee, 2006). There were three overall goals: to provide winter sports venues for elite Russian sport, to establish the region as a world-class winter tourist resort, and to increase the nation's prestige in both domestic and international contexts.

To expand on these motivations: after the collapse of the Soviet Union, Russia was left with no domestic training facilities for many of its winter athletes. Constructing domestic venues would allow Russian athletes to train at home rather than hiring facilities abroad. It also was intended to give the nation the ability to host both Russian and international sports championships in the future. At the same time, this massive infrastructure development would transform Sochi – already long established as a summer seaside resort – into a world-class winter destination (Putin, 2007). In concert with a modernised urban environment, the tourist economy could function year round and thus improve quality of life for the local population. This project signalled an active re-entry of the federal state into regional and urban development, though accompanied with significant human, environmental, and financial costs (Golubchikov, 2017). Finally, there was also a goal to reframe perceptions of the nation, presenting Russia as 'Great, New, Open!' – a slogan emblazoned at the entry to the Olympic park and on billboards and posters around the country. The federal government's ambitions for this image project were mostly achieved in domestic contexts but failed to change western attitudes towards Russia (Wolfe, 2016). These hosting motivations can be understood as broad promises for regeneration: of sporting facilities, of infrastructure overall, of the regional economy, of domestic conceptions of national identity, and of international perceptions of the country as a whole.

112   *Sven Daniel Wolfe*

One of the challenges in accomplishing the infrastructure aspects of this multifaceted regeneration was due to Sochi's natural environment, which is home to a variety of rare and endangered flora, and protected by a slew of national and international laws. The coastal cluster of Olympic venues was sited on the Black Sea shore, whose cleanliness is vital to the continued tourist attractiveness of the region. The mountain cluster was situated within the Sochi National Park, the only undisturbed mountain forest in Europe, adjacent to the Caucasus Nature Reserve, and protected as a UNESCO natural world heritage site. The Sochi Winter Olympic construction project was deployed in this environment, erecting each of the 11 sports venues from scratch, building an entirely new city in the mountains, and linking these developments with existing settlements via extensive transport links. Taking cues from the International Olympic Committee's Agenda 21 (IOC, 1999), which suggested guidelines for hosting sustainable games, the Sochi 2014 Organising Committee set out to build what they called the 'Games in Harmony with Nature' (Sochi 2014 Organizing Committee, 2006). The goal was to 'minimize, and when possible eliminate negative environmental impacts in Sochi during the construction and operation of Olympic venues and infrastructure' (Sochi 2014 Organizing Committee, 2015, 50). In the bid, organisers promised to enhance and increase the size of Sochi's environmental preserves, among numerous other ecological commitments. When the United Nations Environment Program expressed concern that the bobsled and luge facilities were planned within protected environments, Sochi 2014 organisers altered their plans and relocated the developments, earning international praise for their commitment to green games (UNEP, 2008). These green standards were intended to catalyse a sustainable building revolution across Russia and, to some extent, this has indeed come to pass in the post-Olympic period (Telichenko and Benuzh, 2014).

In many instances, however, these environmental aspirations conflicted with the broader infrastructural goals of the Sochi project. As construction progressed it became clear to many Russian and international ecologists and observers that the project's much-touted ecological standards were being violated, leading to claims that the organisers' gestures towards the environment amounted to image politics and greenwashing (EWNC, 2011a; O'Hara, 2015). Construction proceeded in protected areas and resulted in environmental damage (Gazaryan, 2010; and Shevchenko, 2014).

To some degree, these ecological costs should be expected: it is not possible to conduct massive construction projects in such delicate environments without deleterious impacts, particularly when working to meet an inflexible event deadline. This begs the question of why the games were bid for and awarded in the first place, given the almost unavoidable risks to the region's fragile environment. The most plausible explanation is that organisers prioritised the idea of developing Sochi's year-round tourist economy over protecting Sochi's natural environment. The *Lastochka* and New Krasnaya Polyana Highway epitomise these conflicting ideas, as the transit links were aimed at the tourist class and built with little consideration for the long-terms transport needs of residents, nor for the care of the environment. That Russian environmental protection laws were loosened in the run-up to the Olympics in order to facilitate these developments only underscores the importance of the Sochi tourist development idea to the minds of decision makers in Moscow.

Roads that provide and divide

Olga Sidorova holds her 6-year-old daughter's hand and walks down the narrow sidewalk to the bus stop. They are in the village of Kazachiy Brod, across the river from Akhstyr, walking alongside the original arterial road that connects the mountains to the coast (see map – Figure 7.1). For the Olympics, the road was expanded and upgraded with barriers and streetlights. 'The road is better now, but traffic was not so bad before', she says, as cars and trucks roar past. 'There used to be cows and horses on this road, can you imagine?' They sit down on the bus stop bench to wait. There is a digital display that listed bus arrival times during the Olympics but it is not working anymore. Still, Olga knows the schedule and the bus arrives only a few minutes late. They enter and pay the driver – the fare is higher now than it was before the Games – and squeeze into the packed bus. A man gives up his seat and Olga sits with her daughter on her lap. The girl watches the small screen on the ceiling, where snippets of children's cartoons play in between streams of commercials. An automated voice announces the upcoming stops in Russian and English. In less than 30 minutes, Olga and her daughter have travelled all the way down the upgraded original road to the market in Adler.

Overall, attention paid to road infrastructure constitutes substantial improvements to the region's car-system, linking residents to tourist infrastructures, employment, and consumption opportunities (Whitelegg, 1997). The ability to connect to these infrastructures and networks generates increased affordances for residents, and can result in significant economic and population growth; on the contrary, if these transit networks bypass a settlement, this can lead to its decline or demise (Garrison et al., 1959). These divergent potential trajectories are illustrated by the routine travel experiences of people on opposite sides of the Mzymta River. There is a marked advantage in travelling to Adler from Kazachiy Brod as opposed to from Akhshtyr. In Kazachiy Brod, people have always enjoyed better access to both mountains and coast due to their proximity to the original arterial road, and Olympic-related improvements to this road have improved travel times. So even though the *marshrutki* minibus taxis that serviced the village before the Olympics have been removed and replaced by an insufficient number of buses, it is still possible to travel without a car. Travel is noticeably easier for residents who do have their own vehicles, though, and access to the New Krasnaya Polyana Highway on the Akhshtyr side of the river only increases their options.

Previously, before the Olympics were granted to Sochi, a regional project had replaced the old mountain road to Krasnaya Polyana with a larger highway and three new tunnels, cutting Kazachiy Brod's travel time from over two hours to under 30 minutes. This original road was further improved as part of Olympic preparations but, on top of this, Kazachiy Brod drivers were also given a new option. Now, drivers can start on the original road, cross the Mzymta on a new bridge, join up with the New Krasnaya Polyana Highway and dash up to the resorts in around 20 minutes.

The drive is beautiful, through verdant mountain gorges, and across a picturesque cable-stayed bridge. Because this highway was built to handle peak traffic during the Olympics, it is over capacity for the current needs of the region. The unexpected benefit for drivers, however, is that the highway is largely free from the traffic jams that often clog the roads down by the coast. The main problems with this new highway involve poor flow control, corrupt police, and lack of equitable access. In general, signage is poor and entering or exiting the highway can be dangerous. Combined with fast driving, light traffic, and no dividers for oncoming vehicles, this has led to so many collisions, injuries, and deaths that locals have dubbed it 'the cursed highway'. The police maintain a regular presence to dissuade speeding, but they continue to solicit petty bribes from motorists. Finally, there are problems accessing the new highway in the first place. Thanks to the construction of new bridges, residents in Kazachiy Brod and other villages on the west side of the Mzymta have access to highways on both sides of the river. Due to the lack of adequate onramps on the east, however, Akhshtyr residents are largely excluded from either artery.

Akhshtyr is the northernmost eastern settlement along the Mzymta, and the residents there traditionally have been isolated by their position at the end of an old dirt road. At the beginning of Olympic development, the people in Akhshtyr were promised an onramp to access the new highway being built next to their homes, which could have connected their village to the wider region. Instead, despite protests, a court hearing and international news coverage, this project was delayed and then cancelled (Wolfe, 2013). The absence of a proper onramp has left the village more isolated than before, since the highway and *Lastochka* rails cut residents off from their previous pedestrian route across the river to Kazachiy Brod. Combined with the environmental damage caused by Olympic construction, they continue to suffer years after the event. One resident, who has since relocated to Adler, said:

> The Olympics passed us by. They never built the onramp so we just drive on the old road. They cancelled the bus. There's no store anymore. We still don't have water and everyone has to buy 5 liter bottles. All we have is a quarry and a dump instead of a national park … They installed gas lines but you have to pay for hook up and it's too expensive. I don't know how anyone lives there anymore. (Interview with former Akhshtyr resident, March 2017)

On the other side of the river, residents of Kazachiy Brod live substantially easier lives. Their material position – already superior to their neighbours due to the existence of the original road – has largely been improved by Olympic develop-ment. Gas lines have been extended here as well, and while figures for the village were not available, several residents confirmed that they paid the high hookup fees. Drinking water is available on tap and residents generally have enough, despite occasional shut-offs. Further, on the cliffs above Kazachiy Brod stands the Sochi Skypark, a new adventure tourism attraction that opened in 2014. People from all over Russia now come to cross what owners call the longest suspended pedestrian bridge in the world, and to experience Russia's highest bungee jump, 170 metres above the Mzymta River. Tourists pass Kazachiy Brod in order to reach the Skypark and shop in the local stores, which have expanded in order to meet growing demand. While residents are not universally pleased by the influx of strangers, and nor could they be considered wealthy, their material circumstances nevertheless are much improved since the Olympics. New stores have opened, new houses are being built, and there are rumours that the village's bumpy dirt roads might soon be paved. That Kazachiy Brod is thriving can be attributed to their easy access to two major transport arteries, and to the tourists, money and opportunity engendered by this access. In contrast, Akhshtyr is cut off from both roads and is withering.

Restrictions on the rails

The New Krasnaya Polyana Highway is only part of the major transit inter-vention from the coast to the mountains. There is also the new *Lastochka* train that was built for the games. Railway mobility systems provide public connectedness, mobilising people, blurring the lines between private and public spaces, and inducing profound temporal and regulatory changes in society (Thrift, 1990; Thrift, 2007). As with roads, the fate of a settlement can be made or broken by its proximity to rail service, and the right to move through these connected places – and thereby to engage the subsequent social benefits such as improved connectivity, employment and leisure – is con-tingent upon access. With train systems, access is dependent on the location of the rails, the shape of stations and platforms, the means of reaching these transit nodes, and of course on the trains themselves and on the schedules they maintain. Significant exclusions can occur if any of these elements is missing or obstructed.

The *Lastochka* system consists of nine stations, all built for the Olympics (see Figure 7.1). Arranged in a rough T-shape, the tracks run from downtown Sochi along the Black Sea coast to the Olympic park, with a trunk heading up to the two resort stations in the mountains. There is also a short spur that connects the Adler station to the airport. The areas linked by the new stations are significant. Adler and Khosta – two of Sochi's municipal sub-regions – are now connected via *Lastochka* to central Sochi. These are all tied into the tourist hotspots of the Olympic park and the mountain resorts. In this way, tourists who come to Sochi by train could transfer from the central station downtown or from the subregional train stations and wind up easily at a hotel in either of the Olympic clusters. Likewise, tourists arriving by air can walk from the terminal to the airport *Lastochka* station. However, that the airport is located on a spur line creates inconvenience from the outset, as air travellers are forced to transfer in Adler to the main lines and their destination. This makes them dependent on the smooth operation of a regular train schedule to make their transfer. Overlooking that problem for the moment, the *Lastochka* trains are modern, clean, and quiet, and would not look out of place in Western Europe. At the outset, the system was a point of pride for many locals – a sign that Sochi was becoming a world-class destination. In theory, the *Lastochka* system could have remained after the Olympics as a mass transportation system for the overall benefit of the region, as was the case in post-Olympic Sydney and Athens (Kassens-Noor, 2013b). In the legacy period, however, major problems with the train have come to light.

The first problem with the *Lastochka* system occurred not long after the Olympic closing ceremonies, as train service was cut due to intergovernmental squabbles over regulations and ownership of debt (Müller, 2014). The immediate result was such a severe reduction in service as to make the system practically unusable. Though this dispute has since been resolved, the *Lastochka* train remains plagued by irregular service and undependable schedules. Schedule information online is often contradictory and confusing, and does not always correspond to the actual presence of trains. In 2017 an attempt to buy a ticket from Adler station to the resorts in Roza Khutor was thwarted by a five-hour wait for the next train, and the counter attendant suggested that the author take a bus instead. Facing this predicament, tourists to Sochi often avoid the inconvenience of the train and make use of local buses instead. It is not uncommon to see Sochi residents commuting to work, crammed in a single bus alongside tourists with their snowboards, all while the multi-billion dollar train remains underused.

Aside from the irregular, unpredictable service – which in principle is a fixable problem – the second issue with the *Lastochka* is that the stations themselves are not located in areas that best serve the local population. Instead, the system is targeted at bringing visitors from transit hubs to tourist destinations. The majority of *Lastochka* stations are sited at already existing train stations, which are not convenient to where most people live. There are also buses waiting at the train stations, and since *Lastochka* tickets cost twice that of a bus, it is easier in nearly every situation to avoid the train entirely. For locals, who might live far from the train stations, there is little sense in going out of one's way – and paying higher prices as well – to take the *Lastochka*. There is a tremendous missed opportunity for the region's post-Olympics legacy, exemplified by Akhshtyr, Kazachiy Brod and the other villages by the Mzymta. A *Lastochka* station on the river, at a point somewhere midway between the Olympic clusters, could have served as a lifeline for villagers who do not, cannot, or would prefer not to drive, including the elderly and the youth. It would relieve pressure on the buses and reconnect Akhshtyr to the rest of the region. Aside from the river communities, there are numerous other underserved districts in Sochi that could benefit from connection to a well-run local rail system. Organisers did not appear to favour this version of legacy, though, as their plans centred on making the Sochi region attractive for tourists, with apparently little thought given to providing rail access that would serve the local population.

The third problem with the *Lastochka* system involves the ecological damage wrought during construction. This damage was immense and sustained over a period of years, as pylons for the road and rail were built alongside and in the Mzymta River. Chemical and construction waste was discharged into the river several times, with walls of toxic white foam washing downstream past Akhstyr and Kazachiy Brod, past Adler and into the Black Sea (EWNC, 2011b; Titov, 2011). Construction activity polluted the water so severely that nearly all fish life was extinguished from the river, a loss accounting for nearly 20% of the region's endangered Black Sea salmon (WWF, 2013). Driven by local environmental activists, this ecological damage – which by no means was limited only to the Mzymta – attracted national and international attention. In 2010 the United Nations Environment Program submitted a report to the Russian federal government that outlined some of the environmental damage already occurring in the Sochi Olympic construction project. By 2011 the Russian government organised stakeholders in the project to sign a declaration committing themselves to 17 environmental projects, including a restoration of the Mzymta River basin (UNEP, 2011). This restoration was touted as one of the environmental legacies of the Sochi Olympics, while quietly ignoring the fact that the restoration was only necessary due to Olympic construction in the first place.

Five years after the Games, several species of fish have been reintroduced into the Mzymta, but the river environment still had not recovered and locals do not swim anymore, though tourists do participate in rafting. 'I do not swim [in the river] since the foam', said a Kazachiy Brod resident. 'Before, we used to come here all the time every summer.' The riverbank where residents used to swim has been transformed into an exit point for the rafting tours, complete with a café and loudspeakers for music. Construction debris – large concrete blocks and rusted rebar – litters the riverbank. A sign has been hammered into the ground beside the broken concrete: No Fires, No Picnics, No Swimming.

Ecological destruction has continued even after the Olympics, as developers pushed to expand the mountain resorts. In 2018 local environmental groups protested these expansions, arguing that more construction would further damage the protected natural areas (Greenpeace Russia, 2018). UNESCO has threatened to rescind its natural world heritage site classification and recategorise the region as endangered (Chernikh and Nikitina, 2018). This continuing environmental destruction can be understood as a different kind of Olympic legacy, a byproduct of the processes in which mega-events serve to open previously closed territories to neoliberal globalisation (Horne, 2015; Horne, 2014).

Instead of linking the city for the long-term benefit of residents, the *Las-tochka* train was built to service the short-term needs of the Olympics, with the goal of serving tourists in the post-games period – as indicated by the sparse location of stations. With service cut immediately after the Olympics, however, and undependable schedules even years after the games, the *Lastochka* system remains something of an oddity. In contrast to most mega-event related transport projects, it is a transport white elephant: overpriced, underserviced and underused, and caused profound ecological damage as well.

Conclusion: a playground for tourists

Hosting mega-events transforms places and people, linking them to global processes of capitalist modernity (Roche, 2006; 2000). The Sochi Olympics follow this trend, opening up previously closed territories with promises of economic bonanzas amid the goal of transforming the region into a year-round tourist paradise (Baade and Matheson, 2015; 2016; Baade and Matheson 2014 Organizing Committee, 2006). A crucial part of this promise involved the construction and improvement of transport infrastructure in order to circulate visitors from transit hubs to hotels, resorts, shops, nightclubs and other tourist spots. These infrastructures are part of the material legacy of Sochi's transformation towards globalised leisure capitalism. In the bid book, organisers claim that this improved transport infrastructure would benefit the local population in the long term, and indeed, much popular and government discourse in the post-event period highlights these achievements. At the same time, in focusing on expanded and upgraded transit systems, this discourse often elides the selective, exclusionary and ecologically damaging effects of the Sochi project. These inequalities are exemplified by the construction of the new Sochi road and rail, whose legacy is mixed and controversial.

Host nations around the world have tried to use mega-events as a key to unlock processes of global leisure capitalism. Though the attempts are similar across the globe, what happens once these spaces are opened is not universal, but rather locally contingent. In Sochi this took the shape of building new resort cities in the previously protected mountain forests and constructing the new road and rail to connect them with the coast. At a more micro-level, it meant building a bungee jump bridge across the previously undeveloped mountaintops above Kazachiy Brod, and rafting down the poisoned Mzymta River. This transformative opening had consequences on local communities who were ignored in the rush to turn Sochi into a year-round resort, and to complete required projects by the mega-event deadline.

The result of overlooking local communities is that while the road infrastructure from the coast to the mountains has been improved and expanded, access to these improvements is not equal, and many residents – particularly in the cut-off community of Akhshtyr – cannot enjoy the benefits of Olympic transformation. Moreover, doubts have arisen in the post-event years about the quality of these road works overall, after heavy rains resulted in catastrophic flooding due to the lack of adequate drainage – a situation that raises questions about the long-term benefits even for those who can access the roads. The *Lastochka* system, meanwhile, successfully ignores residents on both sides of the river, and largely ignores the local population of Sochi as a whole. With stations positioned at areas that benefit tourists, the entire system is designed for visitors rather than locals. Even here, however, the system fails to provide, as the irregular service and an awkward connection to the airport push tourists to use local buses instead.

Still, visitors come to Sochi in summer and winter from all over Russia, and the increased economic activity has been substantial, buoying Sochi and the region to such a degree that, overall, unemployment has fallen, incomes have risen, and many indicators of quality of life are improving (Nureev et al., 2014). Sochi is portrayed as – and in many ways has in fact become – Russia's year-round playground, and the achievements of this project should not be over-looked. At the same time, the social and environmental impacts of develop-ments in general and the road and rail project in particular, continue to reverberate through the region. And so it is that Olga Sidorova, with her child in the back seat, carefully drives down Kazachiy Brod's bumpy road in her new Mitsubishi. At the bottom of the hill, she waits for a space between the buses of tourists and the huge construction trucks racing up the highway to the moun-tains. Beyond the road, she ignores the *Lastochka* train gliding silently on its tracks, and at this distance it is impossible to see if the train is empty or full.

Note

1 Names and identifying details have been changed to maintain anonymity.

References

Anti-Corruption Foundation (2014) *Sochi 2014 Encyclopedia of Spending: The Cost of Olympics Report by the Anti-Corruption Foundation*. Available online at: http://sochi.fbk.info/en/.

Baade, R. and Matheson, V. (2015) An analysis of drivers of mega-events in emerging economies. Econ. Dep. Work. Pap. Available online at: http://crossworks.holycross.edu/econ_working_papers/153.

Baade, R.A. and Matheson, V.A. (2016) 'Going for the gold: The economics of the Olympics', *J. Econ. Perspect.*, 30, 201–218. Available online at: https://doi.org/10.1257/jep.30.2.201.

Bovy, P. (2010) '"No transport white elephants": Mobility planning for mega-events', *Mag. Intell. Traffic Syst*, 2, 16–18. Available online at: www.mobility-bovy.ch/resources/Resources/03.Transport.no.elephants-2010.PDF.

Brunet, F. (1995) 'An Economic Analysis of the Barcelona '92 Olympic Games: Resources, Financing and Impact'. In M. de Moragas and M. Botella (eds) *The Keys to Success: The Social, Sporting, Economic and Communications Impact of Barcelona '92*. Barcelona: Centre d'Estudis Olímpics i de l'Esport, 203–237.

Cantarelli, C.C., Flybjerg, B., Molin, E.J.E. and van Wee, B. (2010) 'Cost overruns in large- scale transportation infrastructure projects: Explanations and their theoretical embeddedness', *Eur. J. Transp. Infrastruct. Res.* 10, 5–18.

Cashman, R. (2006) *The Bitter-Sweet Awakening: The Legacy of the Sydney (2000) Olympic Games.* Sydney: Walla Walla Press.

Chappelet, J.-L. (2008) 'Olympic environmental concerns as a legacy of the Winter Games', *Int. J. Hist. Sport*, 25, 1884–1902. https://doi.org/10.1080/09523360802438991.

Chernikh, A. and Nikitina, O. (2018) 'UNESCO otsenilo ugrozu "Zapadnomy Kavkazu"' [UNESCO estimates the threat to the Western Caucasus] ЮНЕСКО ёценилё угрёзу «Западнёму Кавказу»'. [WWW Document]. Kommers. No. 112 6350. Available online at: www.kommersant.ru/doc/3670894 (accessed 7. 5. 18).

Coaffee, J. (2010) 'Urban Regeneration and Renewal'. In J.R. Gold and M.M. Gold (eds) *Olympic Cities: City Agendas, Planning, and the World's Games.* London: Routledge, 180–193.

COHRE (2007) 'Fair play for housing rights: Mega-events, Olympic Games and housing rights: Opportunities for the Olympic movement and others'. Centre on Housing Rights and Evictions (COHRE). Available online at: www.ruig-gian.org/ressources/Report%20Fair%20Play%20FINAL%20FINAL%20070531.pdf.

Essex, S. and Chalkley, B. (2004) 'Mega-sporting events in urban and regional policy: A history of the Winter Olympics'. *Plan. Perspect.*, 19, 201–204. Available online at: https://doi.org/10.1080/0266543042000192475.

Essex, S. and Chalkley, B. (1998) 'Olympic Games: Catalyst of urban change', *Leis. Stud.*, 17, 187–206. https://doi.org/10.1080/026143698375123.

EWNC (2011a) 'EWNC raises international concern about the environmental impact of Sochi (2014) Olympics'. [WWW Document]. Available online at: www.governance.bsnn.org/pdf/RU2.pdf (accessed 7. 1. 18).

EWNC (2011b) 'Sochinskaya reka Mzymta vnov otravlena stokami s olympiiskogo obekta [Sochi's Mzymta River poisoned once again by from the Olympic facilities] Сёчинская река Мзымта внёвь ётравлена стёками с ёлимпийскёгё ёбъекта | Экёлёгическая Вахта пё Севернёму Кавказу'. [WWW Document]. Available online at: http://ewnc.org/node/7710 (accessed 7. 1. 18).

Flyvbjerg, B., Holm, M.K.S. and Buhl, S.L. (2004) 'What causes cost overrun in transport infrastructure projects?' *Transp. Rev.*, 24, 3–18. Available online at: https://doi.org/10.1080/0144164032000080494a.

Flyvbjerg, B., Holm, M.K.S. and Buhl, S.L. (2003) 'How common and how large are cost overruns in transport infrastructure projects?' *Transp. Rev.*, 23, 71–88. Available online at: https://doi.org/10.1080/01441640309904.

Flyvbjerg, B., Stewart, A. and Budzier, A. (2016) *The Oxford Olympics Study (2016) Cost and Cost Overrun at the Games* (SSRN Scholarly Paper No. ID 2804554). Rochester, NY: Social Science Research Network.

Gaffney, C. (2015) 'Gentrifications in pre-Olympic Rio de Janeiro', *Urban Geogr.*, 0, 1–22. Available online at: https://doi.org/10.1080/02723638.2015.1096115.

Gaffney, C. (2010) 'Mega-events and socio-spatial dynamics in Rio de Janeiro, 1919–2016', *J. Lat. Am. Geogr.*, 9, 7–29. Available online at: https://doi.org/10.1353/lag.0.0068.

Garrison, W.L., Berry, B.J., Marble, D.F., Nystuen, J.D. and Morrill, R.L. (1959) *Studies of Highway Development and Geographic Change.* Seattle: University of Washington Press.

Gazaryan, S. (2010) 'Sovmeshennaya doroga "Adler-Krasnaya Polyana" unichtozhila mzimtinsky samshitovy les [The combined 'Adler-Krasnaya Polyana' road destroyed

Mzymta's boxwood forests]'. [WWW Document]. Environ. Watch North Cauc. Available online at: www.ewnc.org/node/5634.

Gazaryan, S. and Shevchenko, D. (2014) 'Sochi-2014 independent environmental report'. Available online at: http://ewnc.org/files/sochi/Doklad-Sochi-2014_EWNC-Eng.pdf.

Gold, J.R. and Gold, M.M. (2016) *Olympic Cities: City Agendas, Planning, and the World's Games, 1896–2020*. 3rd edition. London and New York: Routledge.

Golubchikov, O. (2017) 'From a sports mega-event to a regional mega-project: the Sochi winter Olympics and the return of geography in state development priorities', *Int. J. Sport Policy Polit.*, 0, 1–19. Available online at: https://doi.org/10.1080/19406940.2016.1272620.

Greenpeace Russia (2018) 'Greenpeace i WWF prosyat UNESCO ne dopustit razrusheniya mirovovo naslediya na Kavkaze i v Komi [Greenpeace and the WWF ask UNESCO not to allow the destruction of the world heritage of the Caucasus]'. [WWW Document]. Available online at: http://m.greenpeace.org/russia/ru/high/news/2018/28-06-Greenpeace-WWF-Unesco/ (accessed 7. 5. 18).

Hiller, H. (2000) 'Mega-events, urban boosterism and growth strategies: An analysis of the objectives and legitimations of the Cape Town 2004 Olympic bid', *Int. J. Urban Reg. Res.*, 24, 449–458. Available online at: https://doi.org/10.1111/1468-2427.00256.

Horne, J. (2015) 'Assessing the sociology of sport: On sports mega-events and capitalist modernity'. *Int. Rev. Sociol. Sport*, 50, 466–471. Available online at: https://doi.org/10.1177/1012690214538861.

Horne, J. and Manzenreiter, W. (2006) 'An introduction to the sociology of sports mega- events', *Sociol. Rev.*, 54, 1–24. Available online at: https://doi.org/10.1111/j.1467-954X.2006.00650.x.

International Olympic Committee (2016) Host City Contract. Operational Requirements. IOC 1999 Olympic Movement's Agenda 21: Sport for Sustainable Development. Available online at: https://stillmed.olympic.org/media/Document%20Library/OlympicOrg/Documents/Host-City-Elections/XXXIII-Olympiad-2024/Host-City-Contract-2024-Operational-Requirements.pdf.

Kassens-Noor, E. (2013a) 'Transport Legacy of the Olympic Games, 1992–2012', *J. Urban Aff.*, 35, 393–416. Available online at: https://doi.org/10.1111/j.1467-9906.2012.00626.x.

Kassens-Noor, E. (2013b) 'Managing Transport during the Olympic Games'. In S. Frawley and D. Adair (eds) *Managing the Olympics*. New York and Basingstoke: Palgrave Macmillan, 127–146.

Kassens-Noor, E. (2012) *Planning Olympic Legacies: Transport Dreams and Urban Realities*. London and New York: Routledge.

Müller, M. (2015) 'The mega-event syndrome: Why so much goes wrong in mega-event planning and what to do about it', *J. Am. Plann. Assoc.*, 81, 6–17. Available online at: https://doi.org/10.1080/01944363.2015.1038292.

Müller, M. (2014) 'After Sochi 2014 costs and impacts of Russia's Olympic Games', *Eurasian Geogr. Econ.*, 55, 628–655. Available online at: https://doi.org/10.1080/15387216.2015.1040432.

Nureev, R.M., Markin, E.V. and Grechkin, M.A. (2014) 'XXII Olimpiiskie zimnie igri 2014g v Sochi: pervie itogi [The 22nd Winter Olympic Games in Sochi 2014. Initial Results]', *J. Econ. Regul.*, 5, 14–32.

O'Hara, M. (2015) '2014 Winter Olympics in Sochi: An environmental and human rights disaster'. In Francois Gemenne, Caroline Zickgraf and Dina Ionesco (eds)

The State of Environmental Migration 2015: A Review of 2014. Geneva: International Organization for Migration (IOM), 203–220. Available online at: http://labos. ulg.ac.be/hugo/wp-content/uploads/sites/38/2017/11/The-State-of-Environmenta l-Migration-2015-203-220.pdf.

OlympStroy (2013) 'Olympstroy - O Korporatsii [About the Company]' [WWW Document]. Available online at: https://web.archive.org/web/20130904234007/www. sc- os.ru:80/ru/about/ (accessed 2. 5. 18).

Petrova, Y. and Myazina, E. (2013) 'Sochi izbavyat ot probok po retseptu Moskvi [Sochi will do away with traffic by following Moscow's lead]'. [WWW Document]. Available online at: www.vedomosti.ru/business/articles/2013/11/14/ischeznut-li-prob ki-v-sochi (accessed 7. 12. 18).

Poynter, G., Viehoff, V. and Li, Y. (2015) *The London Olympics and Urban Development: The Mega-Event City*. London and New York: Routledge.

Preuss, H. (2004) *The Economics of Staging the Olympics: A Comparison of the Games, 1972–2008*. Cheltenham and Northampton, MA: Edward Elgar Publishing.

Putin, V. (2007) 'Speech at the 119th International Olympic Committee session'. [WWW Document]. Kremlin.ru. Available online at: http://en.kremlin.ru/events/p resident/transcripts/24402.

Roche, M. (2006) 'Mega-events and modernity revisited: Globalization and the case of the Olympics', *Sociol. Rev.*, 54, 27–40.

Roche, M. (2000) *Mega-Events and Modernity*. London: Routledge.

Russian Federal Government (2006) 'O federalnoi tselevoi programme Razvitiya goroda Sochi kak gornoklimaticheskogo kurorta 2006–2014 godi) [Federal target program for the development of Sochi as a mountain climate resort, 2006–2014]'. [WWW Document]. Available online at: http://pravo.gov.ru/proxy/ips/?docview&pa ge=1&print=1&nd=102108469&rdk=3& &empire= (accessed 10. 26. 16).

Sochi (2014) Organizing Committee (2015) *Official Report: Sochi 2014 Olympic Winter Games. The Organizing Committee of the XXII Olympic Winter Games and XI Paralympic Winter Games of (2014) in Sochi*. Moscow.

Sochi (2014) Organizing Committee (2006) *Sochi 2014 Candidature File: Gateway to the Future. The Organizing Committee of the XXII Olympic Winter Games and XI Paralympic Winter Games of 2014 in Sochi*. Moscow.

Telichenko, V.I. and Benuzh, A.A. (2014) 'Sovershenstvovanie printsipov ustoichi- vovo razvitiya na osnove opita primeneniya 'zelyonikh' standartov pri stroitelstve olimpiiskikh obektov v Sochi [Improvement of the principles of sustainable development based on the experiences of introducing 'green' standards during the construction of Olympic facilities in Sochia]'. *Promishlennoe Grazhdanskoe Stroit.* 40–43.

Thrift, N. (1990) 'The Making of a Capitalist Time Consciousness'. In J. Hassard (ed.) *The Sociology of Time*. New York: Palgrave Macmillan, 105–129.

Titov, E. (2011) 'Ekologicheskaya katastrofa na Mzymte mozhet ostavit Sochi bez pitevoi vodi [Ecological catastrophe on the Mzymta may leave Sochi without drinking water]'. [WWW Document]. Нёвая Газета - Novayagazetaru. Available online at: www.novayagazeta.ru/news/2011/08/20/49925-ekologicheskaya-katastrofa -na-mzymte-mozhet-ostavit-sochi-bez-pitevoy-vody (accessed 7. 1. 18).

Toohey, K. and Veal, A.J. (2007) *The Olympic Games: A Social Science Perspective*. Wallingford: CABI.

Trubina, E. (2014) 'Mega-events in the context of capitalist modernity: The case of 2014 Sochi Winter Olympics', *Eurasian Geogr. Econ.*, 55, 610–627. Available online at: https://doi.org/10.1080/15387216.2015.1037780.

UNEP (2011) 'Sochi's 2014 Winter Olympics turn green, adopting UN-backed plans'. [WWW Document]. UN News. Available online at: https://news.un.org/en/story/2011/03/369992-sochis-2014-winter-olympics-turn-green-adopting-un-backed-plans (accessed 7. 1. 18).

UNEP (2008) 'Russia to relocate Olympic sites after UN expresses environmental concerns'. [WWW Document]. UN News. Available online at: https://news.un.org/en/story/2008/07/265442-russia-relocate-olympic-sites-after-un-expresses-environmental-concerns (accessed 7. 5. 18).

Urry, J. (2007) *Mobilities*. Cambridge: Polity.

Watt, P. (2013) 'It's not for us', *City*, 17, 99–118. Available online at: https://doi.org/10.1080/13604813.2012.754190.

Whitelegg, J. (1997) *Critical Mass: Transport, Environment and Society in the Twenty-first Century*. London and Chicago: Pluto Press.

Wolfe, S.D. (2016) 'A silver medal project: The partial success of Russia's soft power in Sochi 2014', *Ann. Leis. Res.*, 19, 481–496. Available online at: https://doi.org/10.1080/11745398.2015.1122534.

Wolfe, S.D. (2013) 'Life on the ground: A comparative analysis of two villages in Sochi during Olympic transformation', *Euxeinos - Online J. Cent. Gov. Cult. Eur.*, 12/2013, 36–46.

Wolfe, S.D. and Müller, M. (2018) 'Crisis neopatrimonialism: Russia's new political economy and the 2018 World Cup', *Probl. Post-Communism*, 65, 101–114. Available online at: https://doi.org/10.1080/10758216.2018.1429934.

WWF (2013) 'Olympiada-2014 v gorode Sochi: oshibki olimpiada [2014 Olympics in Sochi: the mistakes of the Olympics]'. [WWW Document]. WWFru - Всемирный Фёнд Дикёй Прирёды. Available online at: https://wwf.ru/about/positions/sochi2014/ (accessed 7. 1. 18).

Part II

Alternative mega-events strategies

Critiques and responses to failed/serial bids

8 Bidding trepidation

Stockholm's uncertain relationship with the Olympic Games

Erik Olson, Robert Oliver and Luke Juran

Introduction

Stockholm's withdrawal from the 2022 Winter Olympic bid competition resonates with the growing apprehension by potential bid cities (especially those emerging from democratic countries) towards the Olympic Games. This chapter illustrates how Stockholm's Olympic hopes have book-ended a transformative period in the Olympic bidding process. While Sweden's Olympic Committee's approach to selecting a candidate city to compete in the Olympic Games bidding competition has become more decidedly metropolitan, lingering concerns of political accountability, financial uncertainty, as well as the post-event viability of purpose-built infrastructure serves to undermine Stockholm's commitment to the bid process. Recent reforms to the International Olympic Committee's bidding process embodied in Agenda 2020 although signalling a more accommodating bid process, has not yet convinced stakeholders in Stockholm that the IOC is prepared to accommodate a shift in bidding logics that are sensitive to local conditions. Stockholm's reluctance remains instructive because it speaks to a measured assessment of the pace of the IOC's institutional change, as well as the growing dissatisfaction with trying to ascertain and defend the public benefits that are supposedly tied to hosting.

For several decades, sport mega-events have been promoted as a catalyst for urban development, an opportunity to fundamentally re-envision a city through event-led strategic planning, and as an occasion to secure tens of billions of dollars for land investment by tying that vision to a hosting deadline (Hiller, 2000; Essex and Chalkley, 1998, 2003; Broudehoux, 2007; Gaffney, 2010; Andranovich and Burbank, 2011; Grix, 2014; Müller and Pickles, 2015). While it is clear that over the last half-century, multiple cities have coupled sport mega-event development to an urban revitalisation programme (Gold and Gold 2008; Gratton and Preuss 2008; Alberts 2009; Smith 2014; Viehoff and Poynter 2015), it is equally important to recognise that the vast majority of mega-event planning projects 'fail' as bidding cities lose out to their competitors (Oliver and Lauerman, 2017). The results of both bidding for and hosting mega-events have been mixed. The emergence of a number of negative impacts of hosting, stretching an over-investment in infrastructure to a reduction of civil liberties amongst local residents, has caused anti-bid social movements to question the viability of using sport for development (Silk, 2014; Lauermann, 2015; Zimbalist, 2016; Müller and Gaffney, 2018). As Oliver and Lauermann (2017) illustrate, a sense of crisis has permeated both popular and scholarly debate as bids have been abandoned and as the logic of hosting large-scale sporting events is interrogated and shown to be questionable.

The dwindling number of bid cities for recent competitions signals that for many cities the Olympic Games have simply become too risky an endeavour to justify dedicating significant contributions of human, financial and other forms of capital. With increasing evidence that the benefits of hosting are not distributed in an equitable manner and often fall far short of expectations, the viability of the Olympic Games has been pushed to a precipice. Even as the IOC has instituted broad reforms, anti-Olympics dissent continues to expose the 'creative destruction' unleashed by participating in the sport development arena (Gruneau and Horne, 2015). For Lauermann (2016, 313), bid committees/cities are feeling increased pressure, as '[a] proliferation of anti-bid social movements has pursued a form of urban politics, which more aggressively questions the legitimacy of using mega-events to pursue urban development'.

The Swedish Olympic Committee (SOK) has demonstrated a long-standing interest in securing the Olympic Games, having supported bids from Gothenburg, Falun and Östersund. It should be noted, however, that it did not produce a representative city for the 2006, 2010, 2014 or 2018 Winter Olympic Games competitions. Moreover, two efforts emerging from Stockholm ended in defeat (2004 Summer bid) and withdrawal from the bid competition (2022 Winter bid). Another bid from Stockholm would not be unexpected from a regional perspective; the Olympic Games have not been staged in a Scandinavian country since Lillehammer, Norway hosted the 1994 Winter Olympics. Although Sweden is thought of as a major winter sports country, it has never hosted the Winter Olympics. Stockholm was the host of the 1912 Summer Olympics and, intriguingly held the equestrian events for Melbourne's 1956 Summer Olympics when quarantine laws prevented the Australian city from staging those competitions (Dashper, 2012). Despite the historical and recent interest, there exists an apparent trepidation by Stockholm to launch a bid for the 2026 Winter Games.

This chapter focuses on Stockholm's reluctant pursuit of the Olympic Games not just because the city's quest is understudied, but because Stockholm's process of preparing their bids has exposed the incongruences of sport mega-event development. Stockholm's example, while contributing to a broader general narrative of bid decline, is important because it reveals the difficulties of trying to not only adjust to, but shift the logic of mega-event development. By illustrating how Stockholm's Olympic hopes have bookended a transformative period in the Olympic bidding process there is an opportunity to build on the important conversations of mega-event legacies and leveraging literature. Specifically, two interrelated questions concern us: (1) how has Stockholm's bidding logic shifted across a series (2004, 2022, 2026) of Olympic bids? (2) how has the shifting logic been represented? To address these questions, we use the phrase 'Stockholm shift' as a trope, unpacking it in three different domains. First, we trace the emergence of the phrase in the 2004 bid book illustrating how Stockholm has come to singularly represent the hopes of the SOK. Next, we illustrate how the SOK (along with three other Olympic Committees/Sport Associations) played an important role in articulating the underlying frustration with the Olympic Games bidding process and helped to identify circumstances which gave rise to the recommendations embodied by Olympic Agenda 2020. Finally, we explore how the parameters of reform central to IOC's Agenda 2020 have been negotiated by stakeholders in Stockholm. Although we are sensitive to the notion that the revised bidding process remains in its infancy – as only a couple of bidding cycles have been guided by these new procedures – we propose that uncertainty still defines the bidding process, and continues to challenge those cities like Stockholm who are reliant on a shift (or sharing) of risk from the public to the private sector, and between the host city and the IOC.

Beyond literature reviews, the chapter is informed by reporting on Stockholm's bidding process in primary material emerging from the SOK, Stockholm City Council, news agencies – including the daily Swedish newspaper *Aftonbladet* – and international news outlets, as well as documents (i.e. bid books, candidature files) sent to, or produced by the IOC (i.e. Agenda 2020). The chapter also incorporates semi-structured interviews with a select group of informants who were involved with the 2004, 2022 or 2026 Olympic bidding process.

'The Stockholm Shift'

Shift 1: A metropolitan reorientation

Nestled in the pages of Stockholm's 2004 candidate file (Bidding Committee Stockholm, 2004 1995) are a couple of paragraphs drawing attention to a 'Stockholm shift'. This phrase was used to highlight the repositioning of 'the focus of Sweden's Olympic movement toward the Royal Seat of Stockholm' and the value of mobilising the full spectrum of resources located in the capital city (Bidding Committee Stockholm 2004 1995). Previously, Sweden's Olympic Committee had supported bids from smaller urban centres including Gothenburg (1984 Winter Olympic bid), Falun (1988 and 1992 Winter Olympic bids), and Östersund (1994, 1998 and 2002 Winter Olympic bids). For Stefan Lindeberg, President of the SOK from 2000–2016, two salient observations emerged during the preparation of Stockholm's 2004 Summer Olympic bid. First, Lindeberg (2017) notes that it became clear that Summer Games had grown too big for the Stockholm region and 'that by losing 2004, it would not be possible to come back with another bid for the Summer

Games'. The 2004 bid competition was robust, with 11 candidate cities (Athens, Buenos Aires, Istanbul, Cape Town, Lille, Rio de Janeiro, Rome, San Juan, Seville, Stockholm and St Petersburg) (Feddersen et al., 2008; Billings and Holladay, 2011) all espousing their suitability as host. Stockholm was eliminated in the third round of voting having never really challenged the eventual winner, Athens. However, losing out on the 2004 Olympic bid helped to strengthen Stockholm's global appeal. As Olof Zetterberg (2017), former Director of both Sports Culture and City Planning in Stockholm states, losing the bid resulted in bolstering Stockholm's world image: 'nobody knows about Stockholm they say ... the good thing that came out of this is bid was that, of course, we got more attention for ourselves of what has to be done' and were able to 'put Stockholm on the world map'. At the time, Stockholm was a newcomer to the bidding process, as Zetterberg (2017) professes 'we were called the cousins from the rural area so to say; we did not really understand how things were going in the International Committee'.

Lindeberg's (2017) second observation was that it had also become obvious to Sweden's National Olympic Committee that Östersund was 'no longer big enough to host the Winter Games'. Essex and Chalkley (2004) have captured the unique challenge of preparing for the Winter Olympics, highlighting that the infrastructural demands of the Winter Olympics are often more burdensome on host communities than even those of the Summer Games. While the post-event utility of sport infrastructure/event facilities is typically cited as being a major concern, equally important to consider is the challenge of securing the appropriate ratio of hotel rooms/accommodations and the feasibility of investing in transportation and telecommunications infrastructure for the 16-day event (Essex and Chalkley, 2004). Although Östersund had pressed Lillehammer, Norway for the right to host the 1994 Winter Olympics, the Norwegian city had illustrated the difficulties of a small urban centre trying to accommodate the facility and infrastructure demands of the Games. With less than 25,000 inhabitants, Lillehammer not only 'lacked most of the necessary facilities and infrastructure' but the provision of such facilities generated problems for regional development and tourism post-Olympics (Teigland, 1999, 306). In its failing effort for the 2002 Olympic Games, Östersund was praised by the IOC's Evaluation Commission for its compact plan and realistic budget, but was criticised for failing to perform environmental impact assessments on planned facilities and the uncertainties of site plans for several new venues (i.e. ski jumps, bobsleigh and luge track). The IOC obviously went a different direction with Östersund being soundly defeated during the first round of voting gaining only 14 IOC members votes to Salt Lake City's 54. According to Lindeberg (2017), the lopsided results helped to convince the board of the SOK that if Sweden wished to host the Games, 'it must be Winter Games in the region that has the infrastructure and capacity as much as possible in place, and the only place for that is Stockholm'.

While there is no pre-requisite for population size when bidding for either iteration of the Olympic Games, Chappelet (2008, 1897) documents how 'the winter games have moved away from mountain resorts (Chamonix, St Moritz, Lake Placid, Garmisch, Cortina) towards cities in alpine valleys (Innsbruck, Grenoble, Nagano), and then to metropolises on the plains (Calgary, Salt Lake City, Turin) or even seaside cities (Vancouver, Sochi) relatively far away from the mountains'. Chappelet (2008: 1897–1898) also opines: 'the change has come about as a result of the ever-increasing size of the winter games, and could be perceived as a consequence of the very notion of durability, since larger towns are more easily able to guarantee sustainable post-Olympic use for the installations built for the games'. Given the rise of Stockholm's centrality in the Swedish urban system, it is not surprising to find that the city became the locus of a spatially reoriented bidding strategy. While Stockholm's population lags other host cities for recent editions of Summer Games, it compares favourably to recent Winter Olympic hosts.

The largest selling point of shifting the bids away from smaller urban centres like Östersund or Gothenburg is that sport related and other forms of basic urban infrastructure were already *in situ* in Stockholm. Moreover, new infrastructure development for proposed installations like the Olympic Village could also be leveraged to fulfil a need for additional housing and leave a positive legacy. Stockholm's record of post-event use of facilities stemming from its 1912 hosting of the Olympic Games as well as its failed 2004 Olympic bid offers compelling evidence. Many of the sport venues used during the 1912 Olympic Games remain in use, regularly playing host to major national championships and regional competitions (Bairner, 2015). In addition, the redevelopment of a large industrial harbour site located in southern Stockholm, Hammarby Sjöstad, is linked to Sweden's application for the 2004 Olympic Games (Khakee, 2007; Levin and Pandis Iverot, 2014). By shifting to Stockholm, the SOK was espousing the opportunity to leverage competitive forms of urban development through demonstrating alignment between Stockholm's bid objectives and broader urban development goals. Existing urban and stadium infrastructure, globally competitive companies, as well as a growing economy that is having a larger impact within Scandinavia and Europe are all characteristics that highlight Stockholm as *the* site for an Olympic Games in Sweden. Nevertheless, Lindeberg (2017) candidly summarises, it required significant time and effort to not only legitimate the shift to Stockholm to those living in other regions of Sweden (including those in Östersund) but also to convince those who had been willing to back a Stockholm *Summer* Olympic bid to begin to imagine Stockholm playing host to the *Winter* Games.

Shift 2: Framing Agenda 2020: reconsidering bid priorities

In December of 2014, at their 127 Session in Monaco, the IOC unveiled its strategic roadmap for the future of the Olympic Movement: Agenda 2020 (International Olympic Committee 2014). Launched by IOC president,

Thomas Bach, the process that led to the adoption of the recommendations outlined in Agenda 2020 reflects a serious reconsideration of the status of the Olympic Movement and the Olympic brand. With the social and economic concerns of Sochi 2014 and to some extent Beijing 2008 serving as a backdrop, Bach emphasised the need for the IOC to implement meaningful changes to safeguard the future of the Olympic Games. As Oliver and Lauermann (2017, 8) explain, 'Olympic Agenda 2020 comprised a reform package that was built from 40,000 public submissions synthesized by 14 working groups over the course of a year'. The result was 40 specific recommendations designed to 'improve the relationship between Lausanne and host cities' (MacAloon 2016, 776). Some of the recommendations addressed issues of gender equality, discrimination and ethics, while others stressed the need to engage with communities and foster better dialogue and good governance. But it was the IOC's acknowledgement of the need to: (a) reduce the costs of bidding and hosting; (b) improve transparency in terms of Olympic Games delivery requirements; and (c) enhance sustainability in all facets of the Olympic Games, that were likely of interest to potential bid cities seeking greater flexibility to mesh urban development goals with the expectations of being an Olympic Games host. For IOC member Richard Pound (2017, 53) the success of Agenda 2020 hinges on whether or not the Olympic Games 'become more of a collaborative search for tailor-made solutions in the different circumstances of each potential host city than a non-negotiable, all-or-nothing, bid against a static set of IOC-designed criteria'.

Intriguingly, many of the recommendations articulated in Agenda 2020 and the subsequent alterations to the Olympic bidding process were first voiced in a poignant report entitled, *Olympic Agenda 2020: The Bid Experience* (Austrian Olympic Committee et al., 2014). This report, written by the Swedish Olympic Association, in conjunction with the Austrian Olympic Committee, the German Sports Confederation and the Swiss Olympic Association, highlighted the difficulties that many National Olympic Committees face when trying to generate a candidate city from their respective nations. Prompted by Thomas Bach's invitation to contribute to the formation of Agenda 2020, the report was designed to communicate the experience of the *four* committees' involvement in recent bid competitions (Vienna explored a bid for the 2028 Games and Munich, Graubünden and Stockholm all considered the 2022 Olympic Games). The report avoided ambiguity in its assessment of the bidding process:

> The developments in the latest bid race for the 2022 Olympic Winter Games make it very clear that it has become increasingly difficult for established sports nations to communicate the Olympic values and the benefits that arise from bidding and hosting the Games ... As a result, more and more nations, especially European nations, either do not dare to submit an application anymore or withdraw it later on as just happened in Stockholm and Krakow. (Austrian Olympic Committee et al., 2014, 6)

Table 8.1 Participation in Olympic bidding from 1978 to present day

Key Date	Olympic bid activities in Sweden
May 1978	Gothenburg fails to secure 1984 Winter Olympics (Sarajevo)
September 1981	Falun fails to secure 1988 Winter Olympics (Calgary)
October 1986	Falun fails to secure 1992 Winter Olympics (Albertville)
September 1988	Östersund fails to secure 1994 Winter Olympics (Lillehammer)
June 1995	Östersund fails to secure 2002 Winter Olympics (Salt Lake City)
September 1997	Stockholm fails to secure 2004 Summer Olympics (Athens)
November 2013	Stockholm submits bid for 2022 Winter Olympics
January 2014	Stockholm drops bid for 2022 Winter Olympics
October 2014	Swedish Olympic Committee (SOK) expresses regret about withdrawal
July 2015	Stockholm withdraws bid for 2022 Winter Olympic Games
January 2017	Stockholm City Council commissions report for potential 2026 Winter Olympic Games bid
April 2017	Stockholm's Mayor indicates lack of government support for Olympic bid (the SOK continues efforts)
September 2017	Stockholm enter dialogue phase of 2026 Winter Olympic Games bidding competition
April 2018	Stockholm's Mayor reiterates lack of government support for a Stockholm bid
January 2019	Deadline for submission of Candidature File by Candidate Cities for the 2026 Winter Olympic Game

Stressing the need to 'proactively communicate the social and economic benefits of bidding and hosting the Games' the report recommended that 'the IOC enters a dialogue process with a city and it's NOC as soon as a city explains interest in bidding' (Austrian Olympic Committee et al., 2014: 6).

The report emphasised the need to 'rethink the bidding procedure in order to reduce complexity and increase transparency and flexibility for potential bid cities (Austrian Olympic Committee et al., 2014, 4). It was also a reaction to the unprecedented number of withdrawals of bidding cities. At the same time, the report mentioned the need to improve communication between the IOC and the potential bidding cities about expectations and the sharing of potential risks (Austrian Olympic Committee et al. 2014). The report clearly communicated the underlying frustration of the *four* NOCs and concluded by calling on the IOC to provide: '*M*ore support in bidding; More certainty in process; More partnership in risk; More flexibility in scale' (Austrian Olympic Committee et al., 2014, 14).

In terms of Stockholm's experience, voters rejected the idea of pursuing the 2022 Winter Games in January 2014 (see Table 8.1 for a timeline of this process). For Lindeberg (2017) there was a clear 'Sochi effect' at work: 'the situation was when this came forward in December and January 2013/2014, it was Sochi staging the backdrop with the costs, but not only the costs but the environmental impact'. The concerns of the cit*i*zenry were echoed by politicians at all levels of the Swedish government. Although the 2022 bid had initially generated solid political support from both the Social Democrats and Conservatives in the halls of Stockholm's City Council and was viewed to offer a socially and an environmentally sound bid plan, growing anxiety regarding the spiralling costs of staging served to upset commitments of support from senior levels of government. It is important to recognise that 2014 was an election year in Sweden for parliament as well as for Stockholm's City Council, and the environmental, financial and other costs evident in Sochi's preparations generated a negative image that could not be ignored (Lindeberg, 2017; Zetterberg, 2017). In more detail, Lindeberg (2017) explains 'the ruling parties had won their credibility in taking good responsibility for the financial situation in Sweden' and for a politician 'to go out in the streets and say '*H*ey, hey, we are going to stage the Olympic Games, it was not really possible'.

Tellingly, once the details of Agenda 2020 started to become clear, various stakeholders began to express regret about abandoning the bid competition. There were even conversations amongst IOC members about the feasibility of reopening the bidding process, but this prospect was stifled by IOC president Thomas Bach (Agenda 2020: The revolution begins, 2014). For Lindeberg the timing of the IOC's reforms was unfortunate:

> If we had known in January what we know now about the contribution from the IOC, the new Host City contract including new international standards for workers' rights and all these ethical factors, we would have been in a totally different situation in Sweden. If we'd known that in January, we might still be in the race. (Lindeberg quoted in Agenda 2020: The revolution begins, 2014, 7)

In more detail, Lindeberg (2017) explains that the strength of Stockholm's 2022 bid was that it already represented the core objectives of Agenda 2020, incorporating a sensible sustainability strategy that limited the number of Games-related investments, while emphasising the social and environmental benefits that would result from integrating games and city planning.

Shift 3: A political split: municipal reluctance and SOK promotion

What might Agenda 2020 mean for Stockholm? The adoption of Agenda 2020 with its focus on establishing a bidding process that is less 'made in Lausanne' and more concerned with curbing costs and improving sustainability strategies would seem to bode well for Stockholm. Three years removed from pulling the 2022 bid, roughly 24 months since the adoption of Agenda 2020, and shortly following the commissioning of a feasibility study designed to investigate Stockholm's conditions and interest for bidding and hosting the 2026 Winter Olympic Games, Stockholm's City Council issued a press release claiming: '… the Olympic movement's new strategy, Olympic Agenda 2020, is fully in line with Stockholm's ambitions for social, financial, environmental and democratic sustainability' (Stockholm City Council, City Executive Office, 2017).

The feasibility report commissioned by the City of Stockholm claimed that there was the potential to create a new Winter Games model that was forward-looking, reflecting not only Stockholm's track record of developing innovative solutions to enhance sustainable development but also its ambitions regarding human rights and its commitment to civic discourse on how to improve the city's brand. While not ignoring the challenges of hosting, the Winter Games were pitched as an opportunity to make investments that would improve the city's sport and public health objectives while increasing the attractiveness of the region as a tourist destination and business location. Despite these positive statements, a closer reading of the report and particularly the appendices reveals a lingering sense of uncertainty towards the Olympic Games and the IOC. For instance, the report incorporated the results of more than 2,100 web interviews and *four* focus groups (Demoskop AB, 2017). The results of this empirical work reveal a split in attitude towards the Olympic Games in Stockholm. Ackinger (2017) adds clarity:

> the population in Stockholm is divided roughly 50/50 with for and against the Olympics. The pros are talking about the benefits and how the event could help Stockholm position itself in a global arena. The cons are focused on the cost and the risk of overrunning the budget. They are also negative or very negative towards the International Olympic Committee due to scandals regarding corruption and other affairs.

The appendix of the feasibility report indicates that less than 5% of the people involved in the study were actually aware of Olympic Agenda 2020, with even less claiming some understanding of what Agenda 2020 entails. It is further noted that when Agenda 2020 was more thoroughly explained, many felt that if the objectives of Agenda 2020 were adhered to, then it would likely improve Stockholm's chances of securing the Games. At the same time, the information did not actually increase overall support for the Winter Olympics in Stockholm (Demoskop AB, 2017). Here we find that lack of trust in the IOC and the desire for risk reduction continue to trouble many residents of Stockholm. The report reiterates some long-standing concerns including (1) the costs of the Games; (2) Stockholm was not thought to be a winter city; and (3) Stockholm's urban infrastructure, particularly transportation, was thought to be inadequate. Equally important is the articulation of the continuing sentiments of 'low confidence' that Stockholm's residents have in the IOC. While encouraged by Agenda 2020 reforms, the report suggests that people still desire concrete evidence that the IOC has improved its institutional integrity and that it will actually award the Olympic Games to those cities who emphasise more modest and sustainable Games concepts.

Despite the failures of the 2004 and 2022 bids, the SOK remains dedicated to encouraging a submission from Stockholm. In January 2017, the Swedish Olympic Committee posited that a 2026 Olympic bid was 'possible and desirable', and yet, within a few months the effort was seemingly abandoned (*'Sweden wants to host 2026 Olympics', NBC Sports* 27 January 2017; 'Stockholm drops its bids for 2026 Winter Olympics', *USA Today* April 2017). Once again, the lack of clarity on the IOC's financial commitment was cited as being a key intervening obstacle. The IOC had delayed instructions for potential bid cities regarding the implementation of Agenda 2020 by more than a year and as result, Karin Wanngård, Mayor of the City of Stockholm and Social Democrat, was unable to develop cross-party political support (Arwidson, 2017). As Lindeberg (2017) explains: 'the Social Democrats say they are for the bid, but they cannot gather the majority of the city hall they don't trust whether the Conservatives or Liberals being in their position, would support the bid'. Similar to the 2022 effort, the 2026 bid overlaps with an election cycle in Sweden and in Ackinger's estimation moving a bid application forward during the campaign season (Spring–Summer 2018) remains problematic politically and thus unlikely (Ackinger, 2017).

Conclusion

A central concern of this chapter was to expose and explain the apparent municipal reluctance of Stockholm to commit the resources necessary to pursue the Olympic Games. We used the foundation of the 'Stockholm Shift' as a trope, breaking the apparent reluctance into *three* separate, but interconnected sections. First, we inspected the decidedly metropolitan shift that has emerged within the SOK; shifting the bid efforts to Stockholm. This shift reflected the abandonment of a bid strategy that had previously encouraged smaller urban centres such as Östersund, Falun and Gothenburg to pursue the Olympic Games. The rise in prominence of Stockholm as a small European capital with growing significance regionally and a more compelling base of urban infrastructure was determined by the SOK to offer a more attractive bid to an international audience. The metropolitan shift also illustrated that

Stockholm was not suitably equipped to compete for the Summer Games, thus leading the SOK to focus bid ef*forts* on the Winter Games.

The second shift examined the growing necessity of recognising the cultural relativity and context of mega-event bids. Drawing on the Swedish Olympic Committee, and other NOC's criticism of the Olympic bidding process, we explained how hosting the Olympics has come to be considered incompatible with planning objectives of many cities. By tracing the influence of the several Olympic Committees on the IOC's Agenda 2020, we illustrated the underlying need for the IOC to provide a less templated mega-event. Central to the reluctance of many cities from submitting a bid is the notion that it had simply become too difficult to marry local urban development objectives to the requirements imposed by the IOC. Beyond the obvious gigantism that has taken root, recent editions of the Olympic Games had failed to accommodate local contingencies. Put differently, the Olympic Games despite being a global mega-event need to remain locally rooted. For Stockholm to consider mounting a bid, the IOC must take sustainability seriously and be willing to award the Games to a city offering a more modest Games plan.

The last shift exposed the political split that has developed across Stockholm's series of bids. The adoption of Agenda 2020 would appear to improve Stockholm's chance of securing the Olympic Games, but Stockholm's City Council remains unwilling to commit to a project that continues to have a high degree of uncertainty and voices from the grassroots remain sceptical about whether there has been actual existing reform. Inspecting Stockholm's relationship with the Olympic Games reveals the difficult road that many NOCs encounter when attempting to generate a candidate city for the Olympics. In Sweden, the SOK's pursuit of the Olympics has been marred by multiple failures. The constant tinkering and shifting logic of bids illustrates 'the struggle of urban and extra-local actors to legitimate particular forms of urban transformation' (Oliver and Lauermann, 2017, 11). With each additional iteration of the Games, it is plausible to imagine that a distancing effect will curtail the negative connotations associated with previous editions of the Games, but to date there has been very limited proof that Agenda 2020 is altering the sport mega-event landscape. Zimbalist (2016) has highlighted the ongoing difficulties that Pyeongchang 2018, Tokyo 2020 and Beijing 2022 have encountered when trying to ameliorate long-standing concerns of financial security, stadium construction, political protest, as well as environmental and broader issues of social sustainability. For Zimbalist (2016: 164), recent withdrawals from bid competitions, such as Boston 2024, is a useful reminder that: 'it is prudent to be vigilant when dealing with unregulated, international monopolies. And sometimes it is even a good idea to fight back'. The clearest indication that a city can show that reforms must extend beyond rhetoric is to refrain from entering the bid competition. In the absence of *both* the SOK and Stockholm's City Council being convinced that there has been a shift in expectations by the IOC, it remains difficult to imagine a Stockholm Olympics.

References

'Agenda 2020: the revolution begins'. (2014). *Host City*, 50 (Winter), 4–9. Available online at: https://www.hostcity.com.

Alberts, H. (2009) 'Berlin's failed bid to host the 2000 Summer Olympic Games: Urban development and the improvement of sports facilities', *International Journal of Urban and Regional Research*, 33(2), 502–516.

Andranovich, G. and Burbank, M. (2011) 'Contextualizing Olympic legacies', *Urban Geography*, 32(6), 823–844.

Arwidson, P. (2017) 'No OS in Sweden 2026', *Aftonbladet* (accessed online 26 April 2017).

Austrian Olympic Committee, German Sports Confederation, Swedish Olympic Committee, Swiss Olympic Association (2014) *Olympic Agenda 2020: The Bid Experience*. Frankfurt: Proprojekt.

Bairner, A. (2015) 'The Legacy of Memory: The Stockholm and Helsinki Olympic Stadia as Living Memorials'. In R. Holt and D. Ruta (eds) *Routledge Handbook of Sport and Legacy: Meeting the Challenge of Major Sports Events*. New York: Routledge, 120–130.

Bidding Committee Stockholm 2004 (1995) Bid Book, Vols 1–3. Stockholm.

Billings, S. and Holladay, S. (2011). 'Should cities go for the gold? The long-term impacts of hosting the Olympics', *Economic Inquiry*, 50(3), 754–772.

Broudehoux, A. (2007) 'Spectacular Beijing: The conspicuous construction of an Olympic metropolis', *Journal of Urban Affairs*, 29(4), 389–399.

Chappelet, J. (2008) 'Olympic environmental concerns as a legacy of the Winter Games', *The International Journal of the History of Sport*, 25(14), 1884–1902.

Dashper, K. (2012) 'The Olympic Experience from a Distance: The Case of the Equestrian Events at the 2008 Games'. In R. Shipway and A. Fyall (eds) *International Sports Events: Impacts, Experiences and Identities*. London: Routledge, 141–153.

Demoskop AB (2017) 'Attitudes to applying for the Winter Olympics and Paralympics 2026'. Stockholm.

Essex, S. and Chalkley, B. (1998) 'Olympic Games: Catalyst of urban change', *Leisure Studies*, 17(3), 187–206.

Essex, S. and Chalkley, B. (2003) 'Urban transformation from hosting the Olympic Games: university lecture on the Olympics [online article]'. Barcelona Centre d'Estudis Olíímpics (UAB) International Chair of Olympism (IOC-UAB).

Essex, S. and Chalkley, B. (2004) 'Mega-sporting events in urban and regional policy: A history of the Winter Olympics', *Planning Perspectives*, 19(2), 201–204.

Feddersen, A., Maennig, W. & Zimmermann, P. (2008). 'The empirics of key factors in the success of bids for Olympic Games', *Revue d'Économie Politique*, 118(2), 171–187.

Gaffney, C. (2010) 'Mega-events and socio-spatial dynamics in Rio de Janeiro, 1919–2016', *Journal of Latin American Geography*, 9(1), 7–29.

Gold, J. and Gold, M. (2008) 'Olympic Cities: Regeneration, city rebranding and changing urban agendas', *Geography Compass*, 2(1), 300–318.

Gratton, C. and Preuss, H. (2008) 'Maximizing Olympic impacts by building up legacies', *The International Journal of the History of Sport*, 25(14), 1922–1938.

Grix, J. (ed.) (2014). *Leveraging Legacies from Sports Mega-Events: Concepts and Cases*. Basingstoke: Palgrave Macmillan.

Gruneau, R. and Horne, J. (eds) (2015). 'Mega-events and globalization: A critical introduction.' In *Mega-Events and Globalization: Capital and Spectacle in a Changing World Order*. London: Routledge.

Hiller, H. (2000) 'Mega-events, urban boosterism and growth strategies: An analysis of the objectives and legitimations of the Cape Town 2004 Olympic bid', *International Journal of Urban and Regional Research*, 24(2), 439–458.

Khakee, A. (2007) 'From Olympic village to middle-class waterfront housing project: Ethics in Stockholm's development planning', *Planning, Practice & Research*, 22(2), 235–251.

Lauermann, J. (2015) 'Boston's Olympic bid and the evolving urban politics of event-led development', *Urban Geography*, 37(2), 313–321.

Lauermann, J. (2016) 'Temporary projects, durable outcomes: Urban development through failed Olympic Bids?' *Urban Studies*, 53(9), 1885–1901.

Levin, P. and Pandis Iverot, S. (2014) '(Failed) Mega-events and City Transformation: The Green Vision for the 2004 Olympic Village in Stockholm'. In P. Berg and E. Björner (eds) *Branding Chinese Mega-Cities Policies, Practices and Position*. Northampton MA: Edward Elgar Publishing, 155–167.

Lindeberg, S. (2017). Telephone interview, 21 September 2017.

MacAloon, J. (2016) 'Agenda 2020 and the Olympic Movement', *Sport in Society*, 19 (6), 767–785.

Müller, M. and Gaffney, C. (2018) 'Comparing the urban impacts of the FIFA World Cup and Olympic Games from 2010 to 2016', *Journal of Sport and Social Issues*, 42 (4), 247–269.

Müller, M. and Pickles, J. (2015) 'Global Games, local rules: Mega-events in the post-socialist world', *European Urban and Regional Studies*, 22(2), 121–127.

Oliver, R. and Lauermann, J. (2017) *Lasting Legacies? Failed Olympic Bids and the Transformation of Urban Space*. Basingstoke: Palgrave Macmillan.

Pound, R. (2017) 'The Management of Big Games: An Introduction'. In E. Bayle and J. Chappelet (eds) *From Olympic Administration to Olympic Governance*. London: Routledge, 60–69.

Silk, M. (2014) 'The London 2012 Olympics: The cultural politics of urban regeneration', *Journal of Urban Cultural Studies*, 1(2), 273–293.

Smith, A. (2014) 'Leveraging sport mega-events: New model or convenient justification?' *Journal of Policy Research in Tourism, Leisure and Events*, 6(1), 15–30.

Stockholm City Council, City Executive Office. (2017) 'City of Stockholm's Olympic investigation presented'. Press release, 27 January. Available online at: www.stock holm.se/vinterspelen2026.

'Stockholm drops its bid to host the 2022 Winter Olympic Games' (2014) *British Broadcasting Corporation* (accessed online 17 January 2014).

'Sweden wants to Host 2026 Olympics'. *NBC Sports* (accessed online 27 January 2017).

Teigland, J. (1999) 'Mega-events and impacts on tourism: The predictions and realities of the Lillehammer Olympics', *Impact Assessment and Project Appraisal*, 17(4), 305–317.

Viehoff, V. and Poynter, G. (eds) (2015) *Mega-Event Cities: Urban Legacies of Global Sports Events*. New York: Routledge.

Zetterberg, O. (2017) Telephone interview, 19 September.

Zimbalist, A. (2016) *Circus Maximus: The Economic Gamble behind Hosting the Olympics and the World Cup*. Washington, DC: Brookings Institution Press.

9   What Hamburg's HafenCity can learn from the Olympic Games

Mathias Kuhlmann

Stage free: the world as a guest in Hamburg

'Hello World, welcome to Hamburg!' Elphi as a new landmark

The most beautiful way to Hamburg leads over the River Elbe. At the western border of the city, every ship coming from the North Sea and Baltic Sea is greeted with the national anthem of its home country and in its national language. Only a little later the new landmark of the Hanseatic city comes into view, the Elbphilharmonie, lovingly called 'Elphi' by Hamburgers and guests. But not only from the west, from all directions visible from far away, the 110m-high building with its facade made of glass mounts up. When the new temple of culture opened on 11 January 2017 with a grand concert, millions of people around the world followed it live via TV and the Internet. The music in the large hall was translated into a dazzling colour symphony on the Elbe-facing facades using video technology and spotlights. 'Hello World' was projected there at the end of a fantastic evening.

The glass structure of the Elphi rests on a quay warehouse dating from the year 1963 with 3,100m^2 of floor space and a 37m-high brick facade. The location on the western tip of the former harbour area behind the historic Speicherstadt could hardly have been better chosen. A real piece of luck in Hamburg's architectural history, yet nobody half a century ago thought that HafenCity would be home to the largest inner-city urban development project in Europe. The Elphi now welcomes Hamburg's guests to the central piers and directs their attention to the new HafenCity. The slogan of Hamburg has been 'Gateway to the World' for centuries and the largest German port has always been the symbol for it. Since the establishment of HafenCity and Elphi, the slogan is now more modest: 'Welcome to Hamburg'.

The people say 'No' to Olympics on the Elbe islands

Spectacular images and sounds such as those from the Elphi opening are particularly associated with the opening and closing ceremonies of the Olympic and Paralympic Games (subsequently referred to as the 'Olympic Games'), most recently in Rio (Summer 2016) and Sochi (Winter 2014). Hamburg also

Figure 9.1 Structure plan of HafenCity
Source: Free and Hanseatic City of Hamburg, 2015b.

aspired to host the Summer Games. After a first bid, which was defeated in the national competition against Leipzig in 2002, the newly elected red-green Hamburg government announced in spring 2015 that it would re-apply as a key project in the coming legislative period. Its centrepiece was the development of the new OlympiaCity district on the Elbe island Kleiner Grasbrook opposite the HafenCity. In addition to the athletes' village, the Olympic Stadium designed for 60,000 spectators, the Aquatics Stadium for 17,000, and a multifunctional sports hall for 15,000, was to be built on an area of 104 hectares, all embedded in a large park with beach and spectacular views over the Elbe river, with the skyline of Hamburg including St Michel's church, the TV tower, HafenCity and Elphi.

The Olympic Stadium was to be dismantled after the Games, making way for a terraced residential complex around a remaining athletics stadium. After the Games, the Aquatics Stadium would have become a sports and fun pool and the multi-purpose hall would have become a cruise terminal. For the athletes' village, conversion into a mixed-use district with apartments for up to 18,000 people, of which one-third was publicly funded, was planned. Shops, restaurants and service companies were expected to create 7,000 new jobs. Social facilities such as day nurseries, schools, health and facilities for the elderly, two parks and other sports facilities were also planned. The new district was to be developed, in particular via a new underground line, which later would have been extended further south to Wilhelmsburg and Harburg. In addition, several new bridges were designed to improve the accessibility of the city centre by bicycle to the residents of the adjacent old working-class neighbourhoods on the Elbe islands (Free and Hanseatic City of Hamburg, 2015b).

Most of the Hamburgers considered plans for an OlympiaCity as a continuation of HafenCity on the Elbe islands. People with lower income and education (and others), however, viewed HafenCity primarily as a district for corporations, high earners and tourists – but not as their district. In consequence, the governing parties had declared the acceptance of the population in a referendum as a condition for the bid. At numerous events, the plans were presented, advertised and discussed with the active participation of politicians, the public and the media. From the outset, the numerous supporters (according to polls initially up to two-thirds of the population) were opposed by a powerful NOlympics movement (NOlympia Hamburg, 2015). On 29 November 2015, 51.6% of Hamburgers said 'No' to the Olympics. Almost the entire city centre with the left-alternative strongholds St Georg, St Pauli, Old Town Altona, Ottensen and Schanzenviertel and all neighbourhoods around the Kleiner Grasbrook – with the exception of HafenCity itself – had spoken out clearly against the Games. In addition, in a large part of the Borough of Harburg and on the Elbe islands, the rejection reached up to 80 percent. The reason was obvious – the fear of rising rents and land prices, as well as the loss of many jobs in the port businesses, which would have been forced to give way to the OlympiaCity. The prospect of the Olympic Games in the midst of the city and the harbour, against the wishes of the local residents and a considerable degree of scepticism in the port industry – meant that the scheme could not and cannot work (Kuhlmann, 2017).

HafenCity in the context of worldwide waterfront projects

The conversion of former port areas into new neighbourhoods for living, working, culture and leisure began earlier in other cities than in Hamburg – in Europe since the early 1980s notably the Docklands in the East of London, followed by Amsterdam and Copenhagen. The first ideas for the revitalisation of fallow harbour areas had been promoted already in 1973 by the Hamburg architect Volkwin Marg in his study *Hamburg: Building at the Waterfront*. However, it took another 24 years before the HafenCity project was officially launched by the Senate under the First Mayor Henning Voscherau (SPD / Social Democratic Party of Germany). Volkwin Marg grew up in Gdansk, Poland, and spent several years in the Netherlands and was particularly inspired by the development of the port cities there. The draftsman of the 2000 HafenCity Masterplan, the Dutchman Kees Christiaanse, came from Amsterdam, studied in Delft and later became a partner in the Office for Metropolitan Architecture (OMA) of Rem Kohlhaas in Rotterdam. The early waterfront projects in Europe, in turn, were influenced by previous developments in the USA, particularly in Boston and San Francisco. Dirk Schubert, who worked as a professor for housing and neighbourhood development at the Technical University Hamburg-Harburg and later until his retirement at the HafenCity University Hamburg, can be regarded as a pioneer of international waterfront research in German-speaking countries (Kuhlmann, 2009).

The list of cities in which the urban and landscape designers, architects and engineers involved in the HafenCity development were working, reads like a cosmopolitan 'Who's Who': New York, London, Amsterdam, Copenhagen, Barcelona, Vienna, Berlin, Munich, Frankfurt, Stuttgart – and of course Hamburg. The HafenCity was thus inspired by ideas from Germany, Europe and the entire world, and especially from port cities. Since ports, financial districts/CBDs and city centres were rediscovered for urban development in the 1970s, there has been a lively exchange of ideas and experiences, not only of planners but also of other stakeholders such as investors, developers, residents, scientists, non-governmental organisations, city authorities and politicians. The resulting international know-how became impressively visible in the information centre, Kesselhaus, and on the website of HafenCity (HafenCity Hamburg, 2017).

The special quality of the Hamburg HafenCity, like other waterfront projects, is essentially based on the mutual learning of these cities. The wheel does not have to be reinvented at every location. What was planned and tested in one city could be taken up and further developed in the other city. Keeping in mind all the competition that has always existed between port cities, and with every legitimate interest in the protection of good ideas, building on existing knowledge and ability is driving forward innovative developments considerably. Hamburg's plans for an OlympiaCity have also been developed by renowned offices that are involved in major urban development projects and sports facilities worldwide. With the necessary critical eye for weaknesses and mistakes, Hamburg can only benefit from this in the further development of HafenCity in the absence of the OlympiaCity. In its planned eastern and southern extension, in the Billebogen as well as on the Kleiner Grasbrook, there is plenty of opportunity to do so in the coming years.

HafenCity: Europe's largest inner-city urban development project

The masterplan from the year 2000

The political decisions to establish HafenCity in 1997 were largely based on the study: *Development of the Inner City Harbour between Grasbrook and Baakenhafen*, submitted by Volkwin Marg in December 1996. The municipal agency HafenCity Hamburg was commissioned with the key development management role in 1998. It is responsible for the marketing of urban land, the acquisition and support of investors and builders, the development of sites and land for housing, service and recreational use. The agency also leads the coordination and facilitation of all planning and construction projects, the planning and implementation of development measures, the management of the municipal special purpose vehicle 'City and Port' used for the development of HafenCity, cooperation with politicians and public administration, as well as for location marketing, public relations and public participation (Kähler, 2016).

HafenCity, situated between Kehrwiederspitze and Elbphilharmonie in the west and Elbbrücken in the east, covers an area of 157 hectares and will increase the neighbouring inner-city area by about 40% by 2025. A diverse mix of uses from offices, housing, leisure, retail and culture is being realised, broken up by water areas, parks, squares and promenades. Here, up to 45,000 jobs are being created on up to 2.4m^2 of (gross) floor space, as well as 7,000 apartments for 14,000 residents. With the exception of the promenades, the entire area is raised for flood protection up to 8m above sea level. The concept of building on artificial compacted mounds (warfts) allows free access to both the water and the land, and differentiates HafenCity from other waterfront projects that are dyked (HafenCity Hamburg, 2018).

Course correction ten years later

In 2010, the masterplan was substantially revised after intense public debate in the light of changing economic, social and political conditions. Compared with the western and central parts, the three eastern quarters of Oberhafen, Baakenhafen and Elbbrücken (Elbe Bridges) are less spatially integrated into the existing city. In addition, the proximity to the traffic routes requires special noise protection measures. Baakenhafen is to be transformed into a socially mixed neighbourhood, a residential and leisure quarter with several thousand jobs. The Oberhafen becomes a creative and cultural quarter and the Elbe Bridges Neighbourhood becomes a business and residential location with a high degree of innovation. Also, significantly more usable space can now be realised than originally planned.

The number of planned new apartments was also increased at this stage. As the Baakenhafen and Elbbrückenquartier alone are generating more than 3,000 apartments, the total number of apartments has grown from 5,500 to more than 7,000. In addition, the possibilities of a greater social mix are strengthened, as social building ventures (Baugemeinschaften) are given greater consideration in the land allocation and, since 2011, one-third of the resulting living space has received public funding. Another elementary school, a high school with a neighbourhood school and several additional day-care centres strengthen family-oriented living. At the same time, the number of possible jobs increases. The green character was also strengthened, with large and small squares, as well as a networking of places underlining the spatial integration. In the south, an Elbe promenade invites users to stroll, and the Baakenhafen receives an artificially raised peninsula creating a green play and leisure area (HafenCity Hamburg, 2017).

Model for an OlympiaCity?

The economic boom, as consequence of Germany's reunification in the early 1990s, was an essential background for the specification of the plans for HafenCity. Hamburg needed more office space and that was to be created on a large scale in HafenCity. From 1992 to 1997, however, the plans were kept secret in order to avoid price-increasing speculation in connection with the relocation of the remaining port businesses on the site. The plots were mostly owned by the state of Hamburg. However, the companies had lease agreements, the extension of which would probably have delayed the realisation of HafenCity. At the same time, HafenCity was under considerable pressure from the beginning to exploit land sales in commercial and residential construction, not only to finance public infrastructure but also to expand the port in the south. On the site of the former village of Altenwerder, due to its proximity to the A7 motorway and existing railway lines, a large high-tech container terminal was to be built to ensure the long-term competitiveness of Hamburg's port; 232 million euros were to be generated by HafenCity. This coupling business effectively burdened HafenCity until 2013 (Kähler, 2016).

The preparation of HafenCity as a 'secret project',[1] the massive economic pressures, as well as a lack of social infrastructure, in particular the lack of affordable or even publicly subsidised housing, did not correspond to the model of state-of-the-art urban development that had emerged since the 1980s. The new model included transparency and early citizen participation, a broad economically and socially oriented mix of uses as well as a more cautious approach, while avoiding too much dependence on quick profit-taking. These were some of the lessons learned from the Berlin International Building Exhibition (IBA) of the 1980s, which were decisively reflected in the National Building Law, which came into force in 1987, and acted as guiding principle for major projects such as HafenCity (HafenCity University Hamburg, 2015).

The masterplan for the HafenCity was agreed in 1997 by a 'red-green' Senate. This was replaced four years later by a coalition of the CDU (Christian Democratic Union of Germany / Conservative Party) and a right-wing populist law and order party (Schill Party). Many people in the old dockers' quarters on the Elbe islands and large suburban housing estates, which had suffered from the structural change and subsequent unemployment, no longer felt represented by the SPD which had ruled for 44 years. This democratic deficit, a lack of common benefit from an overpowering profit orientation – are also central criticisms of the Olympic Games and their legacy in the host cities. The International Olympic Committee (IOC) has been seeking to counteract this challenge with its reform agenda, adopted in 2014. And so, in 2015, the second red-green Senate's bid for the Hamburg Olympics actually focused on the modernised concepts of HafenCity and the Olympic Games. Nevertheless, it still failed at the referendum.

Olympics in the heart of the city and harbour? Overlooking the skyline

The Olympic Games have often been staged in port cities, but never in the midst of a large seaport and as close to the city centre as planned in Hamburg. The Games of Tokyo 2020 and Los Angeles 2028, like the recent Games of Rio 2016 (Broudehoux – Chapter 6), are located in large port cities, but without (former) port areas being included in the construction of the main sports facilities and the athletes' village. In this respect, Hamburg's plans to develop an OlympiaCity on a former port island have a unique selling point in the history of the Olympic Games. In addition, from the Kleiner Grasbrook, a completely new view of the skyline of the city and HafenCity with old and new landmarks, would be created. In any event, it is worth taking a closer look at the masterplan for the post-Olympic OlympiaCity,

Figure 9.2 Post-Olympic vision, Kleiner Grasbrook and HafenCity
Source: Free and Hanseatic City of Hamburg, 2015b.

Figure 9.3 Follow-up use vision Hamburg Olympic Stadium
Source: Free and Hanseatic City of Hamburg, 2015b.

which was developed in 2015, especially since parts of it are now to be realised independently of the Olympics.

In order to create a lively and socially stable district, a mixture of apartments, workplaces, shops and leisure facilities, as well as social and educational facilities was intended. The aim should have been a socially, culturally and demographically diverse neighbourhood in which the inclusion of people with disabilities is encouraged. A mixed offer of publicly subsidised and privately financed rented flats, as well as privately owned property, should be created, at least one-third of the rented housing should be publicly subsidised. In total, up to 2,200 new social housing units were planned in the OlympiaCity. Public developers, cooperatives and private housing companies should also be involved, as social building ventures or providers of special housing for students and the elderly. The OlympiaCity as a 'city for all' was planned as a bridge to the adjacent old dockers' neighbourhoods with a population that is predominantly not among the 'winners' of Hamburg's city society.

Living, working and leisure in an ideal waterfront situation

The OlympiaCity was planned as a district with a high proportion of public green spaces. A sports park was to have been created on the waterfront, offering a variety of sports and leisure activities. The masterplan pursued the overarching goal of weaving the district with its parks into a Green Network of Hamburg and linking it with the surrounding parks and open spaces – be it in the south with the dyke of the Spree Harbour, in the north with the Lohsepark in the HafenCity, or in the northeast with the Elbpark Entenwerder. The shore areas were intended as public promenades, parks and ecologically upgraded zones. As part of the sustainability strategy of the Olympic planning, the green areas of the OlympiaCity should also help keep rainwater out in the field, thus avoiding flood risk.

In common with other cities, in recent years Hamburg has returned to mixed-use neighbourhoods in the city centre. This applies to the social mix as well as to workplaces. These concepts also promote mobility, environmentally friendly and lively public spaces (Evans, 2007). The urban planning concept for the OlympiaCity followed this guiding principle and suggested that the new district not only had everything in its entirety but that the sub-areas also differed from each other. With the desired variety, it should be easier to attract people of different backgrounds and cultures – of all ages and lifestyles – for a life in the OlympiaCity. Last but not least, in this way the identification of the inhabitants with their neighbourhood should have been strengthened (Free and Hanseatic City of Hamburg, 2015a).

In the end, the citizens have the say

In contrast to HafenCity and the Hamburg International Building Exhibition (IBA), which took place between 2006 and 2013 south of the Kleiner Grasbrook in Wilhelmsburg and Harburg, the planning of the OlympiaCity as an urban planning centrepiece of the Olympic bid was from the beginning subject to the acceptance of the Hamburg population through a referendum held in November 2015. The Bürgerschaft, the Hamburg state parliament, had decided by a large majority for a plebiscite, although only two years earlier Munich and Upper Bavaria had failed with their bid for the Olympic Winter Games in 2022 at a referendum. In particular, the Green Party, ruling jointly with the SPD, had struggled hard and declared the 'Bürgerschaftsreferendum' as a condition of the Olympic bid as one of the most important projects of the coalition. Regarding the scope and risks of the project, the city wanted to make sure that its citizens backed the venture.

Since the Olympic Games, as well as other major sporting events, have become discredited in the eyes of many people, due to problems such as corruption, displacement, doping, tax wastage, as well as excessive commercialisation, the Hamburg bid focused mainly on the hoped-for benefits for urban development. As in London's eastern extension at Stratford (Evans, 2010), the Games – and in particular the OlympiaCity, including the expansion of the public transport infrastructure – should trigger a great development surge at the Elbe and make Hamburg again world famous. Furthermore, because it was always clear that Hamburg could only cover a small part of the estimated 11.2 billion euros costs and that most of the funding had to be contributed by the Federal Government, the bid was presented as a great opportunity to boost the development of the city with considerable support from outside.

So why did people say 'No' to these extraordinary plans in the end – and despite a large-scale information, advertising and participation campaign, both by a large majority of the Bürgerschaft and the Senate and the powerful Chamber of Commerce, and prominent entrepreneurs such as the Otto family or the Braun brothers, the operators of the largest model railway in the world at Speicherstadt? Many people were clearly not convinced that with the Olympic plans, the much-vaunted ecologically, economically and socially sustainable 'City for All' would actually arise. The bid process itself had also been heavily criticised, costing 12 million euros. It was also noticeable that many urban development experts had not joined the debate. The universities, including HafenCity University, were mostly sceptical or even hostile, as well as welfare and environmental associations. The bid company had set up a stakeholder management process and also consulted Klaus Grewe, one of the leading construction site managers of the 2012 London Games, on the subject of citizen participation. However, it did not reach some of the city's key stakeholders, in particular the port industry, which partly publicly opposed the bid. Rather, together with many supporters, the bid predominantly highlighted emotional factors, looking to inspire citizens with 'fire and flame' and the 'largest party on earth', and the appeal of the modern Olympic Games brand. Without other global factors emerging at the time – the growing refugee crisis, FIFA organisation and sports drug scandals, and terrorist threats – it might have been successful. But would that have been a good outcome for the city? (Kuhlmann, 2017).

Leap across the Elbe and International Building Exhibition (IBA)

Divided Hamburg

From the perspective of most Hamburgers and visitors, the Hanseatic city ends at the Landungsbrücken on the northern bank of the Elbe. Everything south of it is a blank spot on the map. The main river Norderelbe acts as a geographical, mental and social border. Both the Elbe islands and the Borough of Harburg on the other side of the Süderelbe are among the poorest districts of Hamburg with a high proportion of unemployed and low-skilled people, many of them from an immigrant background. For a long time, the harbour fed the people in the workers' quarters. In particular, the conversion of goods handling to automated container terminals has left tens of thousands unemployed, including many former immigrant 'guest workers'. For decades, the areas were neglected by the Senate. In addition to the unemployment and lack of prospects of many people, the neglect of the built environment contributed to typical follow-up problems such as alcohol abuse and crime.

In the wake of these developments – the longstanding resistance to a planned waste incineration plant, the enormous traffic burden caused by the road and rail routes running across the Elbe islands, as well as several highway plans – a powerful civic movement was formed in Wilhelmsburg. Their commitment resulted in 2001 in the implementation of a conference on the future, jointly sponsored by citizens and the Senate, followed by an international workshop on the future, two years later. Many ideas flowed into the new urban development concept: 'Leap across the Elbe', a flagship project of the growing city of Hamburg, which was searching for new development opportunities on the Elbe islands and in Harburg. However, the actual catalyst for the renewal of Hamburg's south was the International Building Exhibition (IBA), which took place from 2006 to 2013 on the Elbe islands and the port of Harburg and whose final presentation year was merged with an International Garden Show (IGS) in 2013 (Association Future of Elbinsel Wilhelmsburg, 2012).

The IBA as a source of inspiration

How can living together in an increasingly international urban society be organised? How can spatial and social barriers be overcome in metropolises and how can new quarters be created in places that previously seemed unsuitable for living? How can metropolises become less dependent on fossil fuels? And how can they prepare for the consequences of climate change? These questions were the focus of the IBA Hamburg. At the beginning, these were concentrated into three main topics. The first topic was 'Cosmopolis, making Diversity a Strength'. The IBA was meant to show the benefits that international urban society can bring to a metropolis when looking for new ways of living together. The second theme was 'Metro Zones, new City in the City'. It was intended to show how the inner-city borders, the zones of the infra-structures and industrial areas, can develop into attractive places. The third theme was 'City in Climate Change, Growth in Harmony with the Environment'. It was intended to show how a metropolis can grow without adding to the burden on the environment and the climate. The IBA was supposed to show with which new solutions a city on the water can respond to the consequences of climate change.

The hoped-for image change of the Elbe islands was be promoted by, among others, the IBA Convention. Their goal was to involve essential urban social actors in the process and to win them over as multipliers for the Elbe islands. Over the years, the number of 'IBA Partners' climbed from 46 initial members to more than 140 private and public companies and institutions that maintained their network in working groups and became ambassadors of the 'Leap across the Elbe'. From the beginning, the Wilhelmsburg activists of the IBA met with interest and vigorous criticism. At many meetings, IBA projects were presented to more than 30 local initiatives in the initial phase. A special role was played by the IBA/IGS participation committee, which consisted of 24 citizens and who advised the projects. However, migrants were mostly under-represented. As a result, the IBA sought to engage with representatives of Muslim communities and organisations who act as gatekeepers in their communities. Overall, IBA Hamburg had implemented more than a dozen target group-oriented participation formats, tailored to the respective projects.

Forward-looking projects

The IBA has been able to make the centre of the Elbe Islands into a liveable urban space through numerous projects: modern workplaces, innovative residential buildings, sports facilities, and the new building for the urban development and environmental authority have been forming a new quarter since 2013, located at the modernised S-Bahn station Wilhelmsburg, and at the entrance to the Inselpark, which emerged from the IGS. About one kilometre east, the 'Gate to the World' education centre was built, consisting of a school and business centre, an environment & science centre and a multifunctional building with an event hall, parents' café, parents' school and a number of counselling centres. The new Elbe Island School, with its reform pedagogical concept, joins the education centre, which provides educational opportunities beyond school education and created a community centre for the district.

The citizens' initiatives and the IBA have set the Elbe islands well on their way from the backyard of the city to a point of departure. Although some (experimental) projects did not work as planned, a number of forward-looking initiatives were created. A flip side of the upgrading is the fear of displacement of the original inhabitants. To this day, however, gentrification is rather a felt than an existing phenomenon. Arguably, better social mixing is definitely something good for the Elbe islands. The current and future area developments with their innovative concepts, competition and participation procedures make important contributions to this (IBA Hamburg, 2017).

The key question: a new city for all

HafenCity and Grasbrook

As a result of the growing demand for residential and commercial space close to the city centre, HafenCity's mandate in recent years has been extended to the renewal of the old industrial port and urban areas east and south of HafenCity. This will further advance the realisation of the two major urban development strategies 'Upstream Elbe and Bille' and 'Leap across the Elbe'. The spatial starting point for these area developments is the new business centre Elbbrückenquartier, characterised by a partially spectacular high-rise development including a 200m-high 'Elbtower' with connection of the new underground line 4 to the S-Bahn lines 3 and 31 in the direction of the central station and the centre respectively, Wilhelmsburg and Harburg in the south. With its location, which is also reminiscent of Canary Wharf, London, due to its exposed location on the river and its excellent integration in the regional rail network, HafenCity is expected to complete its eastern end by 2025.

South of the Elbbrückenquartier the new district Grasbrook is planned on the Kleiner Grasbrook island. After the IBA initiated the 'Leap across the Elbe' in the middle of the last decade in Wilhelmsburg and Harburg, the new district Grasbrook, as the southern further development of HafenCity, forms the gap closure on the Elbe islands and strengthens the connections to the adjacent district of Veddel. However, in contrast to the plans for an OlympiaCity, it is no longer expected that there will be a complete evacuation of the harbour area, which today still employs around 1,000 to 2,000 people.[2] Rather, the renewal will be gradually initiated with the conversion of fallow sub-areas on the northern edge and the successive relocation of port operations from 2019.

The right mix?

On the Kleiner Grasbrook, flats for about 6,000 residents are planned, as well as 16,000 jobs, plus shopping facilities, a primary school and day-care centres. The new district will also provide space for new offices, commercial buildings, research facilities and laboratories, with existing buildings also used for this purpose. In total, a project with approximately 880,000m^2 of gross floor space is to be realised on an area of approximately 46 hectares. Several kilometres of publicly accessible waterfront areas will be created, combined with other attractive urban spaces and green spaces. A mixed district is planned, in which old and new activities and spaces can connect, with a good gradation between living, working and port use. Many technical aspects were studied in the same location as the OlympiaCity was planned, and can now be used as the 'legacy' of the bid for further development.

The Grasbrook district is expected to encompass three neighbourhoods and the residential neighbourhood of the Vltava Port in the dual waterfront between the Elbe and the Vltava Port, the mixed-use Free Port Elbe District, and the Harbour Gate District, which encircles the Saale Port and is reserved for commercial use with a mix of new and old buildings. Independent of noise protection issues, individual projects can be created step by step, because the buildings in this area comprise exclusively commercial uses. At the same time, this quarter marks the transition to existing port uses, which will continue to occupy the largest area of the Kleiner Grasbrook with 53 hectares. The connection to the new U-Bahn and S-Bahn station at Elbbrücken, located on the northern banks of the Elbe, will be made firstly by bus. The underground trail from the south remains free to secure the subsequent extension of the U4 coming from the HafenCity.

For the new district of Grasbrook, as with all major housing projects since the return of the SPD in the state government in 2011, one-third of the apartments are publicly funded. For all buildings, high environmental standards based on the eastern HafenCity will apply. These include, for example, the requirement for solar energy generation on or near buildings and high e-mobility standards. For example, 40% of the parking spaces in residential buildings are to be equipped with electric charging stations, and the share of car sharing for dwelling-related parking spaces limited to 30% (Free and Hanseatic City of Hamburg, Senate Chancellery, 2017).

Conclusion: still space for the Olympics?

The Olympic plans of Hamburg as a major urban development project in the centre of the city and harbour have largely failed due to the lack of integration of both the interests of the port industry and the neighbouring districts. The strategy of the Hamburg Parliament, Senate, Bid Company and private 'Fire and Flame Initiative' relied too much on the emotional conviction of the Olympics brand. Due to the problematic circumstances noted above, as well as the unsecured financing of the Federal Government's contribution, the bid had encountered difficult waters. Instead of too much marketing-oriented stakeholder management, it would have required intensive involvement of both local residents and other important players, such as welfare and environmental organisations, in order to gain the trust of the population. Nevertheless, the enthusiasm of the people for the largest sports festival in the world as a symbol of global understanding among nations is an indispensable condition for hosting Olympic Games and their sustainable legacy for urban development.

Of course, good urban development is also possible without the Olympics. However, the examples of Munich 1972, Barcelona 1992, London 2012 (Gold and Gold, 2010) (and Paris 2024) show that the Games can trigger large development leaps, even in dense, cosmopolitan cities. Hamburg's failed Olympic bid has also left a valuable legacy, as the plans for an OlympiaCity and subsequent plans for a new district in the harbour show how the city's division into a prosperous north and a disadvantaged south could be overcome, at least partly. If, in the years to come, the completion of the 'Leap across the Elbe' would indeed create the much-vaunted 'City for All', Hamburg would have achieved more than many successful Olympic host cities. Also, the reconciliation of urban and port planning had long been overdue, so that large projects no longer need to be developed secretly (Marten, 2016). Decisive are the learning processes. Learning from mistakes is as important as the model of good examples. This shows the transformation of port areas as well as the history of international building exhibitions and Olympic Games. A good partnership between the public sector, business and society, especially with regard to the creation of affordable housing and the securing of sustainable jobs, is also key to successful strategies.

Hamburg has also set out to become a good arrival city for refugees. After the initial contrast of a spontaneous welcome, willingness and doubts about the absorption ability exactly at the time of the Olympic bid disappeared, and the civic contracts negotiated between citizens and Senate provided good, decentralised housing for some 30,000 newcomers at 120 locations with a long-term perspective in mixed-use neighbourhoods. Hamburg actually seems to be a successful model in this respect. A new idea for the Olympic Games would therefore be a more sustainable integrated Games. For example, there is still enough space on the Kleiner Grasbrook – a small athletics stadium for clubs and schools could temporarily become a temporary Olympic Stadium; athletes and carers could stay in student apartments; a swimming pool could temporarily become aquatic centre; and a cruise terminal a multifunctional arena. There is still enough time until 2032 or 2036.

Acknowledgements

Many thanks are due to the following interviewees:

Prof. Ingrid Breckner, HafenCity University Hamburg

Dr Nikolas Hill, formerly managing director of the Bid Company for the Olympic and Paralympic Games, Hamburg 2024.

Prof. Marcus Menzl, University of Applied Sciences Lübeck, formerly HafenCity Hamburg.

Michél Slottag, formerly student at HafenCity University Hamburg, and HafenCity Hamburg.

Notes

1 In Kähler's book *Secret Project HafenCity or How to Invent a New Urban District* (2016), he states that, in addition to the then First Mayor Henning Voscherau, five other SPD Senate members justified their behaviour 20 years later 'on the verge of constitutional legality'.

2 During the debate about the OlympiaCity in 2014/15, it was noticed that only rarely were figures given on the number of employees at the Kleiner Grasbrook. While the port economy initially spoke of 2,000, the Senate quoted a figure of 1,000. There was also no information on this issue during the presentation of the plans for the new Grasbrook district in September 2017. The missing or strongly fluctuating

information is reminiscent of the discussion about the clearance of old industrial areas for the London Olympic Park.

References

Association Future of Elbinsel Wilhelmsburg (2012) *A Strong Island in the Middle of the City: Citizen Engagement in Willhelmsburg and on the Veddel as Engine of the Urban District Development*. Hamburg.

Court of Auditors of the Free and Hanseatic City of Hamburg (2015) 'Court of Auditors points to risks of the Olympic bid'. Press release on the Advisory Statement 'Olympic and Paralympic Games', 1. 9. 2015. Accessed on 15. 1. 2018 from: www.hamburg.de/weitere-veroeffentlichungen/nofl/4595950/beratende-aeusser ung-2015-olympia.

Diakonie Hamburg (2015) 'Olympics for all: Diakonie calls for cost-benefit calculation before the referendum'. Press release of 13. 7. 2015. Accessed on 15. 1. 2018 from: www.diakonie-hamburg.de/web/newsarchiv/Olympia-fuer-alle-Diakonie-fordert-Kos ten-Nutzen-Rechnung-vor-Referendum.

Evans, G.L. (2007) 'The Generation of Diversity: Mixed Use and Urban Sustainability'. In K. Thwaites *et al.* (eds) *Urban Sustainability through Environmental Design: Approaches to Time-People-Place Responsive Urban Spaces*. London: Routledge, 95–101.

Evans, G.L. (2010). 'London 2012'. In J. Gold and M. Gold (eds) *Olympic Cities: City Agendas, Planning and the Worlds Games, 1896–2016*. London: Routledge.

Flyvbjerg, B. and Stewart, A. (2012) 'Olympic proportions: Cost and cost overrun at the Olympics 1960–2012'. Said Business School working papers, University of Oxford. Accessed on 15. 1. 2018 from: http://papers.ssrn.com/sol3/papers.cfm?abstra ct_id=2238053.

Free and Hanseatic City of Hamburg, Authority for Urban Development and Housing (2015a) 'Evaluation of the citizen's suggestions for the Hamburg Olympic and Paralympic Summer Games 2024 bid'. Accessed on 15. 1. 2018 from: www.ham burg.de/olympia-1024.

Free and Hanseatic City of Hamburg, Authority for Urban Development and Housing (2015b) 'Olympic and Paralympic Games 2024 in Hamburg: OlympiaCity and sports facilities'. Accessed on 15. 1. 2018 from: www.hamburg.de/pressearchiv-fhh/ 4609722/2015-10-01-masterplan-olympia.

Free and Hanseatic City of Hamburg, Senate Chancellery (2017) 'Grasbrook: A new district for Hamburg'. Press release from 12. 9. 2017. Accessed on 15. 1. 2018 from: www.hamburg.de/pressearchiv-fhh/9491236/2017-09-12-pr-lpk-hafen-city.

Gold, J. and Gold, M. (eds) (2010) *Olympic Cities: City Agendas, Planning and the Worlds Games, 1896–2016*. London: Routledge.

HafenCity Hamburg (2018) 'HafenCity: The genesis of an idea'. Accessed on 15. 01. 2018 from: www.hafencity.com/en/overview/hafencity-the-genesis-of-an-idea.html.

HafenCity Hamburg (2017) 'Themes, quarters, projects, Hamburg'. Accessed on 15. 01. 2018 from: www.hafencity.com/upload/files/files/HafenCityProjekte_March_2017_eng lish.pdf.

HafenCity University Hamburg (2015) *Olympic Games in Hamburg: Learning from Good and Bad Examples. Final Report of a Study Project in the Master Programme Urban Planning*. Hamburg.

Hamburg Business Association (2017) 'Assessment of Olympic-related costs in the port from the point of view of the port industry'. Press release of 1. 12. 2017. Accessed on 15. 1. 2018 from: www.uvhh.de/info/presse/bewertung-der-olympiabedingten-kos ten-im-hafen-aus-sicht-der-hafenwirtschaft.

Hamburg Chamber of Architects (2016) 'Conclusion workshop of the Hamburg Chamber of Architects "Arrival City of Hamburg - but how?"'. Press release of 15. 3. 2016. Accessed on 15. 1. 2018 from: www.akhh.de/aktuell/nachrichten/artikel/fazit-workshop -der-hamburgischen-architektenkammer-ankunftsstadt-hamburg-aber-wie.

IBA Hamburg (2017). 'Information on the International Building Exhibition 2006–2013 and on the current neighbourhood developments'. Accessed on 15. 1. 2018 from: www. iba-hamburg.de/en/iba-hamburg-gmbh/skill-set/holistic-neighbourhood-development. html.

International Olympic Committee (2012) 'Factsheet London 2012: Facts & figures'. Accessed on 15. 1. 2018 from: www.olympic.org/Documents/Reference_documents_ Factsheets/London_2012_Facts_and_Figures-eng.pdf.

Kähler, G. (2016) 'New publication illustrates Hamburg's development: Secret project HafenCity or How to invent a new district?' Accessed from: www.gmp-architekten.com/ news/2128new-publication-illustrates-hamburgs-development.html?tx_gmpnews_pi1% 5BshowYear_2%5D=2013&tx_gmpnews_pi1%5BshowYear_1%5D=2015&cHash=2c3 9d8dc2fb746111c3cdec9631fa59e.

Kuhlmann, M. (2009) 'Hamburg's HafenCity as a project of regional structural policy in an international comparison'. Accessed from: www.ectp-ceu.eu/images/stories/ PDF-docs/biennal2017/HafenCityKuhlmannFinal15012018.pdf.

Kuhlmann, M. (2015) 'How London benefited from the Olympics'. *Hamburger Abendblatt*. Accessed on 15. 1. 2018 from: www.abendblatt.de/hamburg/a rticle206724129/Wie-London-von-Olympischen-Spielen-profitierte.html.

Kuhlmann, M. (2017) 'Success factors for Olympic Games in Hamburg as beacon project of European urban development'. Presentation during the 12th Biennal of European Towns and Town Planners on 29 June 2017. Accessed on 15. 1. 2018 from: www.ectp-ceu.eu/index.php/en/biennal-31.

Marten, F. (2016) 'Port City and City Port: A Complex Relationship Box with Acute Therapy Needs'. In Hamburg Chamber of Architects (eds) *Architecture in Hamburg: Yearbook 2016/17*. Hamburg, 154–161.

NOlympia Hamburg (2015). 'Something better than Olympia!' Accessed on 15. 1. 2018 from: www.nolympia-hamburg.de.

Schubert, D. (ed.) (2007) 'Ports and Shore Zones in Transition: Analyses and Plans for the Revitalization of the Waterfront in Port Cities'. In C. Hein (ed.) *Routledge Handbook of Planning History*. 3rd edition. London: Routledge, 338–349.

Seifert, D. (2015) 'Fair play'. Accessed on 15. 1. 2018 from: http://fairspielen.de.

Senate Chancellery of the Free and Hanseatic City of Hamburg (2015) *Olympic and Paralympic Games 2024 in Hamburg. Financial Report: Status of Costing and Revenue Expectations.* Hamburg.

Vöpel, H. (2014) 'Olympic Games in Hamburg: Productive vision or expensive fiction?' HWWI Policy Paper 84. Accessed on 15. 1. 2018 from: www.hwwi.org/p ublikationen/policy-report/publikationen-einzelansicht/olympische-spiele-in-ham burg-produktive-vision-oder-teure-fiktion.html.

Zurawski, N.*et al.* (2015) 'Olympic criticism from science'. Position paper of Hamburg scientists on the bid for the Olympic and Paralympic Summer Games 2024. Accessed on 15. 1. 2018 from: www.olympiakritik-aus-der-wissenschaft.de.

10 A 'host of priorities'

Toronto's pursuit of urban waterfront development through Olympic bidding

Robert Oliver

Introduction: rethinking Olympic bid failure

This chapter explores the confluence of sport development and land politics across a series of Olympic bids emerging from Toronto, Canada. Taking a longitudinal perspective, I illustrate how Toronto's engagement with sport development exposes the embedded conflict between public and private interests during the Olympic bidding process as a diversity of interests struggle to develop and respond to the shifting relationships and expectations of local and extra-local agencies. The struggle to leverage urban development objectives through bidding has raised important questions regarding the legitimate use of public waterfront land and the representation of public interest, and requires us to reconsider the lasting legacies of bid failure.

This chapter emerges from my nearly two-decade-long academic interest in Toronto's pursuit of sport development as a means to bring clarity to the city's waterfront development agenda. I have previously argued that '[t]he process of bidding remains crucial to the process of urban redevelopment even in the event of a failed bid' (Oliver 2011, 768). Through a series of articles I have sought to:

1 Highlight the legacies of one of Toronto's failed bid efforts; and
2 llustrate the implications of Toronto's failure for the city's urban politics (Oliver 2011, 2014, 2017; Bellas and Oliver 2016; Oliver and Lauermann 2017).

In this chapter, my aim is to illustrate why a broader set of urban policy and governance questions must be considered when investigating the failure of an Olympic bid. In the following paragraphs I demonstrate that Toronto's multiple bid efforts have been an opportunity for various public and private interests to make assertions and lay claim to the right to define the use of public waterfront land. Specifically, I argue that Toronto's participation in the 2008 Olympic bid competition forced a rethinking of urban waterfront development in Toronto. As will be shown, this is most evident in the city's commitment to a public–private partnership with Waterfront Toronto, an agency formed during the 2008 Olympic bid, but it is also reflected in the city's continued reliance on mega-projects (i.e. the 2015 Pan American Games) and a willingness to have corporate interests (i.e. Sidewalk Labs) spur urban waterfront transformation.

Toronto's Olympic bidding history provides a unique case example not just because it is a clear example of a city being a serial mega event bidder (Lauermann, 2016) but because the bidding logic employed by Toronto across its various bid efforts raises questions about whether the objective of securing the Olympic Games has remained the primary goal. The notion that finishing *second* in the bid competition might actually be a welcomed result has begun to percolate from the vast literature on mega-events (Oliver and Lauermann, 2017; Leopkey et al. 2019; Bason and Grix, 2018). For example, Torres (2012) has indicated the importance of recognising the 'utilitarian' objectives of many bidding cities, arguing that while bids might not be specifically designed to fail, they are being used for a multitude of purposes that are often, at best, only weakly linked to the Olympic project.

Several authors have indicated the importance of (re)considering the legacies that can emerge from failed bids (Masterman, 2008; Oliver, 2011; Girginov, 2011; Horne and Whannel, 2012; Smith, 2012; Oliver and Lauermann, 2017; Leopkey et al. 2019). According to Westerbeek (2009), developing a 'legacy intent' should be a key aspect of a city's bid strategy, where the aim is to win legacies even when losing a bid. Put another way, it has become increasingly useful to view the pursuit of mega-events as 'the opportunity rather than the intervention itself, and leveraging is the intermingling of resources to activate the opportunity afforded by the event' (Misener et al., 2015, 138). Even a brief survey of the growing literature on failed bids reveals how many bids are trea-ted as policy experiments or as a governance strategy (Oliver and Lauermann, 2017) and can be leveraged to encourage sport participation, national and community building, urban development and raise a city's global profile (Bason and Grix, 2018). It is clear that some bidding cities have moved beyond limit-ing the transformative power of the Olympic Games as an opportunity to make changes to the built environment, and now see sport mega-events as an occa-sion to (re)configure institutional arrangements. The implications of this more nuanced approach to bidding are enormous, with Cochrane et al. (2002: 95) positing that Manchester's pursuit of the Olympic Games was a key moment that contributed to a 'dramatic shift in the means and ends of urban politics' in the city. Elsewhere, the reverberations stemming from the changes to zoning laws, the emergence of new municipal redevelopment corporations, and the implementation of innovative financing schemes during New York City's 2012 are just beginning, but are clearly evident in new stadium projects that followed the bid, as well as in the Hudson Yards redevelopment scheme. Likewise, in Toronto the creation of a new development agency sparked by the bidding process has continued to operate in the post-bid period, with echoes of the Olympic bid's objectives periodically resurfacing. While I concur with Preuss (2007) that we have to be careful when attributing specific results or legacies to the bidding process, I do feel that investigations that reveal how the bidding process is being leveraged are becoming increasingly relevant given the recent decision of the International Olympic Committee (IOC) through Olympic Agenda 2020 to encourage bid cities to align Olympic legacy goals to urban development objectives. Intriguingly, the revised bidding procedure now includes an IOC's Candidate Questionnaire that asks: 'What will be the benefits of bidding for the Olympic Games for your city/region, irrespective of the out-come of the bid?' (IOC, 2009, 66). As Bason and Grix (2018) show, viewing the bidding process as 'leverageable resource' requires not only a close examination of strategic objectives but also an investigation of the mechanics or means by which these objectives are pursued and/or achieved.

   Given the length of the bidding process it is also not uncommon for bid cities to shift bid strategies and employ different or hybridised bid logics as the process evolves. It is clear that many cities have employed erudite bid logics during the bidding process in order to realise urban development objectives that are, at best, only tangentially related to the Olympic Games (Smith, 2012, 2014; Grix, 2014; Grix et al.. 2015; Oliver and Lauermann, 2017). From this perspective, the IOC's bidding reforms may be read as simply conforming to a paradigm shift that had *already* been instigated by bid cities. While the IOC may be desirous of more robust bid competitions having struggled to attract candidate cities for recent Olympiads, the emergence of Olympic Agenda 2020 lends credence to claims that the Olympics – and the bidding process – have become as much about cities and urban development as they are sport development (Hiller, 2006). The current struggle by the IOC to entice cities to submit bids creates a unique situation where those cities that do remain interested in hosting the Olympic Games find themselves in a position to: (1) negotiate a more favourable hosting contract (where risks are more broadly shared); and (2) leverage the situation by proposing more creative bid plans that address much longer urban planning horizons. Toronto's bidding history provides evidence that city-building and Olympic bidding are intimately related, whereby bid failure can still result in achieving important compromises that have enormous implications for urban planning, policy, and land use in the post-bid period.

The backbone of Toronto's bids: waterfront development

Toronto's interest in securing the Olympic Games emerged in the mid-twentieth century when the city's was unable to secure the 1954 British Empire and Com-monwealth Games. Having lost to Vancouver, Toronto's then mayor, Allan Lamport, and former mayor/IOC membership nominee Robert Hood Saunders, shifted attention to the 1960 Olympic bid competition. Although the 1960 bid never materialised, more concerted efforts followed for the 1976, 1996 and 2008 Olympic Games competitions (Oliver, 2011). Although each Olympic bid has offered a different assortment of facilities, common among them has been an underlying blueprint for waterfront development (see Figure 10.1 for a general layout of Toronto's waterfront).

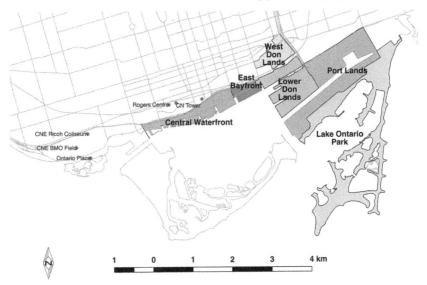

Figure 10.1 Toronto's waterfront

For example, the 1976 bid favoured a domed stadium to be located on the water's edge with an Athletes Village slated to occupy a series of islands (Harbour City) comprising a new mixed-use community. The 1996 bid sought to capitalise on the building of a domed stadium (initially called SkyDome but now referred to as Rogers Centre) just blocks from the waterfront by improving sport facilities and transportation linkages at Ontario Place, and by infilling former railway lands with residential development that would begin as an Olympic Village. The 2008 bid book proposed a large number of infrastructure projects to be spread across three proposed rings or hubs of Olympic activity. Once again waterfront renewal remained the core objective as all but 3 of the 28 proposed Olympic venues were distributed along the lake's edge. Moreover, as the 2008 bid's master plan evolved, a specific emphasis was placed on the development of the eastern portion of the city's waterfront including the city's Port Lands as well as the West Don Lands (Toronto 2008 Olympic Bid Corporation; Oliver, 2011).

It is quite common for Olympic bids to propose to redevelop an urban district. In Toronto's case, the success of Barcelona's refashioning of its harbour district for the 1992 Olympic Games provided a tempting template to consider emulating. But, as a number of authors have shown, public waterfront land in Toronto has a long history of mismanagement and the failure to represent the public interest is a defining narrative of the city's waterfront story (Goheen, 2003; Oliver, 2008, 2011; Desfor and Laidley, 2011; Eidelman 2011, 2013). For Eidelman (2013), the degree of historical inaction on Toronto's waterfront results from a specific blend of implementation failure and jurisdictional gridlock. Specifically, he informs us: '[f]rom 1961–1998, no less than 81% of all land in the central waterfront was owned by one public body or another, dispersed across a patchwork of public agencies, corporations, and special purpose authorities nestled within multiple levels of government' (Eidelman, 2013, ii). In Eidelman's (2013, 173) estimation, it is the amount of public waterfront land in Toronto combined with the number of authorities with rights or jurisdiction to its use, that has resulted in a form of 'multilevel *non*-governance'. As such, the desire of the Olympic bid teams to locate high-profile facilities and sport venues along the waterfront, requires confronting a complicated political history that has on numerous occasions scuttled water-front redevelopment plans. Nevertheless, Toronto's 2008 Olympic bid was initially championed by a former mayor, David Crombie, who believed that the only way to stimulate waterfront renewal in Toronto was to pursue a mega-project (Oliver, 2011). Crombie knew that political support and finan-cial backing would need to emerge from senior levels of government should the city ever expect to commence on a large-scale waterfront renewal scheme. So, while Crombie was not opposed to hosting the Olympics, his ultimate goal was to leverage the bidding process to concentrate attention and direct resources towards the city's waterfront land (Oliver, 2011).

Crombie's intuition proved astute and the city's 2008 Olympic bid has been credited with: (1) triggering the formation of a new waterfront Task Force that eventually resulted in a new waterfront development corporation (now called Waterfront Toronto); and (2) helping serve as a catalyst to generate a shared vision between various public and private stakeholders (Lehrer and Laidley, 2008; Laidley, 2011; Oliver, 2011; White, 2016). Intriguingly over the course of two years and through the release of several key documents (*Our Toronto Waterfront: Wave of the Future!; Our Toronto Waterfront: Gateway to the New Canada; Our Toronto Waterfront: Building Momentum*), the 2008 Olympic bid was enveloped into a bold waterfront vision that would require the formation of an intergovernmental task force to address the jurisdictional challenges that the pattern of waterfront land ownership presented.

Lehrer and Laidley (2008) have documented the significance of the forma-tion of the Waterfront Redevelopment Task Force and the Waterfront Rede-velopment Corporation that followed, drawing attention to the agreement between the municipal, provincial and federal governments to proceed with waterfront revitalisation – backed by a CDN$500 million commitment from each level of government. As Lehrer and Laidley (2008, 791) describe, the tripartite agreement that resulted in the creation of the Toronto Waterfront Revitalisation Corporation (TWRC) might best be thought of as a 'jurisdic-tional compromise' that reflected 'a changing understanding of the role of waterfront land in the urban economy and of the various uses to which it should be put ...'. The task force had called for more planning and financial power to be invested in a new waterfront corporation that could operate in more corporatist style, but this devolution of power was rejected by the three governments. It was clear that what was at stake was the capacity to create and manage a waterfront vision that went well beyond the Olympic bid. As a result, the three of governments remained wary about losing control of their influence on waterfront planning and relinquishing public land holdings, and consequently limited the power of the TWRC by forcing it rely on contribution agreements (Eidelman, 2011; White, 2016).

At the same time, the value of the Olympic bid was linked to its ability to create a 'definitive timeline', offer 'a focus and sense of urgency' and act as 'catalyst for the transformation of the Portlands' (Toronto Waterfront Revitalization Task Force, 2000: 40, 21, 46). Even after the 2008 bid was lost, several of the projects that were considered Olympic priorities were still funded, consuming precious capital and raising questions about the transparency and accountability of the TWRC (White, 2016; Lehrer and Laidley, 2008). Instead of lamenting the loss as had happened during previous bids, the local newspapers reported the necessity of seizing the momentum generated by the bid. It is important to note that it was only a couple of weeks after Toronto lost the bid to Beijing that Toronto's City Council approved the conversion of the Task Force to the interim TWRC. As White (2016, 14) summarises, '[f]or the supporters of the Task Force this proved a pivotal moment in the saga of Toronto's waterfront redevelopment because the three governments had kept to their promise and supported the ambitious project despite the disappointing Olympic result'.

The bid sparked other changes as well. Most prominent were the zoning changes that accompanied the bidding process as land designated as industrial shifted to mixed-use to accommodate Olympic purposes (Lehrer and Laidley, 2008). It was also a period of extraordinary policy alignment, as each level of government embraced the notion that Toronto had to increase its inter-urban competitiveness. Like countless other cities seeking to cater to globalising markets, Toronto began shifting to the logic of neoliberalism. The onset of neoliberalism first began with senior levels of governments in the 1980s and early 1990s, but by the mid-1990s the presumed necessity of shifting towards market-oriented and market dependent approaches of economic restructuring had become, as Keil (1998) puts it, common-sense (Keil, 1998; Donald, 2002a, 2002b; Frisken, 2007; Sancton, 2008; Fanelli, 2009; Evans and Smith, 2015; Fanelli and Thomas, 2011). Having been launched in 1996, Toronto's 2008 Olympic bid emerged precisely when the language and logic of a New Urban Politics (UAP) based on public–private partnerships, inter-urban competition, urban entrepreneurialism, government-sponsored intervention, had become orthodoxy (Harvey, 1989; Cochrane et al., 1996; Jessop, 1997; Peck and Tickell, 2002; Smith and Fox, 2007; Sager, 2011; Raco, 2014; Shin, 2014). For Mayor Mel Lastman and other bid boosters, it was clear that Toronto was not better off having lost the 1996 bid, with the city continuing to struggle to provide affordable housing, upgrade the transportation network, and offer sporting opportunities for the citizenry. In contrast to the 1996 bid, Toronto was no longer in a building frenzy and the city was still recovering from a recession of the early 1990s. From this perspective, an Olympic bid was a means for Toronto to engage with the symbolic economy and communicate the city's aspiration of playing a more important role in the world city hierarchy.

For many, the bid was an important lever to draw attention to a city that had come to function as Canada's economic engine, but lacked the revenue tools to deal with ageing infrastructure and population growth. Put simply, the Olympic bid was increasingly being viewed as an opportunity to recapture some of the billions of tax revenues that flowed out of Toronto to subsidise government services (i.e. health care and social security) across the country. For example, John Barber (2000: A23) noted: '[p]ersonally, I can't think of a single good reason to play host to an Olympics if that's all we get – an Olympics. But if the stupendous cash flows of the Games can be leveraged to create concrete and permanent improvements of benefit to all Torontonians, bring'em on'. Royson James (2000, B01) was even more succinct, '[i]t doesn't play well outside of Toronto, but it would be nice to hear someone stand up and say: We're going to use the Olympics as a grand excuse to pour money into Toronto'. Rusk (1999) claimed that the Olympic bid was the exact political tonic needed to remedy the waterfront.

Without question, the 2008 bid's Olympic Master Plan provided many with an exciting image. For Cam Cole (1999, B10) there was 'an undeniable allure to this vision that, if even half of it came true, might actually be a turning point for a city that seems to be losing the fight to stay ahead of its exploding population'. Other commentators, while not denying Toronto's need for overdue investment, were keen to point out that while the bid was principally about land development, the bid plans failed to offer details on how public lands would be managed throughout the process (Reguly, 2001). Gord Garland, a former policy analyst with the Royal Commission on the Future of Toronto Waterfront, was even less enthusiastic about a potential victory:

> Olympic construction requires a central command structure and the subjugation of democracy ... Our waterfront will be reconstructed according to ToBid's image of it, as dictated by Olympic-venue requirements. This means very limited community involvement in shaping the type of waterfront we want and need. It means that the public is left to respond to proposals from on high, or to absent itself from a debate that it was never intended to enter. Waterfront land is too valuable to be left in the control of any single-purpose group. To plan and construct a waterfront without real community participation is shortsighted. To construct it at one point in time for one purpose, the Olympics, is myopic. (Garland 2000, A11)

The desire to make the bid competitive and demonstrate intent to the IOC meant that the city had to illustrate that it backed the bid vision. The support went far beyond public relations soundbites. For example, the city released a policy document entitled 'Unlocking Toronto's Port Lands: Directions for the Future' that essentially opened up significant acreage of waterfront land in the eastern waterfront to accommodate the diversity of facilities designated by the Olympic bid's master plan. This document communicated the city's willingness to have private sector investment combine with public sector/state involvement to dictate Toronto's waterfront future (Oliver, 2011; Lehrer and Laidley, 2008). What remained unclear however, was: (a) how broadly mixed-use would be defined and how much would be tolerated; (b) how much soil remediation and flood protection would cost; (c) how public interest would be protected; and (d) how consenting the government partners would be to the TWRC. Put another way, the Olympic bid had aided the garnering of seed funding for waterfront development but the thorny issue of ownership fragmentation remained unresolved. When the bid was lost, the 'serious public debate about urban waterfront renewal in Toronto' (Oliver, 2011, 783) and schemes for waterfront development based on bid conversations continued; yet, without the symbolic power of the bid serving as a convenient political excuse, there was a real threat that the three layers of government, despite having agreed to the formation of the TWRC, would revert to previous habits of parsimony.

Avoiding post-bid inertia

In this section, I highlight the lingering influence of Toronto's 2008 bid effort on the politics of waterfront development. It is ironic that the series of sport mega event bids designed to transform Toronto's waterfront have actually contributed to the stalling of waterfront development as lands targeted for Olympic facilities become 'frozen' during the bidding period in the event of a potential victory. With Vancouver having won the right to host the 2010 Winter Olympics, Toronto was not in a favourable position to submit a bid for the 2012 or 2016 Olympic competitions. The city also considered applying for the 2020 and 2024 Olympic Games but the business community did not communicate strong support (Bellas and Oliver, 2016) and the escalating costs of hosting of Olympics dampened the appeal. The city did eventually agree to support a provincially led 2015 Pan American Games because the newly elected Mayor of Toronto, David Miller, saw the potential to build an aquatic facility and improve the city's transportation infrastructure among other benefits (Bellas and Oliver, 2016). But, the 2015 Pan American Games also offered an important reminder about the weak political status of Canadian municipalities as the Province of Ontario made site and funding decisions that reflected its privileged scalar hierarchy. Similar to the stated goals of the Olympic bids, the 2015 Pan American Games effort was designed to improve Toronto's sport capacity and develop the city's infrastructure along the waterfront, but, since the Province of Ontario took charge of the management of the bid the effort, 'Toronto's urban fabric was retrofitted to accommodate the needs of the Pan American Games without being subject to deeper social commentary' (Oliver, 2017, 297). It should be noted that most of the sport and supporting facilities built for the Pan American Games lack the capacity to accommodate the Olympic Games. Meanwhile, city-led initiatives to improve options for community sport and recreation, such as a proposal to build a stacked four pad ice hockey arena in the Port Lands, were abandoned because of cost concerns. Other initiatives such Mayor Rob Ford's proposal in 2011 to build a giant Ferris wheel, mega-mall and monorail along the waterfront sparked community outrage before being soundly defeated by a vote of city council (Doolittle, 2011; White, 2016).

In the aftermath of the 2008 bid failure, and with the formation of the TWRC, one of important narratives that emerged was the struggle of the TWRC to lay the groundwork for long-term waterfront change while facing pressure to meet the short-term political priorities that were voiced during the recent episode of Olympic imagineering. As mentioned, the TWRC had an ambitious mandate, but suffered from limited empowerment. Both the Olympic bid and the larger waterfront development vision envisioned connecting the Port Lands to the urban fabric, and creating coherence across the patchwork of former industrial sites that had been both physically and psychologically abandoned. The Olympic bid's Master Plan had outlined the value of working towards: (1) a cleaner environment; (2) the provision of more housing; (3) a more effective transportation network; (4) improved infrastructure; (5) fostering a prosperous economy; (6) the enhancement of parks and open spaces; (6) greater accessibility; and (7) strategic land assembly. With the release of new planning and policy documents, Toronto's citizenry had been told repeatedly that the waterfront needed to, and would, be revitalised even if the Olympic bid was not secured. Yet, without the bid's timeline, the impetus to spearhead change in a timely fashion was lost. Complicating the situation were broad changes to political leadership during both the municipal and provincial elections, as centre-left politicians (Mayor David Miller and Premier Dalton McGuinty) replaced right-leaning governments (White, 2016). Locally, the new mayor expressed concern about the degree of detachment that the TWRC had from the City of Toronto, while arguing that the 'politicians should be allowed to serve as board members' (White 2016, 18). Meanwhile, the TWRC struggled to secure stable funding – even flirting with bankruptcy in 2004–as each level of government remained unwilling to release their land holdings to the new corporation. As White (2016, 18) explains, the City of Toronto also remained reluctant 'to grant planning powers to an independent entity fearing this would undermine its citywide planning decision-making powers'. In many ways, early concerns about the operations of the TWRC were similar to criticisms typically levied at organising committees for an Olympic Games, with decisions being shielded from public input and issues of accountability and transparency generating consternation. Eventually, the TWRC was recognised as the lead developer of waterfront land and the city transferred some of the lands held by its economic development agency (TEDCO) and the Province of Ontario negotiated an agreement to transfer responsibility of the West Don Lands to the agency (White, 2016).

Several scholars have shown that increased privatisation as well as greater centralisation of the planning process has been the result of Olympic success

(Searle and Bounds, 1999; Kipfer and Keil, 2002; Owen, 2002; Gaffney, 2010; Raco, 2014). In Toronto's case, claims concerning the centralisation of decision-making and democratic deficiency can be extended to the bidding process (Lensky, 2000; Kipfer and Keil 2002; Lehrer and Laidley 2008; Oliver 2017). In particular, Kipfer and Keil (2002: 229) argue that the 2008 bid both reflected and aided the growing alliance between 'city planners, developers, architects and business lobbies with connections to transnational capital and the provincial and federal governments'. Likewise, Lehrer and Laidley (2008, 796) argue that 2008 bid helped to entrench 'networked relationships' and 'new governance structures' that began to dictate waterfront development. The early development decisions of the TWRC were criticised by Lehrer and Laidley (2008, 792) for 'circumscribing public accountability' and operating with 'an almost complete lack of disclosure of the ways in which it spen[t] public funds'. However, reflecting on the performance of the TWRC (which was renamed Waterfront Toronto in 2007) over a longer time period does yield a more sympathetic evaluation. For example, White (2016) has indicated that as the TWRC evolved into Waterfront Toronto, the corporation matured, transforming its practice and improving its public engagement strategy. It is also prudent to consider how informal networking that occurred during the bid process held potential to reshape stakeholder relationships in the city moving forward. Although the public consultation process for Toronto's 2008 Olympic bid has been criticised for failing to extend meaningful agency to a broad spectrum of Toronto's citizenry during the bid process (Lensky, 1996; Oliver, 2017), there *was* far more public consultation for the 2008 bid than conducted during the 1996 bid (Oliver, 2017). So, while I am confident that Toronto's public remained relatively powerless to dictate the terms of the bid, I am also convinced that individuals from across the city's socio-ethnic-cultural communities did have the opportunity to meet on multiple occasions to discuss ideas and concerns.

The TWRC's has constantly had to legitimate its performance while delicately negotiating the demands of both sides of a public–private partnership. Despite its weak governance model, according to White (2016) the corporation's focus on: (a) developing waterfront precinct plans; (b) establishing a discretionary urban design peer review panel; and (c) exhibiting a strong commitment to public participation, has had a positive influence on the local community's sense of ownership of waterfront land and has broader based city-scale public benefit. White (2016: 33) does not deny that Waterfront Toronto continues to struggle to engage disenfranchised populations, but he maintains that it has demonstrated a commitment to fostering an 'iterative relationship' that 'now meets many of the basic conditions for collaborative decision-making'. Intriguingly, White (2016) roots this more community sensitive approach to the 2008 Olympic bid, and specifically to the efforts of local neighbourhood association called the West Don Lands Committee (WDLC). Seeking to exercise a degree of community input into the development of the West Don Lands, the site chosen by the 2008 bid team for the Olympic media village, the WDLC conducted a planning workshop in the fall of 1999 to discuss various development scenarios (White, 2016; Bellas and Oliver, 2016).

Crucial to the WDLC vision for the area was the blending of public space and mixed-use residential development (White, 2016). When Waterfront Toronto launched their precinct planning process for the West Don Lands several years later, it incorporated the WDLC's suggestion of establishing a stakeholder advisory committee to help 'allow the community's local knowledge to be integrated into the decision making process' (White, 2016, 31). To its credit, Waterfront Toronto now combines 'public meetings with stakeholder advisory committees (SACs) – that are unique to each precinct – on all of its projects' (White, 2016, 31).

Conclusions: lingering dilemmas of democratic engagement

Waterfront Toronto has built a good deal of community support through a series of projects designed to enhance the public's connection to the water's edge over the past decade. While these projects lack the comprehensive development that the Olympic Games represented, the dedication to piecemeal improvements has helped Waterfront Toronto gain credibility with Toronto's citizenry in a sustained manner while simultaneously building institutional confidence that comes from a stronger portfolio of completed projects. The drawback of the heavy investment by Waterfront Toronto in smart public space design in the form of public beaches, wavedecks/boardwalks, plazas and park spaces, is that although frequently receiving architectural and design awards, these spaces have limited potential to generate revenue.

Another dilemma emerges when the logic of Waterfront Toronto strategy is applied to vacant waterfront industrial land that lacks a dedicated residential community. Here we find that despite a plethora of engineering, environmental and fiscal reviews, city-building on vast tracts of industrial lands continues to operate with a democratic deficit. Consider, for example, the recent announcement of a partnership between Waterfront Toronto and Google's Sidewalk Labs. What we find is a different style of mega-project that echoes many of the concerns raised during Toronto's Olympic bids. As before, an important section of Toronto's waterfront is slated to become a testbed, this time for a style of smart city development that is being advocated by a number of large tech companies (i.e. Google, Facebook, Microsoft, Amazon and Apple) looking to expand their influence into the physical realm. What is being offered is the opportunity to build futuristic high-tech neighbourhoods as both a panacea to some of the difficulties of urban growth, while simultaneously challenging the bureaucratic sluggishness that often impairs urban innovation (i.e. inefficient zoning laws, rigid building codes). For many, the partnership between Waterfront Toronto and Sidewalk Labs is premised on a form of urbanism that relies on the erosion of communal decision-making with the future of Toronto's waterfront being outsourced to extra-local interests. As with the 2008 Olympic bid, a large public consultation process has been launched to gather opinions and share ideas. What remains unclear is whether or not any progress has been made on how to incorporate those expressions of public opinion.

Although Toronto has never won the right to host the Olympic Games, the desire to connect bid efforts to longer-term urban planning objectives makes the city an important case example of how mega event failure can still influence urban policy making. As noted, the IOC's launch of Agenda 2020 only deepens the relevance of Toronto's participation in Olympic bid competitions.

References

Barber, J. (2000) 'Olympic benefits must be permanent', *The Globe and Mail*, 14 September, A23.

Bason, T., and Grix, J. (2018). 'Planning to fail? Leveraging the Olympic bid', *Marketing Intelligence and Planning*, 36(1), 138–151.

Bellas, L. and Oliver, R. (2016) 'Rescaling ambitions: Waterfront governance and Toronto's 2015 Pan American Games', *Journal of Urban Affairs*, 38(5), 676–691.

Cochrane, A., Peck, J. and Tickell, A. (1996) 'Manchester plays games: Exploring the local politics of globalisation', *Urban Studies*, 33(8), 1319–1336.

Cochrane, A., Peck, J. and Tickell, A. (2002) 'Olympic Dreams: Visions of Partnership'. In J. Peck and K. Ward (eds) *City of Revolution: Restructuring Manchester*. Manchester: Manchester University Press, 95–115.

Cole, C. (1999) 'Olympian dreams in the bid city', *National Post*, 10 November, B10.

Desfor, G. and Laidley, J. (eds) (2011) *Reshaping Toronto's Waterfront*. Toronto, ON: University of Toronto Press.

Donald, B. (2002a) 'Spinning Toronto's golden age: The making of a "city that worked"', *Environment and Planning A*, 34, 2127–2154.

Donald, B. (2002b) 'The permeable city: Toronto's spatial shift at the turn of the millennium', *The Professional Geographer*, 54(2), 190–203.

Doolittle, R. (2011) 'There's fog in Doug Ford's waterfront vision', *Toronto Star*, 31 August.

Eidelman, G. (2011) 'Who's in Charge? Jurisdictional Gridlock and the Genesis of Waterfront Toronto'. In G. Desfor and J. Laidley (eds) *Reshaping Toronto's Waterfront*. Toronto, ON: University of Toronto Press, 263–286.

Eidelman, G. (2013) 'Landlocked: Politics, property, and the Toronto waterfront, 1960–2000'. Doctoral dissertation, University of Toronto, Toronto, Ontario, Canada.

Evans, B., and Smith, C. (2015) 'The Transformation of Ontario Politics: The Long Ascent of Neoliberalism'. In B. Evans and C. Smith (eds) *Transforming Provincial Politics: The Political Economy of Canada's Provinces and Territories in the Neoliberal Era*. Toronto, ON: University of Toronto Press, pp. 162–191.

Fanelli, C. (2009) 'The city of Toronto fiscal crisis: Neoliberal urbanism and the reconsolidation of class power', *Interdisciplinary Themes Journal*, 1(1), 11–18.

Fanelli, C. and Thomas, M. (2011) 'Austerity, competitiveness and neoliberalism redux: Ontario responds to the great recession', *Socialist Studies*, 7(1/2), 141–170.

Frisken, F. (2007) *The Public Metropolis: The Political Dynamics of Urban Expansion in the Toronto Region, 1924–2003*. Toronto, ON: Canadian Scholars Press.

Gaffney, C. (2010) 'Mega-events and socio-spatial dynamics in Rio de Janeiro, 1919–2016', *Journal of Latin American Geography*, 9(1), 7–29.

Garland, G. (2000) 'Don't let the Games begin', *The Globe and Mail*, 28 August, A11.

168   *Robert Oliver*

Girginov, V. (2011) 'Governance of London 2012 Olympic Games legacy', *International Review for the Sociology of Sport*, 47(5), 543–558.

Goheen, P. (2003) 'The assertion of middle-class claims to public space in late Victorian Toronto', *Journal of Historical Geography*, 29(1), 73–92.

Grix, J. (ed.) (2014) *Leveraging Legacies from Sports Mega-events: Concepts and Cases*. Basingstoke: Palgrave Macmillan.

Grix, J., Brannagan, P.M. and Houlihan, B. (2015) '"Interrogating states" soft power strategies: A case study of sports mega-events in Brazil and the UK', *Global Society*, 29(3), 463–479.

Harvey, D. (1989) 'From managerialism to entrepreneurialism: The transformation in urban governance in late capitalism', *Geografiska Annaler. Series B. Human Geography*, 71(1), 3–17.

Hiller, H. (2006) 'Post-event outcomes and the post-modern turn: The Olympics and urban transformations', *European Sport Management Quarterly*, 6(4), 317–332.

Horne, J., and Whannel, G. (2012) *Understanding the Olympics*. New York: Routledge.

IOC (2009) *2016 Candidature Procedure and Questionnaire*. Lausanne: IOC.

James, R. (2000) 'Get the Games and the goodies will follow', *The Toronto Star*, 6 September, B01.

Jessop, B. (1997) 'The Entrepreneurial City: Re-imaging Localities, Redesigning Economic Governance or Restructuring Capital?' In N. Jewson and S. MacGregor (eds) *Transforming Cities: Contested Governance and New Spatial Divisions*. London: Routledge, 28–41.

Keil, R. (1998) 'Toronto in the 1990s: Dissociated governance?', *Studies in Political Economy*, 56(1), 151–167.

Kipfer, S., and Keil, R. (2002). 'Toronto Inc? Planning the competitive city in the new Toronto', *Antipode*, 34(2), 227–264.

Laidley, J. (2011) 'Creating an Environment for Change: The "Ecosystem Approach" and the Olympics on Toronto's Waterfront'. In G. Desfor and J. Laidley (eds),*Transforming Toronto's Waterfront*. Toronto, ON: University of Toronto Press, 203–223.

Lauermann, J. (2016). 'Temporary projects, durable outcomes: Urban development through failed Olympic bids?' *Urban Studies*, 53, 1885–1901.

Lehrer, U., and Laidley, J. (2008) 'Old mega-projects newly packaged? Waterfront redevelopment in Toronto', *International Journal of Urban and Regional Research*, 32(4), 786–803.

Lensky, H. (1996). 'When winners are losers: Toronto and Sydney bids for the Summer Olympics', *Journal of Sport and Social Issues*, 20(4), 392–410.

Lensky, H. (2000). *Inside the Olympic Industry: Power, Politics, and Activism*. New York: State University of New York Press.

Leopkey, B., Salisbury, P. and Tinaz, C. (2019). 'Examining legacies of unsuccessful Olympic bids: Evidence from a cross-case analysis', *Journal of Global Sport Management*, 1–28.

Masterman, G. (2008) 'Losing Bids, Winning Legacies: An Examination of the Need to Plan for Olympic Legacies Prior to the Bidding'. In R. Barney, M. Heine, K. Wamsley and G. MacDonald (eds) *Pathways: Critiques and Discourse in Olympic Research. Ninth International Symposium of Olympic Research*. London, ON: International Centre for Olympic Studies, 171–178.

Misener, L., Taks, M., Chalip, L. and Green, C. (2015) 'The elusive "trickledown effect" of sport events: Assumptions and missed opportunities', *Managing Sport and Leisure*, 20(2), 135–156.

Oliver, R. (2008). 'Bidding for the Future: Toronto's 2008 Olympic Bid and the Regulation of Waterfront Land'. Unpublished PhD dissertation, Queen's University, Kingston, Ontario, Canada.

Oliver, R. (2011) 'Toronto's Olympic aspirations: A bid for the waterfront', *Urban Geography*, 32(6), 767–787.

Oliver, R. (2014) 'The legacies of losing: Rethinking the "failure" of Toronto's Olympic Games bids', *Sport in Society*, 17(2), 204–217.

Oliver, R. (2017) 'Sport mega event planning in Toronto: From a democratic demand to a democratic demise', *The Canadian Geographer / Le Geographe canadien*, 61(2), 292–299.

Oliver, R. and Lauermann, J. (2017) *Failed Olympic Bids and the Transformation of Urban Space*. Basingstoke: Palgrave Macmillan.

Owen, K. (2002) 'The Sydney 2000 Olympics and urban entrepreneurialism: Local variations in urban governance', *Geographical Research*, 40(3), 323–336.

Peck, J. and Tickell, A. (2002) 'Neoliberalizing space', *Antipode*, 34(3), 380–404.

Preuss, H. (2007) 'The conceptualisation and measurement of mega sport event legacies', *Journal of Sport & Tourism*, 12(3–4), 207–228.

Raco, M. (2012) 'The privatisation of urban development and the London Olympics 2012', *City*, 16(4), 452–460.

Raco, M. (2014) 'Delivering flagship projects in an era of regulatory capitalism: State-led privatization and the London Olympics 2012', *International Journal of Urban and Regional Research*, 38(1), 176–197.

Reguly, E. (2001) 'Toronto wins if it loses Olympics', *The Globe and Mail*, 25 June.

Rusk, J. (1999) 'Lakefront facelift costing billions unveiled today', *The Globe and Mail*, 3 November, A11.

Sager, T. (2011) 'Neo-liberal urban planning policies: A literature survey 1990–2010', *Progress in Planning*, 76(4), 147–199.

Sancton, A. (2008) *The Limits of Boundaries: Why City-regions Cannot be Self-governing*. Montreal and Kingston: McGill-Queen's University Press.

Searle, G. and Bounds, M. (1999) 'State powers, state land and competition for global entertainment: The case of Sydney', *International Journal of Urban and Regional Research*, 23(1), 165–172.

Shin, H. (2014) 'Urban spatial restructuring, event-led development and scalar politics', *Urban Studies*, 51(14), 2961–2978.

Smith, A. (2012) *Events and Urban Regeneration: The Strategic Use of Events to Revitalise Cities*. New York: Routledge.

Smith, A. (2014) 'Leveraging sport mega-events: New model or convenient justification?', *Journal of Policy Research in Tourism, Leisure and Events*, 6(1), 15–30.

Smith, A. and Fox, T. (2007) 'From "event-led" to "event-themed" regeneration: The 2002 Commonwealth Games legacy programme', *Urban Studies* 44(5–6), 1125–1143.

Toronto 2008 Olympic Bid Corporation (2000) *Toronto 2008: Expect the World*. Toronto: Toronto 2008 Olympic Bid Corporation.

Toronto Waterfront Revitalization Task Force (2000) *Our Toronto Waterfront: Gateway to the New Canada*. Toronto, ON: Toronto Waterfront Revitalization Task Force.

Torres, C. (2012) *On the Merit of the Legacy of a Failed Olympic Bid*. Lausanne: International Olympic Committee.

Westerbeek, H. (2009) 'The Amsterdam Olympic Games of 1928 and 2028: Will city heritage inform legacy intent?', *Sport in Society*, 12(6), 776–791.

White, J.T. (2016) 'Pursuing design excellence: Urban design governance on Toronto's waterfront', *Progress in Planning*, 110, 1–41.

Index

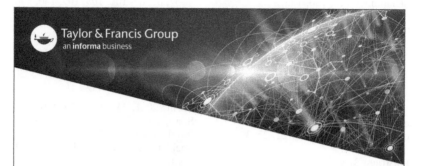